H. DE BALZAC

COMÉDIE HUMAINE

Edited by

GEORGE SAINTSBURY

H. DE BALZAC

THE UNKNOWN MASTERPIECE

(Le Chef-d'œuvre inconnu)

AND OTHER STORIES

Translated by

ELLEN MARRIAGE

with a Preface by

GEORGE SAINTSBURY

LONDON

J. M. DENT AND CO.

PHILADELPHIA : THE GEBBIE PUBLISHING CO., LTD.

MDCCCXCVI

Edinburgh: T. and A. Constable, Printers to Her Majesty

CONTENTS

LIST OF ETCHINGS

Drawn and Etched by W. Boucher.

PREFACE

THE volume of short stories which, in the first complete edition of the *Comédie*, opens with *Les Marana*, contains, with that in which *La Recherche de l'Absolu* leads off, the very finest productions of the author on a small scale; and they now appear together, *La Recherche* excepted. Almost all the pieces herein contained were early work, written when Balzac was under the combined excitement of his emergence from the valley of the shadow in which he had toiled so long, and of the heat and stress of the political and literary Revolution of 1830. All of them show his very freshest matured power, not as yet in the slightest degree sicklied o'er by any excessive attempt to codify or systematise. It is true that they are called *Études Philosophiques*, and that it puzzles the adroitest advocate to make out any very particular claim that they have to the title. But 'philosophy,' a term pretty freely abused in all languages, had in French been treated during the eighteenth century and earlier as a sort of 'blessed word,' which might mean anything, from the misbeliefs and disbeliefs of those who did not believe in the devil to the pursuits of those who meddled with test-tubes and retorts. Balzac seems generally to have meant by it something that was not mere surface-literature—that was intended to make the reader think and feel. In this sense very little of his own work is unworthy of the title, and we certainly need not refuse it to *Les Marana* and its companions.

The only objection that I can think of to the title-tale is a kind of uncertainty in the plan of the character of Juana. It is perfectly proper that she should fall an unsophisticated victim to the inherited tendencies (let it be remembered that Balzac worked this vein with discretion long before it was tediously overworked by literary Darwinians), to her own genuine affection, and to the wiles of Montefiore. It is quite right, as well as satisfactory, that she should refuse her seducer when she discovers the baseness of his motives. It is natural enough, especially in a southern damsel, that she should submit to the convenient cloak of marriage with Diard, and even make him a good and affectionate wife afterwards. But Balzac seems to me—perhaps I am wrong

to have left us in undue doubt whether she killed Diard purely out of Castilian honour, or partly as a sort of revenge for the sufferings she had undergone in enduring his love. A mixture of the two would be the finer and the truer touch, and therefore it is probable that Balzac meant it ; but I think he should have indicated it, not by any clumsy labelling or explanation, but by something 'leading up.' It may, however, seem that this is a hypercriticism, and certainly the tale is fine enough.

The fantastic horror of *Adieu* may seem even fine to some, but a trifle overwrought to others. Balzac, who had very little literary jealousy in his own way and school, made a confession of enthusiastic regret afterwards that he, Balzac, could not attain to the perfection of description of the Russian retreat which Beyle had achieved. Both were observer-idealists, and required some touch of actual experience to set their imaginations working, an advantage which, in this case, Balzac did not possess, and Beyle did. But I do not think that any one can reasonably find fault with the scenes on the Beresina here. The induction (to use Sackville's good old word) of the story is excellent : and there is no part of a short story, hardly even the end, which is so important as the beginning ; for if it fails to lay a grip on the reader, it is two to one that he will not go on with it. The character of Philippe de Sucy is finely touched, and the contrast of the unconscious selfishness of his love with the uncle's affection is excellent, and not in the least (as it might be) obtrusive. But the point of danger, of course, is in the representation of the pure animalised condition of the unhappy Countess, and her monkey-like tricks. It is never quite certain that a thing of this kind will not strike the reader, in some variable mood, with a sense of the disgusting, of the childish, of the merely fantastic, and any such sense in a tale appealing so strongly to the sense of ' the pity of it ' is fatal. I can only say that I have read *Adieu* at long intervals of time and in very different circumstances, and have not felt anything of the kind, or anything but the due pity and terror. The style, perhaps, is not entirely Balzac's own ; the interest is a little simple and elementary for him ; but he shows that he can handle it as well as things more complicated and subtler.

Le Réquisitionnaire, El Verdugo, and *Un Drame au bord de la Mer* may be called, assuredly in no uncomplimentary or slighting sense, anecdotes rather than stories. The hinge, the centre, the climax, or the catastrophe (as from different points of view we may call it), is in all cases more important than the details and the thread of narrative. They are all good, but *El Verdugo* is far the best: the great incident of the father blessing his son and executioner in the words 'Marquis [his own title] frappe sans peur, tu es sans reproche,' being worthy of Hugo himself.

I do not know that I admire *L'Auberge Rouge* quite so much as some of the other contents of the volume. It has interest; and it may be observed that, as indicating the origin of Taillefer's wealth, it connects itself with the general scheme of the *Comédie*, as few of the others do. But it is an attempt, like one or two others of Balzac's, at a style very popular in 1830, a sort of combination of humour and terror, of Sterne and Monk Lewis, which is a little doubtful in itself, which has very rarely been done well, and for which he himself was not quite completely equipped. *L'Elixir de longue Vie*, in which Balzac acknowledges (I do not know whether by trick or not) indebtedness to Hoffmann or somebody else, is also 'style 1830,' and, to speak with perfect frankness, would have been done much better by Mérimée or Gautier than by Balzac. But it is done well. *Maître Cornélius*, which, by the way, is interesting in its dedication to Count Georges Mniszech, partakes of the character of a 'Conte drolatique' thrown out of the scheme of those *Contes*. But it very worthily completes in its own way one of the most remarkable volumes of the old collection.

The tales now added take equal rank. The *Chef-d'œuvre inconnu*, a masterpiece in two senses, has been noticed in connection with *La Recherche*. *Jésus-Christ en Flandre* is good, and *Melmoth réconcilié*, inferior in itself, has a special and adventitious interest. Maturin, whose most famous book (quite recently reprinted after long forgetfulness, but one of European interest in its time, and of special influence on Balzac) can hardly be said to receive here a continuation which is exactly *en suite*, and the odd thing is that nothing was further from Balzac's mind than to parody his original. The thing, therefore, is a curious example of the difference of point of view, of the way in which an English conception travesties itself when it gets into French hands. Maturin was an infinitely smaller man than Shakespeare, and Balzac was an infinitely greater man than Ducis; but 'equals aquals,' as they say, or used to say, in Maturin's country, I do not know that Maturin fared much better at the hands of Balzac than Shakespeare has fared at the hands of Ducis and a long succession of adapters down to the present day in France.

All the *Marana* group of stories appeared together in the fourth edition of the *Études Philosophiques*, 1835-1837, and have not since been separated, with one exception (see below), either before or after their entry into the *Comédie*. Most of them, however, had earlier appearances in periodicals and in the *Romans et Contes Philosophiques*, which preceded the *Études*. And in these various appearances they were subjected to their author's usual processes of division and unification, of sub-titling and cancelling sub-titles. *Les Marana* appeared first in the *Revue de Paris* for the last month of 1832 and the first of 1833; while it next made a show, oddly enough, as a *Scène de la vie Parisienne*. *Adieu* appeared in the *Mode* during June 1830, and was afterwards for a time a *Scène de la vie privée*. *Le Réquisitionnaire* was issued by the *Revue de Paris* of February 23, 1831; *El Verdugo* by the *Mode* for January 29, 1830; *L'Auberge Rouge* in the *Revue de Paris*, August 1831; *L'Elixir de longue Vie*, by the same periodical for October 1830; *Maître Cornélius*, again by the same for December 1831. *Un Drame au bord de la Mer* alone appeared nowhere except in book form with its companions; but in 1843 it left them for a time (afterwards to return), and as *La Justice Paternelle* accompanied *La Muse du Département*, *Albert Savarus*, and *Facino Cane* in a separate publication.

Of those here added, *Jésus-Christ en Flandre* was one of the *Romans et Contes Philosophiques*, which Gosselin published in 1831, and remained as such till the constitution of the *Comédie*. It is a sort of Aaron's rod among Balzac's stories, and swallowed up a minor one called *L'Église*. *Melmoth réconcilié*, dating from 1835, first appeared in a miscellany, *Le Livre des Contes*; then it was an *Étude Philosophique*; and in 1845 it received its class in the *Comédie*. *Le Chef-d'œuvre inconnu* appeared in the *Artiste* of 1831, before its present date, as a 'Conte fantastique,' in two parts. It almost immediately became one of the *Romans et Contes Philosophiques*, passed in 1837 to the *Études Philosophiques*, was most unequally yoked for a time with *Les Comédiens sans le savoir*, and took definite rank in 1845 as usual.

G. S.

NOTE.—*Maître Cornelius* has been omitted, and postponed to a future volume, owing to exigencies of space.

THE UNKNOWN MASTERPIECE

To a Lord

. . . . . .

1845

I. GILLETTE

On a cold December morning in the year 1612, a young man, whose clothing was somewhat of the thinnest, was walking to and fro before a gateway in the Rue des Grands-Augustins in Paris. He went up and down the street before this house with the irresolution of a gallant who dares not venture into the presence of the mistress whom he loves for the first time, easy of access though she may be ; but after a sufficiently long interval of hesitation, he at last crossed the threshold and inquired of an old woman, who was sweeping out a large room on the ground floor, whether Master Porbus was within. Receiving a reply in the affirmative, the young man went slowly up the staircase, like a gentleman but newly come to court, and doubtful as to his reception by the king. He came to a stand once more on the landing at the head of the stairs, and again he hesitated before raising his hand to the grotesque knocker on the door of the studio, where doubtless the painter was at work—Master Porbus, sometime painter in ordinary to Henri iv. till Mary de' Medici took Rubens into favour.

The young man felt deeply stirred by an emotion that must thrill the hearts of all great artists when, in the

A

pride of their youth and their first love of art, they come into the presence of a master or stand before a master-piece. For all human sentiments there is a time of early blossoming, a day of generous enthusiasm that gradually fades until nothing is left of happiness but a memory, and glory is known for a delusion. Of all these delicate and short-lived emotions, none so resemble love as the passion of a young artist for his art, as he is about to enter on the blissful martyrdom of his career of glory and disaster, of vague expectations and real disappointments.

Those who have missed this experience in the early days of light purses; who have not, in the dawn of their genius, stood in the presence of a master and felt the throbbing of their hearts, will always carry in their in-most souls a chord that has never been touched, and in their work an indefinable quality will be lacking, a some-thing in the stroke of the brush, a mysterious element that we call poetry. The swaggerers, so puffed up by self-conceit that they are confident oversoon of their success, can never be taken for men of talent save by fools. From this point of view, if youthful modesty is the measure of youthful genius, the stranger on the staircase might be allowed to have something in him; for he seemed to possess the indescribable diffidence, the early timidity that artists are bound to lose in the course of a great career, even as pretty women lose it as they make progress in the arts of coquetry. Self-distrust vanishes as triumph succeeds to triumph, and modesty is, perhaps, distrust of self.

The poor neophyte was so overcome by the conscious-ness of his own presumption and insignificance, that it began to look as if he was hardly likely to penetrate into the studio of the painter, to whom we owe the wonder-ful portrait of Henri IV. But fate was propitious; an old man came up the staircase. From the quaint costume of this new-comer, his collar of magnificent lace, and a certain serene gravity in his bearing, the first arrival thought that this personage must be either a patron or a friend of the court painter. He stood aside therefore upon the landing to allow the visitor to pass, scrutinising him curiously the while. Perhaps he might hope to find the good nature of an artist or to receive the good offices of an amateur not unfriendly to the arts ; but besides an almost diabolical expression in the face that met his gaze, there was that indescribable something which has an irresistible attraction for artists.

Picture that face. A bald high forehead and rugged jutting brows above a small flat nose turned up at the end, as in the portraits of Socrates and Rabelais, deep lines about the mocking mouth ; a short chin, carried proudly, covered with a grizzled pointed beard ; sea-green eyes that age might seem to have dimmed were it not for the contrast between the iris and the surrounding mother-of-pearl tints, so that it seemed as if under the stress of anger or enthusiasm there would be a magnetic power to quell or kindle in their glances. The face was withered beyond wont by the fatigue of years, yet it seemed aged still more by the thoughts that had worn away both soul and body. There were no lashes to the deep-set eyes, and scarcely a trace of the arching lines of the eyebrows above them. Set this head on a spare and feeble frame, place it in a frame of lace wrought like an engraved silver fish-slice, imagine a heavy gold chain over the old man's black doublet, and you will have some dim idea of this strange personage, who seemed still more fantastic in the sombre twilight of the staircase. One of Rembrandt's portraits might have stepped down from its frame to walk in an appropriate atmosphere of gloom, such as the great painter loved. The older man gave the younger a shrewd glance, and knocked thrice at the door. It was opened by a man of forty or thereabouts, who seemed to be an invalid.

'Good-day, Master.'

Porbus bowed respectfully, and held the door open for the younger man to enter, thinking that the latter accompanied his visitor; and when he saw that the neophyte stood awhile as if spellbound, feeling, as every artist-nature must feel, the fascinating influence of the first sight of a studio in which the material processes of art are revealed, Porbus troubled himself no more about this second comer.

All the light in the studio came from a window in the roof, and was concentrated upon an easel, where a canvas stood untouched as yet save for three or four outlines in chalk. The daylight scarcely reached the remoter angles and corners of the vast room; they were as dark as night, but the silver ornamented breastplate of a Reiter's corselet, that hung upon the wall, attracted a stray gleam to its dim abiding-place among the brown shadows; or a shaft of light shot across the carved and glistening surface of an antique sideboard covered with curious silver-plate, or struck out a line of glittering dots among the raised threads of the golden warp of some old brocaded curtains, where the lines of the stiff heavy folds were broken, as the stuff had been flung carelessly down to serve as a model.

Plaster *écorchés* stood about the room; and here and there, on shelves and tables, lay fragments of classical sculpture — torsos of antique goddesses, worn smooth as though all the years of the centuries that had passed over them had been lovers' kisses. The walls were covered, from floor to ceiling, with countless sketches in charcoal, red chalk, or pen and ink. Amid the litter and confusion of colour boxes, overturned stools, flasks of oil, and essences, there was just room to move so as to reach the illuminated circular space where the easel stood. The light from the window in the roof fell full upon Porbus's pale face and on the ivory-tinted forehead of his strange visitor. But in another moment the younger man heeded nothing but a picture that had already become famous even in those stormy days of political and religious revolution, a picture that a few of the zealous worshippers, who have so often kept the sacred fire of art alive in evil days, were wont to go on pilgrimage to see. The beautiful panel represented a Saint Mary of Egypt about to pay her passage across the seas. It was a masterpiece destined for Mary de' Medici, who sold it in later years of poverty.

'I like your saint,' the old man remarked, addressing Porbus. 'I would give you ten golden crowns for her over and above the price the Queen is paying; but as for putting a spoke in that wheel . . . the devil take it!'

'It is good then?'

'Hey! hey!' said the old man; 'good, say you?— Yes and no. Your good woman is not badly done, but she is not alive. You artists fancy that when a figure is correctly drawn, and everything in its place according to the rules of anatomy, there is nothing more to be done. You make up the flesh tints beforehand on your palettes according to your formulæ, and fill in the outlines with due care that one side of the face shall be darker than the other; and because you look from time to time at a naked woman who stands on the platform before you, you fondly imagine that you have copied nature, think yourselves to be painters, believe that you have wrested His secret from God. Pshaw! You may know your syntax thoroughly and make no blunders in your grammar, but it takes that and something more to make a great poet. Look at your saint, Porbus! At a first glance she is admirable; look at her again, and you see at once that she is glued to the background, and that you could not walk round her. She is a silhouette that turns but one side of her face to all beholders, a figure cut out of canvas, an image with no power to move nor change her position. I feel as if there were no air between that arm and the background, no space, no sense of distance in your canvas. The perspective is perfectly correct, the strength of the colouring is accurately diminished with the distance; but, in spite of these praiseworthy efforts, I could never bring myself to believe that the warm breath of life comes and goes in that beautiful body. It seems to me that if I laid my hand on the firm rounded throat, it would be cold as marble to the touch. No, my friend, the blood does not flow beneath that ivory skin, the tide of life does not flush those delicate fibres, the purple veins that trace a network beneath the transparent amber of her brow and breast. Here the pulse seems to beat, there it is motionless, life and death are at strife in every detail; here you see a woman, there a statue, there again a corpse. Your creation is incomplete. You had only power to breathe a portion of your soul into your beloved work. The fire of Prometheus died out again and again in your hands; many a spot in your picture has not been touched by the divine flame.'

'But how is it, dear master?' Porbus asked respectfully, while the young man with difficulty repressed his strong desire to beat the critic.

'Ah!' said the old man, 'it is this! You have halted between two manners. You have hesitated between drawing and colour, between the dogged attention to detail, the stiff precision of the German masters and the dazzling glow, the joyous exuberance of Italian painters. You have set yourself to imitate Hans Holbein and Titian, Albrecht Dürer and Paul Veronese in a single picture. A magnificent ambition truly, but what has come of it? Your work has neither the severe charm of a dry execution nor the magical illusion of Italian *chiaroscuro*. Titian's rich golden colouring poured into Albrecht Dürer's austere outlines has shattered them, like molten bronze bursting through the mould that is not strong enough to hold it. In other places the outlines have held firm, imprisoning and obscuring the magnificent glowing flood of Venetian colour. The drawing of the face is not perfect, the colouring is not perfect; traces of that unlucky indecision are to be seen everywhere. Unless you felt strong enough to fuse the two opposed manners in the fire of your own genius, you should have cast in your lot boldly with the one or the other, and so have obtained the unity which simulates one of the conditions of life itself. Your work is only true in the centres; your outlines are false, they project nothing, there is no hint of anything behind them. There is truth here,' said the old man, pointing to the breast of the Saint, 'and again here,' he went on, indicating the rounded shoulder. 'But there,' once more returning to the column of the throat, 'everything is false. Let us go no farther into detail; you would be disheartened.'

The old man sat down on a stool, and remained a while without speaking, with his face buried in his hands.

'Yet I studied that throat from the life, dear master,' Porbus began; 'it happens sometimes, for our misfortune, that real effects in nature look improbable when transferred to canvas——'

'The aim of art is not to copy nature, but to express it. You are not a servile copyist, but a poet!' cried the old man sharply, cutting Porbus short with an imperious gesture. 'Otherwise a sculptor might make a plaster cast of a living woman and save himself all further trouble. Well, try to make a cast of your mistress's hand, and set up the thing before you. You will see a monstrosity, a dead mass, bearing no resemblance to the living hand; you would be compelled to have recourse to the chisel of a sculptor who, without making an exact copy, would represent for you its movement and its life. We must detect the spirit, the informing soul in the appearances of things and beings. Effects! What are effects but the accidents of life, not life itself? A hand, since I have taken that example, is not only a part of a body, it is the expression and extension of a thought that

must be grasped and rendered.   Neither painter nor
poet nor sculptor may separate the effect from the cause,
which are inevitably contained the one in the other.
There begins the real struggle!   Many a painter
achieves success instinctively, unconscious of the task
that is set before art.   You draw a woman, yet you do
not see her!   Not so do you succeed in wresting nature's
secrets from her!   You are reproducing mechanically
the model that you copied in your master's studio.   You
do not penetrate far enough into the inmost secrets of
the mystery of form; you do not seek with love enough
and perseverance enough after the form that baffles
and eludes you.   Beauty is a thing severe and un-
approachable, never to be won by a languid lover.   You
must lie in wait for her coming and take her unawares,
press her hard and clasp her in a tight embrace, and force
her to yield.   Form is a Proteus more intangible and
more manifold than the Proteus of the legend; compelled, only after long wrestling, to stand forth manifest
in his true aspect.   Some of you are satisfied with the first
shape, or at most by the second or the third that appears.
Not thus wrestle the victors, the unvanquished painters
who never suffer themselves to be deluded by all those
treacherous shadow-shapes; they persevere till nature at
the last stands bare to their gaze, and her very soul is
revealed.

'In this manner worked Rafael,' said the old man,
taking off his cap to express his reverence for the King
of Art.   'His transcendent greatness came of the intimate sense that, in him, seems as if it would shatter
external form.   Form in his figures (as with us) is a
symbol, a means of communicating sensations, ideas,
the vast imaginings of a poet.   Every face is a whole
world.   The subject of the portrait appeared for him
bathed in the light of a divine vision; it was revealed by
an inner voice, the finger of God laid bare the sources
of expression in the past of a whole life.

'You clothe your women in fair raiment of flesh, in gracious veiling of hair; but where is the blood, the source of passion and of calm, the cause of the particular effect? Why, this brown Egyptian of yours, my good Porbus, is a colourless creature! These figures that you set before us are painted bloodless phantoms; and you call that painting, you call that art!

'Because you have made something more like a woman than a house, you think that you have set your fingers on the goal; you are quite proud that you need not to write *currus venustus* or *pulcher homo* beside your figures, as early painters were wont to do, and you fancy that you have done wonders. Ah! my good friend, there is still something more to learn, and you will use up a great deal of chalk and cover many a canvas before you will learn it. Yes, truly, a woman carries her head in just such a way, so she holds her garments gathered into her hand; her eyes grow dreamy and soft with that expression of meek sweetness, and even so the quivering shadow of the lashes hovers upon her cheeks. It is all there, and yet it is not there. What is lacking? A nothing, but that nothing is everything.

'There you have the semblance of life, but you do not express its fulness and effluence, that indescribable something, perhaps the soul itself, that envelopes the outlines of the body like a haze; that flower of life, in short, that Titian and Rafael caught. Your utmost achievement hitherto has only brought you to the starting-point. You might now perhaps begin to do excellent work, but you grow weary all too soon; and the crowd admires, and those who know smile.

'Oh, Mabuse! oh, my master!' cried the strange speaker, 'thou art a thief! Thou hast carried away the secret of life with thee!

'Nevertheless,' he began again, 'this picture of yours is worth more than all the paintings of that rascal Rubens, with his mountains of Flemish flesh raddled with vermilion, his torrents of red hair, his riot of colour. You, at least, have colour there, and feeling and drawing —the three essentials in art.'

The young man roused himself from his deep musings.

'Why, my good man, the Saint is sublime!' he cried. 'There is a subtlety of imagination about those two figures, the Saint Mary and the Shipman, that cannot be found among Italian masters; I do not know a single one of them capable of imaging the Shipman's hesitation.'

'Did that little malapert come with you?' asked Porbus of the older man.

'Alas! master, pardon my boldness,' cried the neophyte, and the colour mounted to his face. 'I am unknown— a dauber by instinct, and but lately come to this city— the fountainhead of all learning.'

'Set to work,' said Porbus, handing him a bit of red chalk and a sheet of paper.

The new-comer quickly sketched the Saint Mary line for line.

'Aha!' exclaimed the old man. 'Your name?' he added.

The young man wrote 'Nicolas Poussin' below the sketch.

'Not bad that for a beginning,' said the strange speaker, who had discoursed so wildly. 'I see that we can talk of art in your presence. I do not blame you for admiring Porbus's saint. In the eyes of the world she is a masterpiece, and those alone who have been initiated into the inmost mysteries of art can discover her short-comings. But it is worth while to give you the lesson, for you are able to understand it, so I will show you how little it needs to complete this picture. You must be all eyes, all attention, for it may be that such a chance of learning will never come in your way again.—Porbus! your palette.'

Porbus went in search of palette and brushes. The little old man turned back his sleeves with impatient energy, seized the palette, covered with many hues, that Porbus handed to him, and snatched rather than took a handful of brushes of various sizes from the hands of his acquaintance. His pointed beard suddenly bristled—a menacing movement that expressed the prick of a lover's fancy. As he loaded his brush, he muttered between his teeth, 'These paints are only fit to fling out of the window, together with the fellow who ground them, their crudeness and falseness are disgusting! How can one paint with this?'

He dipped the tip of the brush with feverish eagerness in the different pigments, making the circuit of the palette several times more quickly than the organist of a cathedral sweeps the octaves on the keyboard of his clavier for the *O Filii* at Easter.

Porbus and Poussin, on either side of the easel, stood stock-still, watching with intense interest.

'Look, young man,' he began again, 'see how three or four strokes of the brush and a thin glaze of blue let in the free air to play about the head of the poor Saint, who must have felt stifled and oppressed by the close atmosphere! See how the drapery begins to flutter; you feel that it is lifted by the breeze! A moment ago it hung as heavily and stiffly as if it were held out by pins. Do you see how the satin sheen that I have just given to the breast rends the pliant, silken softness of a young girl's skin, and how the brown red, blended with burnt ochre, brings warmth into the cold grey of the deep shadow where the blood lay congealed instead of coursing through the veins? Young man, young man, no master could teach you how to do this that I am doing before your eyes. Mabuse alone possessed the secret of giving life to his figures; Mabuse had but one pupil—that was I. I have had none, and I am old. You have sufficient intelligence to imagine the rest from the glimpses that I am giving you.'

While the old man was speaking, he gave a touch here

and there; sometimes two strokes of the brush, sometimes a single one; but every stroke told so well, that the whole picture seemed transfigured—the painting was flooded with light. He worked with such passionate fervour, that beads of sweat gathered upon his bare forehead; he worked so quickly, in brief, impatient jerks, that it seemed to young Poussin as if some familiar spirit inhabiting the body of this strange being took a grotesque pleasure in making use of the man's hands against his own will. The unearthly glitter of his eyes, the convulsive movements that seemed like struggles, gave to this fancy a semblance of truth which could not but stir a young imagination. The old man continued, saying as he did so—

'Paf! paf! that is how to lay it on, young man!—Little touches! come and bring a glow into those icy cold tones for me! Just so! Pon! pon! pon!' and those parts of the picture that he had pointed out as cold and lifeless flushed with warmer hues, a few bold strokes of colour brought all the tones of the pictures into the required harmony with the glowing tints of the Egyptian, and the differences in temperament vanished.

'Look you, youngster, the last touches make the picture. Porbus has given it a hundred strokes for every one of mine. No one thanks us for what lies beneath. Bear that in mind.'

At last the restless spirit stopped, and turning to Porbus and Poussin, who were speechless with admiration, he spoke—

'This is not as good as my *Belle Noiseuse*; still one might put one's name to such a thing as this.—Yes, I would put my name to it,' he added, rising to reach for a mirror, in which he looked at the picture.—'And now,' he said, 'will you both come and breakfast with me. I have a smoked ham and some very fair wine! . . . Eh! eh! the times may be bad, but we can still have some talk about art! We can talk like equals. . . . Here is a little fellow who has aptitude,' he added, laying a hand on Nicolas Poussin's shoulder.

In this way the stranger became aware of the thread-bare condition of the Norman's doublet. He drew a leather purse from his girdle, felt in it, found two gold coins, and held them out.

'I will buy your sketch,' he said.

'Take it,' said Porbus, as he saw the other start and flush with embarrassment, for Poussin had the pride of poverty. 'Pray take it; he has a couple of king's ransoms in his pouch!'

The three came down together from the studio, and, talking of art by the way, reached a picturesque wooden house hard by the Pont Saint-Michel. Poussin wondered a moment at its ornament, at the knocker, at the frames of the casements, at the scroll-work designs, and in the next he stood in a vast low-ceiled room. A table, covered with tempting dishes, stood near the blazing fire, and (luck unhoped for) he was in the company of two great artists full of genial good humour.

'Do not look too long at that canvas, young man,' said Porbus, when he saw that Poussin was standing, struck with wonder, before a painting. 'You would fall a victim to despair.'

It was the *Adam* painted by Mabuse to purchase his release from the prison where his creditors had so long kept him. And as a matter of fact, the figure stood out so boldly and convincingly, that Nicolas Poussin began to understand the real meaning of the words poured out by the old artist, who was himself looking at the picture with apparent satisfaction, but without enthusiasm. 'I have done better than that!' he seemed to be saying to himself.

'There is life in it,' he said aloud; 'in that respect my poor master here surpassed himself, but there is some lack of truth in the background. The man lives indeed; he is rising, and will come towards us; but the atmosphere, the sky, the air, the breath of the breeze—you look and feel for them, but they are not there. And then the man himself is, after all, only a man! Ah! but the one man in the world who came direct from the hands of God must have had a something divine about him that is wanting here. Mabuse himself would grind his teeth and say so when he was not drunk.'

Poussin looked from the speaker to Porbus, and from Porbus to the speaker, with restless curiosity. He went up to the latter to ask for the name of their host; but the painter laid a finger on his lips with an air of mystery. The young man's interest was excited; he kept silence, but hoped that sooner or later some word might be let fall that would reveal the name of his entertainer. It was evident that he was a man of talent and very wealthy, for Porbus listened to him respectfully, and the vast room was crowded with marvels of art.

A magnificent portrait of a woman, hung against the dark oak panels of the wall, next caught Poussin's attention.

'What a glorious Giorgione!' he cried.

'No,' said his host, 'it is an early daub of mine——'

'Gramercy! I am in the abode of the god of painting, it seems!' cried Poussin ingenuously.

The old man smiled as if he had long grown familiar with such praise.

'Master Frenhofer!' said Porbus, 'do you think you could send me a little of your capital Rhine wine?'

'A couple of pipes!' answered his host; 'one to discharge a debt, for the pleasure of seeing your pretty sinner, the other as a present from a friend.'

'Ah! if I had my health,' returned Porbus, 'and if you would but let me see your *Belle Noiseuse*, I would paint some great picture, with breadth in it and depth; the figures should be life-size.'

'Let you see my work!' cried the painter in agitation. 'No, no! it is not perfect yet; something still remains

for me to do.   Yesterday, in the dusk,' he said, 'I
thought I had reached the end.   Her eyes seemed moist,
the flesh quivered, something stirred the tresses of her
hair.   She breathed !   But though I have succeeded in
reproducing Nature's roundness and relief on the flat
surface of the canvas, this morning, by daylight, I
found out my mistake.   Ah ! to achieve that glorious
result I have studied the works of the great masters of
colour, stripping off coat after coat of colour from
Titian's canvas, analysing the pigments of the king of
light.   Like that sovereign painter, I began the face in
a slight tone with a supple and fat paste—for shadow
is but an accident ;   bear that in mind, youngster !
—Then I began afresh, and by half-tones and thin
glazes of colour less and less transparent, I gradually
deepened the tints to the deepest black of the strongest
shadows.   An ordinary painter makes his shadows something entirely different in nature from the high lights ;
they are wood or brass, or what you will, anything but
flesh in shadow.   You feel that even if those figures
were to alter their position, those shadow stains would
never be cleansed away, those parts of the picture would
never glow with light.

'I have escaped one mistake, into which the most
famous painters have sometimes fallen ; in my canvas the
whiteness shines through the densest and most persistent
shadow. I have not marked out the limits of my figure in
hard, dry outlines, and brought every least anatomical detail
into prominence (like a host of dunces, who fancy that they
can draw because they can trace a line elaborately smooth
and clean), for the human body is not contained within
the limits of line.   In this the sculptor can approach the
truth more nearly than we painters.   Nature's way is a
complicated succession of curve within curve.   Strictly
speaking, there is no such thing as drawing.—Do not
laugh, young man ; strange as that speech may seem to
you, you will understand the truth in it some day.—A

line is a method of expressing the effect of light upon an object; but there are no lines in nature, everything is solid. We draw by modelling, that is to say, that we disengage an object from its setting; the distribution of the light alone gives to a body the appearance by which we know it. So I have not defined the outlines; I have suffused them with a haze of half-tints warm or golden, in such a sort that you cannot lay your finger on the exact spot where background and contours meet. Seen from near, the picture looks a blur; it seems to lack definition; but step back two paces, and the whole thing becomes clear, distinct, and solid; the body stands out, the rounded form comes into relief; you feel that the air plays round it. And yet—I am not satisfied; I have misgivings. Perhaps one ought not to draw a single line; perhaps it would be better to attack the face from the centre, taking the highest prominences first, proceeding from them through the whole range of shadows to the heaviest of all. Is not this the method of the sun, the divine painter of the world? Oh, Nature, Nature! who has surprised thee, fugitive? But, after all, too much knowledge, like ignorance, brings you to a negation. I have doubts about my work.'

There was a pause. Then the old man spoke again. 'I have been at work upon it for ten years, young man; but what are ten short years in a struggle with Nature? Do we know how long Sir Pygmalion wrought at the one statue that came to life?'

The old man fell into deep musings, and gazed before him with wide unseeing eyes, while he played unheedingly with his knife.

'Look, he is in converse with his *dæmon*!' murmured Porbus.

At the word, Nicolas Poussin felt himself carried away by an unaccountable accession of artist's curiosity. For him the old man, at once intent and inert, the seer with the unseeing eyes, became something more than a man—a fantastic spirit living in a mysterious world, and countless vague thoughts awoke within his soul. The effect of this species of fascination upon his mind can no more be described in words than the passionate longing awakened in an exile's heart by the song that recalls his home. He thought of the scorn that the old man affected to display for the noblest efforts of art, of his wealth, his manners, of the deference paid to him by Porbus. The mysterious picture, the work of patience on which he had wrought so long in secret, was doubtless a work of genius, for the head of the Virgin which young Poussin had admired so frankly was beautiful even beside Mabuse's *Adam*—there was no mistaking the imperial manner of one of the princes of art. Everything combined to set the old man beyond the limits of human nature.

Out of the wealth of fancies in Nicolas Poussin's brain an idea grew, and gathered shape and clearness. He saw in this supernatural being a complete type of the artist nature, a nature mocking and kindly, barren and prolific, an erratic spirit intrusted with great and manifold powers which she too often abuses, leading sober reason, the Philistine, and sometimes even the amateur forth into a stony wilderness where they see nothing ; but the white-winged maiden herself, wild as her fancies may be, finds epics there and castles and works of art. For Poussin, the enthusiast, the old man, was suddenly transfigured, and became Art incarnate, Art with its mysteries, its vehement passion and its dreams.

' Yes, my dear Porbus,' Frenhofer continued, ' hitherto I have never found a flawless model, a body with outlines of perfect beauty, the carnations—Ah ! where does she live ?' he cried, breaking in upon himself, ' the undiscoverable Venus of the older time, for whom we have sought so often, only to find the scattered gleams of her beauty here and there ? Oh ! to behold once and for one moment, Nature grown perfect and divine, the Ideal at

B

last, I would give all that I possess. . . . Nay, Beauty
divine, I would go to seek thee in the dim land of the
dead ; like Orpheus, I would go down into the Hades of
Art to bring back the life of art from among the shadows
of death.'

'We can go now,' said Porbus to Poussin. 'He
neither hears nor sees us any longer.'

'Let us go to his studio,' said young Poussin, wondering greatly.

'Oh ! the old fox takes care that no one shall enter
it. His treasures are so carefully guarded that it is
impossible for us to come at them. I have not waited
for your suggestion and your fancy to attempt to lay
hands on this mystery by force.'

'So there is a mystery ?'

'Yes,' answered Porbus. 'Old Frenhofer is the only
pupil Mabuse would take. Frenhofer became the
painter's friend, deliverer, and father ; he sacrificed the
greater part of his fortune to enable Mabuse to indulge in
riotous extravagance, and in return Mabuse bequeathed to
him the secret of relief, the power of giving to his figures
the wonderful life, the flower of Nature, the eternal
despair of art, the secret which Mabuse knew so well that
one day when he had sold the flowered brocade suit in
which he should have appeared at the Entry of Charles v.,
he accompanied his master in a suit of paper painted to
resemble the brocade. The peculiar richness and splendour of the stuff struck the Emperor ; he complimented
the old drunkard's patron on the artist's appearance, and
so the trick was brought to light. Frenhofer is a
passionate enthusiast, who sees above and beyond other
painters. He has meditated profoundly on colour, and
the absolute truth of line ; but by the way of much
research he has come to doubt the very existence of the
objects of his search. He says, in moments of despondency, that there is no such thing as drawing, and that
by means of lines we can only reproduce geometrical

figures; but that is overshooting the mark, for by outline and shadow you can reproduce form without any colour at all, which shows that our art, like Nature, is composed of an infinite number of elements. Drawing gives you the skeleton, the anatomical framework, and colour puts the life into it; but life without the skeleton is even more incomplete than a skeleton without life. But there is something else truer still, and it is this—for painters, practice and observation are everything; and when theories and poetical ideas begin to quarrel with the brushes, the end is doubt, as has happened with our good friend, who is half crack-brained enthusiast, half painter. A sublime painter! but, unluckily for him, he was born to riches, and so he has leisure to follow his fancies. Do not you follow his example! Work! painters have no business to think, except brush in hand.'

'We will find a way into his studio!' cried Poussin confidently. He had ceased to heed Porbus's remarks. The other smiled at the young painter's enthusiasm, asked him to come to see him again, and they parted.

Nicolas Poussin went slowly back to the Rue de la Harpe, and passed the modest hostelry where he was lodging without noticing it. A feeling of uneasiness prompted him to hurry up the crazy staircase till he reached a room at the top, a quaint, airy recess under the steep, high-pitched roof common among houses in old Paris. In the one dingy window of the place sat a young girl, who sprang up at once when she heard some one at the door; it was the prompting of love; she had recognised the painter's touch on the latch.

'What is the matter with you?' she asked.

'The matter is . . . is . . . Oh! I have felt that I am a painter! Until to-day I have had doubts, but now I believe in myself! There is the making of a great man in me! Never mind, Gillette, we shall be rich and happy! There is gold at the tips of those brushes——'

He broke off suddenly. The joy faded from his

powerful and earnest face as he compared his vast hopes with his slender resources. The walls were covered with sketches in chalk on sheets of common paper. There were but four canvases in the room. Colours were very costly, and the young painter's palette was almost bare. Yet in the midst of his poverty he possessed and was conscious of the possession of inexhaustible treasures of the heart, of a devouring genius equal to all the tasks that lay before him.

He had been brought to Paris by a nobleman among his friends, or perchance by the consciousness of his powers; and in Paris he had found a mistress, one of those noble and generous souls who choose to suffer by a great man's side, who share his struggles and strive to understand his fancies, accepting their lot of poverty and love as bravely and dauntlessly as other women will set themselves to bear the burden of riches and make a parade of their insensibility. The smile that stole over Gillette's lips filled the garret with golden light, and rivalled the brightness of the sun in heaven. The sun, moreover, does not always shine in heaven, whereas Gillette was always in the garret, absorbed in her passion, occupied by Poussin's happiness and sorrow, consoling the genius which found an outlet in love before art engrossed it.

'Listen, Gillette. Come here.'

The girl obeyed joyously, and sprang upon the painter's knee. Hers was perfect grace and beauty, and the loveliness of spring; she was adorned with all luxuriant fairness of outward form, lighted up by the glow of a fair soul within.

'Oh! God,' he cried; 'I shall never dare to tell her——'

'A secret?' she cried; 'I must know it!'

Poussin was absorbed in his dreams.

'Do tell it me!'

'Gillette, . . . poor beloved heart! . . .'

'Oh ! do you want something of me ? '

'Yes.'

'If you wish me to sit once more for you as I did the other day,' she continued with playful petulance, 'I will never consent to do such a thing again, for your eyes say nothing all the while. You do not think of me at all, and yet you look at me——'

'Would you rather have me draw another woman ? '

'Perhaps—if she were very ugly,' she said.

'Well,' said Poussin gravely, 'and if, for the sake of my fame to come, if to make me a great painter, you must sit to some one else ? '

'You may try me,' she said ; 'you know quite well that I would not.'

Poussin's head sank on her breast ; he seemed to be overpowered by some intolerable joy or sorrow.

'Listen,' she cried, plucking at the sleeve of Poussin's threadbare doublet. 'I told you, Nick, that I would lay down my life for you ; but I never promised you that I in my lifetime would lay down my love.'

'Your love ? ' cried the young artist.

'If I showed myself thus to another, you would love me no longer, and I should feel myself unworthy of you. Obedience to your fancies was a natural and simple thing, was it not ? Even against my own will, I am glad and even proud to do thy dear will. But for another, out upon it ! '

'Forgive me, my Gillette,' said the painter, falling upon his knees ; 'I would rather be beloved than famous. You are fairer than success and honours. There ; fling the pencils away, and burn these sketches ! I have made a mistake. I was meant to love and not to paint. Perish art and all its secrets ! '

Gillette looked admiringly at him, in an ecstasy of happiness ! She was triumphant ; she felt instinctively that art was laid aside for her sake, and flung like a grain of incense at her feet.

'Yet he is only an old man,' Poussin continued ; 'for him you would be a woman, and nothing more. You—so perfect !'

'I must love you indeed !' she cried, ready to sacrifice even love's scruples to the lover who had given up so much for her sake ; 'but I should bring about my own ruin. Ah ! to ruin myself, to lose everything for you ! . . . It is a very glorious thought ! Ah ! but you will forget me. Oh ! what evil thought is this that has come to you ?'

'I love you, and yet I thought of it,' he said, with something like remorse. 'Am I so base a wretch ?'

'Let us consult Père Hardouin,' she said.

'No, no ! let it be a secret between us.'

'Very well ; I will do it. But you must not be there,' she said. 'Stay at the door with your dagger in your hand ; and if I call, rush in and kill the painter.'

Poussin forgot everything but art. He held Gillette tightly in his arms.

'He loves me no longer !' thought Gillette when she was alone. She repented of her resolution already.

But to these misgivings there soon succeeded a sharper pain, and she strove to banish a hideous thought that arose in her own heart. It seemed to her that her own love had grown less already, with a vague suspicion that the painter had fallen somewhat in her eyes.

II. CATHERINE LESCAULT

Three months after Poussin and Porbus met, the latter went to see Master Frenhofer. The old man had fallen a victim to one of those profound and spontaneous fits of discouragement that are caused, according to medical logicians, by indigestion, flatulence, fever, or enlargement of the spleen ; or, if you take the opinion of the Spiritualists, by the imperfections of our moral nature. The good man had simply overworked himself in putting the finishing touches to his mysterious picture. He was lounging in a huge carved oak chair, covered with black leather, and did not change his listless attitude, but glanced at Porbus like a man who has settled down into low spirits.

'Well, master,' said Porbus, 'was the ultramarine bad that you sent for to Bruges? Is the new white difficult to grind? Is the oil poor, or are the brushes recalcitrant?'

'Alas!' cried the old man, 'for a moment I thought that my work was finished; but I am sure that I am mistaken in certain details, and I cannot rest until I have cleared my doubts. I am thinking of travelling. I am going to Turkey, to Greece, to Asia, in quest of a model, so as to compare my picture with the different living forms of Nature. Perhaps,' and a smile of contentment stole over his face, 'perhaps I have Nature herself up there. At times I am half afraid that a breath may waken her, and that she will escape me.'

He rose to his feet as if to set out at once.

'Aha!' said Porbus, 'I have come just in time to save you the trouble and expense of a journey.'

'What?' asked Frenhofer in amazement.

'Young Poussin is loved by a woman of incomparable and flawless beauty. But, dear master, if he consents to lend her to you, at the least you ought to let us see your work.'

The old man stood motionless and completely dazed.

'What!' he cried piteously at last, 'show you my creation, my bride? Rend the veil that has kept my happiness sacred? It would be an infamous profanation. For ten years I have lived with her; she is mine, mine alone; she loves me. Has she not smiled at me, at each stroke of the brush upon the canvas? She has a soul— the soul that I have given her. She would blush if any

eyes but mine should rest on her. To exhibit her!
Where is the husband, the lover so vile as to bring the
woman he loves to dishonour? When you paint a
picture for the court, you do not put your whole soul
into it; to courtiers you sell lay figures duly coloured.
My painting is no painting, it is a sentiment, a passion.
She was born in my studio, there she must dwell in
maiden solitude, and only when clad can she issue thence.
Poetry and women only lay the last veil aside for their
lovers. Have we Rafael's model, Ariosto's Angelica,
Dante's Beatrice? Nay, only their form and semblance.
But this picture, locked away above in my studio, is an
exception in our art. It is not a canvas, it is a woman—
a woman with whom I talk. I share her thoughts, her
tears, her laughter. Would you have me fling aside
these ten years of happiness like a cloak? Would you
have me cease at once to be father, lover, and creator?
She is not a creature, but a creation.

'Bring your young painter here. I will give him my
treasures; I will give him pictures by Correggio and
Michel Angelo and Titian; I will kiss his footprints in
the dust; but—make him my rival! Shame on me. Ah!
ah! I am a lover first, and then a painter. Yes, with
my latest sigh I could find strength to burn my *Belle
Noiseuse*; but—compel her to endure the gaze of a stranger,
a young man and a painter!—Ah! no, no! I would
kill him on the morrow who should sully her with a
glance! Nay, you, my friend, I would kill you with
my own hands in a moment if you did not kneel in
reverence before her! Now, will you have me submit my idol to the careless eyes and senseless criticisms
of fools? Ah! love is a mystery; it can only live
hidden in the depths of the heart. You say, even to
your friend, " Behold her whom I love," and there is
an end of love.'

The old man seemed to have grown young again;
there was light and life in his eyes, and a faint flush of

red in his pale face. His hands shook. Porbus was so amazed by the passionate vehemence of Frenhofer's words that he knew not what to reply to this utterance of an emotion as strange as it was profound. Was Frenhofer sane or mad? Had he fallen a victim to some freak of the artist's fancy? or were these ideas of his produced by that strange lightheadedness which comes over us during the long travail of a work of art. Would it be possible to come to terms with this singular passion?

Harassed by all these doubts, Porbus spoke—'Is it not woman for woman?' he said. 'Does not Poussin submit his mistress to your gaze?'

'What is she?' retorted the other. 'A mistress who will be false to him sooner or later. Mine will be faithful to me for ever.'

'Well, well,' said Porbus, 'let us say no more about it. But you may die before you will find such flawless beauty as hers, even in Asia, and then your picture will be left unfinished.

'Oh! it is finished,' said Frenhofer. 'Standing before it you would think that it was a living woman lying on the velvet couch beneath the shadow of the curtains. Perfumes are burning on a golden tripod by her side. You would be tempted to lay your hand upon the tassel of the cord that holds back the curtains; it would seem to you that you saw her breast rise and fall as she breathed; that you beheld the living Catherine Lescault, the beautiful courtesan whom men called *La Belle Noiseuse*. And yet—if I could but be sure——'

'Then go to Asia,' returned Porbus, noticing a certain indecision in Frenhofer's face. And with that Porbus made a few steps towards the door.

By that time Gillette and Nicolas Poussin had reached Frenhofer's house. The girl drew away her arm from her lover's as she stood on the threshold, and shrank back as if some presentiment flashed through her mind.

'Oh! what have I come to do here?' she asked of her lover in low vibrating tones, with her eyes fixed on his.

'Gillette, I have left you to decide; I am ready to obey you in everything. You are my conscience and my glory. Go home again; I shall be happier, perhaps, if you do not——'

'Am I my own when you speak to me like that? No, no; I am like a child.—Come,' she added, seemingly with a violent effort; 'if our love dies, if I plant a long regret in my heart, your fame will be the reward of my obedience to your wishes, will it not? Let us go in. I shall still live on as a memory on your palette; that shall be life for me afterwards.'

The door opened, and the two lovers encountered Porbus, who was surprised by the beauty of Gillette, whose eyes were full of tears. He hurried her, trembling from head to foot, into the presence of the old painter.

'Here!' he cried, 'is she not worth all the master-pieces in the world!'

Frenhofer trembled. There stood Gillette in the artless and childlike attitude of some timid and innocent Georgian, carried off by brigands, and confronted with a slave merchant. A shame-fast red flushed her face, her eyes drooped, her hands hung by her side, her strength seemed to have failed her, her tears protested against this outrage. Poussin cursed himself in despair that he should have brought his fair treasure from its hiding-place. The lover overcame the artist, and countless doubts assailed Poussin's heart when he saw youth dawn in the old man's eyes, as, like a painter, he discerned every line of the form hidden beneath the young girl's vesture. Then the lover's savage jealousy awoke.

'Gillette!' he cried, 'let us go.'

The girl turned joyously at the cry and the tone in which it was uttered, raised her eyes to his, looked at him, and fled to his arms.

'Ah! then you love me,' she cried; 'you love me!' and she burst into tears.

She had spirit enough to suffer in silence, but she had no strength to hide her joy.

'Oh! leave her with me for one moment,' said the old painter, 'and you shall compare her with my *Catherine* ... yes—I consent.'

Frenhofer's words likewise came from him like a lover's cry. His vanity seemed to be engaged for his semblance of womanhood; he anticipated the triumph of the beauty of his own creation over the beauty of the living girl.

'Do not give him time to change his mind!' cried Porbus, striking Poussin on the shoulder. 'The flower of love soon fades, but the flower of art is immortal.'

'Then am I only a woman now for him?' said Gillette. She was watching Poussin and Porbus closely.

She raised her head proudly; she glanced at Frenhofer, and her eyes flashed; then as she saw how her lover had fallen again to gazing at the portrait which he had taken at first for a Giorgione—

'Ah!' she cried; 'let us go up to the studio. He never gave me such a look.'

The sound of her voice recalled Poussin from his dreams.

'Old man,' he said, 'do you see this blade? I will plunge it into your heart at the first cry from this young girl; I will set fire to your house, and no one shall leave it alive. Do you understand?'

Nicolas Poussin scowled, every word was a menace. Gillette took comfort from the young painter's bearing, and yet more from that gesture, and almost forgave him for sacrificing her to his art and his glorious future.

Porbus and Poussin stood at the door of the studio and looked at each other in silence. At first the painter of the Saint Mary of Egypt hazarded some exclamations: 'Ah! she has taken off her clothes; he told her to come into the light—he is comparing the two!' but the sight of the deep distress in Poussin's face suddenly silenced him; and though old painters no longer feel these scruples, so petty in the presence of art, he admired them because they were so natural and gracious in the lover. The young man kept his hand on the hilt of his dagger, and his ear was almost glued to the door. The two men standing in the shadow might have been conspirators waiting for the hour when they might strike down a tyrant.

'Come in, come in,' cried the old man. He was radiant with delight. 'My work is perfect. I can show her now with pride. Never shall painter, brushes, colours, light, and canvas produce a rival for *Catherine Lescault*, the beautiful courtesan!'

Porbus and Poussin, burning with eager curiosity, hurried into a vast studio. Everything was in disorder and covered with dust, but they saw a few pictures here and there upon the wall. They stopped first of all in admiration before the life-sized figure of a woman partially draped.

'Oh! never mind that,' said Frenhofer; 'that is a rough daub that I made, a study, a pose, it is nothing. These are my failures,' he went on, indicating the enchanting compositions upon the walls of the studio.

This scorn for such works of art struck Porbus and Poussin dumb with amazement. They looked round for the picture of which he had spoken, and could not discover it.

'Look here!' said the old man. His hair was disordered, his face aglow with a more than human exaltation, his eyes glittered, he breathed hard like a young lover frenzied by love.

'Aha!' he cried, 'you did not expect to see such perfection! You are looking for a picture, and you see a woman before you. There is such depth in that canvas, the atmosphere is so true that you cannot distinguish it from the air that surrounds us. Where is

art ?   Art has vanished, it is invisible !   It is the form
of a living girl that you see before you.   Have I not
caught the very hues of life, the spirit of the living line that
defines the figure.   Is there not the effect produced there
like that which all natural objects present in the atmosphere about them, or fishes in the water ?   Do you see how
the figure stands out against the background ?   Does it
not seem to you that you could pass your hand along the
back ?   But then for seven years I studied and watched
how the daylight blends with the objects on which it falls.
And the hair, the light pours over it like a flood, does it
not ? . . . Ah ! she breathed, I am sure that she breathed !
Her breast—ah, see !   Who would not fall on his knees
before her ?   Her pulses throb.   She will rise to her
feet.   Wait !'

'Do you see anything ?' Poussin asked of Porbus.

'No . . . do you ?'

'I see nothing.'

The two painters left the old man to his ecstasy, and
tried to ascertain whether the light that fell full upon
the canvas had in some way neutralised all the effect for
them.   They moved to the right and left of the picture ;
then they came in front, bending down and standing
upright by turns.

'Yes, yes, it is really canvas,' said Frenhofer, who
mistook the nature of this minute investigation.

'Look ! the canvas is on a stretcher, here is the easel ;
indeed, here are my colours, my brushes,' and he took up
a brush and held it out to them, all unsuspicious of their
thought.

'The old *lansquenet* is laughing at us,' said Poussin,
coming once more towards the supposed picture.   'I
can see nothing there but confused masses of colour
and a multitude of fantastical lines that go to make a
dead wall of paint.'

'We are mistaken, look !' said Porbus.

In a corner of the canvas as they came nearer, they

distinguished a bare foot emerging from the chaos of colour, half-tints and vague shadows that made up a dim formless fog. Its living delicate beauty held them spell-bound. This fragment that had escaped an incomprehensible, slow, and gradual destruction seemed to them like the Parian marble torso of some Venus emerging from the ashes of a ruined town.

'There is a woman beneath,' exclaimed Porbus, calling Poussin's attention to the coats of paint with which the old artist had overlaid and concealed his work in the quest of perfection.

Both artists turned involuntarily to Frenhofer. They began to have some understanding, vague though it was, of the ecstasy in which he lived.

'He believes it in all good faith,' said Porbus.

'Yes, my friend,' said the old man, rousing himself from his dreams, 'it needs faith, faith in art, and you must live for long with your work to produce such a creation. What toil some of those shadows have cost me. Look! there is a faint shadow there upon the cheek beneath the eyes—if you saw that on a human face, it would seem to you that you could never render it with paint. Do you think that that effect has not cost unheard-of toil?

'But not only so, dear Porbus. Look closely at my work, and you will understand more clearly what I was saying as to methods of modelling and outline. Look at the high lights on the bosom, and see how by touch on touch, thickly laid on, I have raised the surface so that it catches the light itself and blends it with the lustrous whiteness of the high lights, and how by an opposite process, by flattening the surface of the paint, and leaving no trace of the passage of the brush, I have succeeded in softening the contours of my figure and enveloping them in half-tints until the very idea of drawing, of the means by which the effect is produced, fades away, and the picture has the roundness and relief of nature.

Come closer. You will see the manner of working better; at a little distance it cannot be seen. There! Just there, it is, I think, very plainly to be seen,' and with the tip of his brush he pointed out a patch of transparent colour to the two painters.

Porbus, laying a hand on the old artist's shoulder, turned to Poussin with a 'Do you know that in him we see a very great painter?'

'He is even more of a poet than a painter,' Poussin answered gravely.

'There,' Porbus continued, as he touched the canvas, 'lies the utmost limit of our art on earth.'

'Beyond that point it loses itself in the skies,' said Poussin.

'What joys lie there on that piece of canvas!' exclaimed Porbus.

The old man, deep in his own musings, smiled at the woman he alone beheld, and did not hear.

'But sooner or later he will find out that there is nothing there!' cried Poussin.

'Nothing on my canvas!' said Frenhofer, looking in turn at either painter and at his picture.

'What have you done?' muttered Porbus, turning to Poussin.

The old man clutched the young painter's arm and said, 'Do you see nothing? clodpate! Huguenot! varlet! cullion! What brought you here into my studio? —My good Porbus,' he went on, as he turned to the painter, 'are you also making a fool of me? Answer! I am your friend. Tell me, have I ruined my picture after all?'

Porbus hesitated and said nothing, but there was such intolerable anxiety in the old man's white face that he pointed to the easel.

'Look!' he said.

Frenhofer looked for a moment at his picture, and staggered back.

'Nothing! nothing! After ten years of work . . .'

He sat down and wept.

'So I am a dotard, a madman, I have neither talent nor power! I am only a rich man, who works for his own pleasure, and makes no progress. I have done nothing after all!'

He looked through his tears at his picture. Suddenly he rose and stood proudly before the two painters.

'By the body and blood of Christ,' he cried with flashing eyes, 'you are jealous! You would have me think that my picture is a failure because you want to steal her from me! Ah! I see her, I see her,' he cried, 'she is marvellously beautiful . . .'

At that moment Poussin heard the sound of weeping; Gillette was crouching forgotten in a corner. All at once the painter once more became the lover. 'What is it, my angel?' he asked her.

'Kill me!' she sobbed. 'I must be a vile thing if I love you still, for I despise you. . . . I admire you, and I loathe you! I love you, and I feel that I hate you even now.'

While Gillette's words sounded in Poussin's ears, Frenhofer drew a green serge covering over his *Catherine* with the sober deliberation of a jeweller who locks his drawers when he suspects his visitors to be expert thieves. He gave the two painters a profoundly astute glance that expressed to the full his suspicions and his contempt for them, saw them out of his studio with impetuous haste and in silence, until from the threshold of his house he bade them 'Good-bye, my young friends!'

That farewell struck a chill of dread into the two painters. Porbus, in anxiety, went again on the morrow to see Frenhofer, and learned that he had died in the night after burning his canvases.

Paris, *February* 1832.

CHRIST IN FLANDERS

To Marcelline Desbordes-Valmore, a daughter of Flanders, of whom these modern days may well be proud, I dedicate this quaint legend of old Flanders.
De Balzac.

At a dimly remote period in the history of Brabant, communication between the Island of Cadzand and the Flemish coast was kept up by a boat which carried passengers from one shore to the other. Middelburg, the chief town in the island, destined to become so famous in the annals of Protestantism, at that time only numbered some two or three hundred hearths; and the prosperous town of Ostend was an obscure haven, a straggling village where pirates dwelt in security among the fishermen and the few poor merchants who lived in the place.

But though the town of Ostend consisted altogether of some score of houses and three hundred cottages, huts or hovels built of the driftwood of wrecked vessels, it nevertheless rejoiced in the possession of a governor, a garrison, a forked gibbet, a convent, and a burgomaster, in short, in all the institutions of an advanced civilisation.

Who reigned over Brabant and Flanders in those days? On this point tradition is mute. Let us confess at once that this tale savours strongly of the marvellous, the mysterious, and the vague; elements which Flemish narrators have infused into a story retailed so often to gatherings of workers on winter evenings, that the versions vary widely in poetic merit and incongruity of

c

detail. It has been told by every generation, handed
down by grandames at the fireside, narrated night and
day, and the chronicle has changed its complexion somewhat in every age. Like some great building that has
suffered many modifications of successive generations of
architects, some sombre weather-beaten pile, the delight
of a poet, the story would drive the commentator
and the industrious winnower of words, facts, and dates
to despair. The narrator believes in it, as all superstitious
minds in Flanders likewise believe; and is not a whit
wiser nor more credulous than his audience. But as it
would be impossible to make a harmony of all the
different renderings, here are the outlines of the story;
stripped, it may be, of its picturesque quaintness, but with
all its bold disregard of historical truth, and its moral
teaching approved by religion -a myth, the blossom of
imaginative fancy; an allegory that the wise may interpret to suit themselves. To each his own pasturage,
and the task of separating the tares from the wheat.

The boat that served to carry passengers from the
Island of Cadzand to Ostend was upon the point of
departure; but before the skipper loosed the chain that
secured the shallop to the little jetty, where people
embarked, he blew a horn several times, to warn late
lingerers, this being his last journey that day. Night
was falling. It was scarcely possible to see the coast of
Flanders by the dying fires of the sunset, or to make out
upon the hither shore any forms of belated passengers
hurrying along the wall of the dykes that surrounded the
open country, or among the tall reeds of the marshes.
The boat was full.

'What are you waiting for? Let us put off!' they
cried.

Just at that moment a man appeared a few paces from
the jetty, to the surprise of the skipper, who had heard
no sound of footsteps. The traveller seemed to have

sprung up from the earth, like a peasant who had laid himself down on the ground to wait till the boat should start, and had slept till the sound of the horn awakened him. Was he a thief? or some one belonging to the custom-house or the police?

As soon as the man appeared on the jetty to which the boat was moored, seven persons who were standing in the stern of the shallop hastened to sit down on the benches, so as to leave no room for the new-comer. It was the swift and instinctive working of the aristocratic spirit, an impulse of exclusiveness that comes from the rich man's heart. Four of the seven personages belonged to the most aristocratic families in Flanders. First among them was a young knight with two beautiful greyhounds; his long hair flowed from beneath a jewelled cap; he clanked his gilded spurs, curled the ends of his moustache from time to time with a swaggering grace, and looked round disdainfully on the rest of the crew. A high-born damsel, with a falcon on her wrist, only spoke with her mother or with a churchman of high rank, who was evidently a relation. All these persons made a great deal of noise, and talked among themselves as though there were no one else in the boat; yet close beside them sat a man of great importance in the district, a stout burgher of Bruges, wrapped about with a vast cloak. His servant, armed to the teeth, had set down a couple of bags filled with gold at his side. Next to the burgher came a man of learning, a doctor of the University of Louvain, who was travelling with his clerk. This little group of folk, who looked contemptuously at each other, was separated from the passengers in the forward part of the boat by the bench of rowers.

The belated traveller glanced about him as he stepped on board, saw that there was no room for him in the stern, and went to the bows in quest of a seat. They were all poor people there. At first sight of the bare-headed man in the brown camlet coat and trunk-hose,

and plain stiff linen collar, they noticed that he wore
no ornaments, carried no cap nor bonnet in his hand,
and had neither sword nor purse at his girdle, and one
and all took him for a burgomaster sure of his authority, a worthy and kindly burgomaster like so many
a Fleming of old times, whose homely features and
characters have been immortalised by Flemish painters.
The poorer passengers, therefore, received him with
demonstrations of respect that provoked scornful titter-
ing at the other end of the boat.   An old soldier, inured
to toil and hardship, gave up his place on the bench to
the new-comer, and seated himself on the edge of the
vessel, keeping his balance by planting his feet against
one of those transverse beams, like the backbone of a
fish, that hold the planks of a boat together.   A young
mother, who bore her baby in her arms, and seemed to
belong to the working class in Ostend, moved aside to
make room for the stranger.   There was neither servility
nor scorn in her manner of doing this; it was a simple
sign of the goodwill by which the poor, who know by
long experience the value of a service and the warmth
that fellowship brings, give expression to the openhearted-
ness and the natural impulses of their souls ; so artlessly do
they reveal their good qualities and their defects.   The
stranger thanked her by a gesture full of gracious dignity,
and took his place between the young mother and the old
soldier.   Immediately behind him sat a peasant and his
son, a boy ten years of age.   A beggar woman, old,
wrinkled, and clad in rags, was crouching, with her
almost empty wallet, on a great coil of rope that lay in
the prow.   One of the rowers, an old sailor, who had
known her in the days of her beauty and prosperity, had
let her come in 'for the love of God,' in the beautiful
phrase that the common people use.

'Thank you kindly, Thomas,' the old woman had said.
'I will say two *Paters* and two *Aves* for you in my
prayers to-night.'

The skipper blew his horn for the last time, looked along the silent shore, flung off the chain, ran along the side of the boat, and took up his position at the helm. He looked at the sky, and as soon as they were out in the open sea, he shouted to the men : 'Pull away, pull with all your might! The sea is smiling at a squall, the witch! I can feel the swell by the way the rudder works, and the storm in my wounds.'

The nautical phrases, unintelligible to ears unused to the sound of the sea, seemed to put fresh energy into the oars; they kept time together, the rhythm of the movement was still even and steady, but quite unlike the previous manner of rowing; it was as if a cantering horse had broken into a gallop. The gay company seated in the stern amused themselves by watching the brawny arms, the tanned faces, and sparkling eyes of the rowers, the play of the tense muscles, the physical and mental forces that were being exerted to bring them for a trifling toll across the channel. So far from pitying the rowers' distress, they pointed out the men's faces to each other, and laughed at the grotesque expressions on the faces of the crew who were straining every muscle; but in the fore part of the boat the soldier, the peasant, and the old beggar woman watched the sailors with the sympathy naturally felt by toilers who live by the sweat of their brow and know the rough struggle, the strenuous excitement of effort. These folk, moreover, whose lives were spent in the open air, had all seen the warnings of danger in the sky, and their faces were grave. The young mother rocked her child, singing an old hymn of the Church for a lullaby.

'If we ever get there at all,' the soldier remarked to the peasant, ' it will be because the Almighty is bent on keeping us alive.'

'Ah! He is the Master,' said the old woman, ' but I think it will be His good pleasure to take us to Himself.

Just look at that light down there . . .' and she nodded her head as she spoke towards the sunset.

Streaks of fiery red glared from behind the masses of crimson-flushed brown cloud that seemed about to unloose a furious gale. There was a smothered murmur of the sea, a moaning sound that seemed to come from the depths, a low warning growl, such as a dog gives when he only means mischief as yet. After all, Ostend was not far away. Perhaps painting, like poetry, could not prolong the existence of the picture presented by sea and sky at that moment beyond the time of its actual duration. Art demands vehement contrasts, wherefore artists usually seek out Nature's most striking effects, doubtless because they despair of rendering the great and glorious charm of her daily moods; yet the human soul is often stirred as deeply by her calm as by her emotion, and by silence as by storm.

For a moment no one spoke on board the boat. Every one watched that sea and sky, either with some presentiment of danger, or because they felt the influence of the religious melancholy that takes possession of nearly all of us at the close of the day, the hour of prayer, when all nature is hushed save for the voices of the bells. The sea gleamed pale and wan, but its hues changed, and the surface took all the colours of steel. The sky was almost overspread with livid grey, but down in the west there were long narrow bars like streaks of blood; while lines of bright light in the eastern sky, sharp and clean as if drawn by the tip of a brush, were separated by folds of cloud, like the wrinkles on an old man's brow. The whole scene made a background of ashen greys and half-tints, in strong contrast to the bale-fires of the sunset. If written language might borrow of spoken language some of the bold figures of speech invented by the people, it might be said with the soldier that ' the weather had been routed,' or, as the peasant would say, ' the sky glowered like an executioner.' Suddenly a wind arose from the quarter of the sunset, and the skipper, who never took his eyes off the sea, saw the swell on the horizon line, and cried—

'Stop rowing!'

The sailors stopped immediately, and let their oars lie on the water.

'The skipper is right,' said Thomas coolly. A great wave caught up the boat, carried it high on its crest, only to plunge it, as it were, into the trough of the sea that seemed to yawn for them. At this mighty upheaval, this sudden outbreak of the wrath of the sea, the company in the stern turned pale, and sent up a terrible cry.

'We are lost!'

'Oh, not yet!' said the skipper calmly.

As he spoke, the clouds immediately above their heads were torn asunder by the vehemence of the wind. The grey mass was rent and scattered east and west with ominous speed, a dim uncertain light from the rift in the sky fell full upon the boat, and the travellers beheld each other's faces. All of them, the noble and the wealthy, the sailors and the poor passengers alike, were amazed for a moment by the appearance of the last comer. His golden hair, parted upon his calm, serene forehead, fell in thick curls about his shoulders; and his face, sublime in its sweetness and radiant with divine love, stood out against the surrounding gloom. He had no contempt for death; he knew that he should not die. But if at the first the company in the stern forgot for a moment the implacable fury of the storm that threatened their lives, selfishness and their habits of life soon prevailed again.

'How lucky that stupid burgomaster is, not to see the risks we are all running! He is just like a dog, he will die without a struggle,' said the doctor.

He had scarcely pronounced this highly judicious dictum when the storm unloosed all its legions. The wind blew from every quarter of the heavens, the boat span round like a top, and the sea broke in.

'Oh! my poor child! My poor child! . . . Who will save my baby?' the mother cried in a heartrending voice.

'You yourself will save it,' the stranger said.

The thrilling tones of that voice went to the young mother's heart and brought hope with them; she heard the gracious words through all the whistling of the wind and the shrieks of the passengers.

'Holy Virgin of Good Help, who art at Antwerp, I promise thee a thousand pounds of wax and a statue, if thou wilt rescue me from this!' cried the burgher, kneeling upon his bags of gold.

'The Virgin is no more at Antwerp than she is here,' was the doctor's comment on this appeal.

'She is in heaven,' said a voice that seemed to come from the sea.'

'Who said that?'

''Tis the devil!' exclaimed the servant. 'He is scoffing at the Virgin of Antwerp.'

'Let us have no more of your Holy Virgin at present,' the skipper cried to the passengers. 'Put your hands to the scoops and bale the water out of the boat.—And the rest of you,' he went on, addressing the sailors, 'pull with all your might! Now is the time; in the name of the devil who is leaving you in this world, be your own Providence! Every one knows that the channel is fearfully dangerous; I have been to and fro across it these thirty years. Am I facing a storm for the first time to-night?'

He stood at the helm, and looked, as before, at his boat and at the sea and sky in turn.

'The skipper always laughs at everything,' muttered Thomas.

'Will God leave us to perish along with those wretched creatures?' asked the haughty damsel of the handsome cavalier.

'No, no, noble maiden. . . . Listen!' and he caught

her by the waist and said in her ear, ' I can swim ; say nothing about it ! I will hold you by your fair hair and bring you safely to the shore ; but I can only save you.'

The girl looked at her aged mother. The lady was on her knees entreating absolution of the Bishop, who did not heed her. In the beautiful eyes the knight read a vague feeling of filial piety, and spoke in a smothered voice.

' Submit yourself to the will of God. If it is His pleasure to take your mother to Himself, it will doubtless be for her happiness—in the other world,' he added, and his voice dropped still lower. ' And for ours in this,' he thought within himself.

The Dame of Rupelmonde was lady of seven fiefs beside the barony of Gâvres.

The girl felt the longing for life in her heart, and for love that spoke through the handsome adventurer, a young miscreant who haunted churches in search of a prize, an heiress to marry, or ready money. The Bishop bestowed his benison on the waves, and bade them be calm ; it was all that he could do. He thought of his concubine, and of the delicate feast with which she would welcome him ; perhaps at that very moment she was bathing, perfuming herself, robing herself in velvet, fastening her necklace and her jewelled clasps, and the perverse Bishop so far from thinking of the power of Holy Church, of his duty to comfort Christians and exhort them to trust in God, that worldly regrets and lover's sighs mingled with the holy words of the breviary. By the dim light that shone on the pale faces of the company, it was possible to see their differing expressions as the boat was lifted high in air by a wave, to be cast back into the dark depths; the shallop quivered like a fragile leaf, the plaything of the north wind in the autumn; the hull creaked, it seemed ready to go to pieces. Fearful shrieks went up, followed by an awful silence.

There was a strange difference between the behaviour

of the folk in the bows and that of the rich or great people at the other end of the boat. The young mother clasped her infant tightly to her breast every time that a great wave threatened to engulf the fragile vessel; but she clung to the hope that the stranger's words had set in her heart. Each time that her eyes turned to his face she drew fresh faith at the sight, the strong faith of a helpless woman, a mother's faith. She lived by that divine promise, the loving words from his lips; the simple creature waited trustingly for them to be fulfilled, and scarcely feared the danger any longer.

The soldier, holding fast to the vessel's side, never took his eyes off the strange visitor. He copied on his own rough and swarthy features the imperturbability of the other's face, applying to this task the whole strength of a will and intelligence but little corrupted in the course of a life of mechanical and passive obedience. So emulous was he of a calm and tranquil courage greater than his own, that at last, perhaps unconsciously, something of that mysterious nature passed into his own soul. His admiration became an instinctive zeal for this man, a boundless love for and belief in him, such a love as soldiers feel for their leader when he has the power of swaying other men, when the halo of victories surrounds him, and the magical fascination of genius is felt in all that he does. The poor outcast was murmuring to herself—

'Ah! miserable wretch that I am! Have I not suffered enough to expiate the sins of my youth? Ah! wretched woman, why did you lead the gay life of a frivolous Frenchwoman? why did you devour the goods of God with churchmen, the substance of the poor with extortioners and fleecers of the poor? Oh! I have sinned indeed!—Oh my God! my God! let me finish my time in hell here in this world of misery.'

And again she cried, 'Holy Virgin, Mother of God, have pity upon me!'

'Be comforted, mother. God is not a Lombard

usurer. I may have killed people good and bad at random in my time, but I am not afraid of the resurrection.'

'Ah! master lancepesade, how happy those fair ladies are, to be so near to a bishop, a holy man! They will get absolution for their sins,' said the old woman. 'Oh! if I could only hear a priest say to me, "Thy sins are forgiven!" I should believe it then.'

The stranger turned towards her, and the goodness in his face made her tremble.

'Have faith,' he said, 'and you will be saved.'

'May God reward you, good sir,' she answered. 'If what you say is true, I will go on pilgrimage barefooted to Our Lady of Loretto to pray to her for you and for me.'

The two peasants, father and son, were silent, patient, and submissive to the will of God, like folk whose wont it is to fall in instinctively with the ways of Nature like cattle. At the one end of the boat stood riches, pride, learning, debauchery, and crime—human society, such as art and thought and education and worldly interests and laws have made it; and at this end there was terror and wailing, innumerable different impulses all repressed by hideous doubts—at this end, and at this only, the agony of fear.

Above all these human lives stood a strong man, the skipper; no doubts assailed him, the chief, the king, the fatalist among them. He was trusting in himself rather than in Providence, crying, 'Bale away!' instead of 'Holy Virgin,' defying the storm, in fact, and struggling with the sea like a wrestler.

But the helpless poor at the other end of the wherry! The mother rocking on her bosom the little one who smiled at the storm, the woman once so frivolous and gay, and now tormented with bitter remorse; the old soldier covered with scars, a mutilated life the sole reward of his unflagging loyalty and faithfulness. This veteran could scarcely count on the morsel of bread soaked in tears to keep the life in him, yet he was always

ready to laugh, and went his way merrily, happy when
he could drown his glory in the depths of a pot of beer,
or could tell tales of the wars to the children who
admired him, leaving his future with a light heart in the
hands of God.   Lastly, there were the two peasants, used
to hardships and toil, labour incarnate, the labour by
which the world lives. These simple folk were indifferent
to thought and its treasures, ready to sink them all in a
belief; and their faith was but so much the more vigorous because they had never disputed about it nor
analysed it. Such a nature is a virgin soil, conscience
has not been tampered with, feeling is deep and strong;
repentance, trouble, love, and work have developed,
purified, concentrated, and increased their force of will a
hundred times, the will—the one thing in man that
resembles what learned doctors call the Soul.

The boat, guided by the well-nigh miraculous skill of
the steersman, came almost within sight of Ostend, when,
not fifty paces from the shore, she was suddenly struck by
a heavy sea and capsized. The stranger with the light
about his head spoke to this little world of drowning
creatures—

'Those who have faith shall be saved; let them follow
me!'

He stood upright, and walked with a firm step upon
the waves. The young mother at once took her child
in her arms, and followed at his side across the sea. The
soldier too sprang up, saying in his homely fashion, 'Ah!
nom d'un pipe! I would follow *you* to the devil'; and
without seeming astonished by it, he walked on the
water. The old worn-out sinner, believing in the
omnipotence of God, also followed the stranger.

The two peasants said to each other, 'If they are
walking on the sea, why should we not do as they do?'
and they also arose and hastened after the others. Thomas
tried to follow, but his faith tottered; he sank in the sea
more than once, and rose again, but the third time he

also walked on the sea. The bold steersman clung like a remora to the wreck of his boat. The miser had had faith, and had risen to go, but he tried to take his gold with him, and it was his gold that dragged him down to the bottom. The learned man had scoffed at the charlatan and at the fools who listened to him ; and when he heard the mysterious stranger propose to the passengers that they should walk on the waves, he began to laugh, and the ocean swallowed him. The girl was dragged down into the depths by her lover. The Bishop and the older lady went to the bottom, heavily laden with sins, it may be, but still more heavily laden with incredulity and confidence in idols, weighted down by devotion, into which alms-deeds and true religion entered but little.

The faithful flock, who walked with a firm step high and dry above the surge, heard all about them the dreadful whistling of the blast ; great billows broke across their path, but an irresistible force cleft a way for them through the sea. These believing ones saw through the spray a dim speck of light flickering in the window of a fisherman's hut on the shore, and each one, as he pushed on bravely towards the light, seemed to hear the voice of his fellow crying, 'Courage !' through all the roaring of the surf ; yet no one had spoken a word—so absorbed was each by his own peril. In this way they reached the shore.

When they were all seated near the fisherman's fire, they looked round in vain for their guide with the light about him. The sea washed up the steersman at the base of the cliff on which the cottage stood ; he was clinging with might and main to the plank as a sailor can cling when death stares him in the face ; the MAN went down and rescued the almost exhausted seaman ; then he said, as he held out a succouring hand above the man's head—

'Good, for this once ; but do not try it again ; the example would be too bad.'

He took the skipper on his shoulders, and carried him to the fisherman's door, knocked for admittance for the exhausted man; then, when the door of the humble refuge opened, the Saviour disappeared.

The Convent of Mercy was built for sailors on this spot, where for long afterwards (so it was said) the footprints of Jesus Christ could be seen in the sand; but in 1793, at the time of the French invasion, the monks carried away this precious relic, that bore witness to the Saviour's last visit to earth.

There at the convent I found myself shortly after the Revolution of 1830. I was weary of life. If you had asked me the reason of my despair, I should have found it almost impossible to give it, so languid had grown the soul that was melted within me. The west wind had slackened the springs of my intelligence. A cold, grey light poured down from the heavens, and the murky clouds that passed overhead gave a boding look to the land; all these things, together with the immensity of the sea, said to me, 'Die to-day or die to-morrow, still must we not die?' And then——. I wandered on, musing on the doubtful future, on my blighted hopes. Gnawed by these gloomy thoughts, I turned mechanically into the convent church, with the grey towers that loomed like ghosts through the sea mists. I looked round with no kindling of the imagination at the forest of columns, at the slender arches set aloft upon the leafy capitals, a delicate labyrinth of sculpture. I walked with careless eyes along the side aisles that opened out before me like vast portals, ever turning upon their hinges. It was scarcely possible to see, by the dim light of the autumn day, the sculptured groinings of the roof, the delicate and clean-cut lines of the mouldings of the graceful pointed arches. The organ pipes were mute. There was no sound save the noise of my own footsteps to awaken the mournful echoes lurking in the dark

chapels. I sat down at the base of one of the four
pillars that supported the tower, near the choir. Thence
I could see the whole of the building. I gazed, and no
ideas connected with it arose in my mind. I saw without seeing the mighty maze of pillars, the great rose
windows that hung like a network suspended as by a
miracle in air above the vast doorways. I saw the
doors at the end of the side aisles, the aerial galleries, the
stained glass windows framed in archways, divided by
slender columns, fretted into flower forms and trefoil by
fine filigree work of carved stone. A dome of glass at
the end of the choir sparkled as if it had been built of
precious stones set cunningly. In contrast to the roof
with its alternating spaces of whiteness and colour, the
two aisles lay to right and left in shadow so deep that the
faint grey outlines of their hundred shafts were scarcely
visible in the gloom. I gazed at the marvellous arcades,
the scroll-work, the garlands, the curving lines, and arab-
esques interwoven and interlaced, and strangely lighted,
until by sheer dint of gazing my perceptions became confused, and I stood upon the borderland between illusion
and reality, taken in the snare set for the eyes, and almost
light-headed by reason of the multitudinous changes of
the shapes about me.

Imperceptibly a mist gathered about the carven stone-
work, and I only beheld it through a haze of fine golden
dust, like the motes that hover in the bars of sunlight
slanting through the air of a chamber. Suddenly the
stone lacework of the rose windows gleamed through
this vapour that had made all forms so shadowy. Every
moulding, the edges of every carving, the least detail of
the sculpture was dipped in silver. The sunlight kindled
fires in the stained windows, their rich colours sent out
glowing sparks of light. The shafts began to tremble,
the capitals were gently shaken. A light shudder as of
delight ran through the building, the stones were loosened
in their setting, the wall-spaces swayed with graceful

caution.   Here and there a ponderous pier moved as
solemnly as a dowager when she condescends to complete
a quadrille at the close of a ball.   A few slender and
graceful columns, their heads adorned with wreaths of
trefoil, began to laugh and dance here and there.   Some
of the pointed arches dashed at the tall lancet windows,
who, like ladies of the Middle Ages, wore the armorial
bearings of their houses emblazoned on their golden
robes.   The dance of the mitred arcades with the slender
windows became like a fray at a tourney.

In another moment every stone in the church vibrated,
without leaving its place ; for the organ-pipes spoke, and
I heard divine music mingling with the songs of angels,
an unearthly harmony, accompanied by the deep notes of
the bells, that boomed as the giant towers rocked and
swayed on their square bases.   This strange sabbath
seemed to me the most natural thing in the world ; and
I, who had seen Charles x. hurled from his throne, was
no longer amazed by anything.   Nay, I myself was
gently swaying with a see-saw movement that influenced
my nerves pleasurably in a manner of which it is impossible to give any idea.   Yet in the midst of this heated
riot, the cathedral choir felt cold as if it were a winter
day, and I became aware of a multitude of women, robed
in white, silent, and impassive, sitting there.   The sweet
incense smoke that arose from the censers was grateful
to my soul.   The tall wax candles flickered.   The
lectern, gay as a chanter undone by the treachery of
wine, was skipping about like a peal of Chinese bells.

Then I knew that the whole cathedral was whirling
round so fast that everything appeared to be undisturbed.
The colossal Figure on the crucifix above the altar smiled
upon me with a mingled malice and benevolence that
frightened me ; I turned my eyes away, and marvelled
at the bluish vapour that slid across the pillars, lending
to them an indescribable charm.   Then some graceful
women's forms began to stir on the friezes.   The cherubs

who upheld the heavy columns shook out their wings. I
felt myself uplifted by some divine power that steeped
me in infinite joy, in a sweet and languid rapture. I
would have given my life, I think, to have prolonged
these phantasmagoria for a little, but suddenly a shrill
voice clamoured in my ears—

'Awake and follow me!'

A withered woman took my hand in hers; its icy cold-
ness crept through every nerve. The bones of her face
showed plainly through the sallow, almost olive-tinted
wrinkles of the skin. The shrunken, ice-cold, old woman
wore a black robe, which she trailed in the dust, and
at her throat there was something white, which I
dared not examine. I could scarcely see her wan and
colourless eyes, for they were fixed in a stare upon the
heavens. She drew me after her along the aisles, leaving
a trace of her presence in the ashes that she shook from
her dress. Her bones rattled as she walked, like the
bones of a skeleton; and as we went I heard behind me
the tinkling of a little bell, a thin, sharp sound that rang
through my head like the notes of a harmonica.

'Suffer!' she cried, 'suffer! So it must be!'

We came out of the church; we went through the
dirtiest streets of the town, till we came at last to a
dingy dwelling, and she bade me enter in. She dragged
me with her, calling to me in a harsh, tuneless voice like
a cracked bell—

'Defend me! defend me!'

Together we went up a winding staircase. She
knocked at a door in the darkness, and a mute, like some
familiar of the Inquisition, opened to her. In another
moment we stood in a room hung with ancient, ragged
tapestry, amid piles of old linen, crumpled muslin, and
gilded brass.

'Behold the wealth that shall endure for ever!' said
she.

I shuddered with horror; for just then, by the light of

D

a tall torch and two altar candles, I saw distinctly that this woman was fresh from the graveyard. She had no hair. I turned to fly. She raised her fleshless arm and encircled me with a band of iron set with spikes, and as she raised it a cry went up all about us, the cry of millions of voices—the shouting of the dead!

'It is my purpose to make thee happy for ever,' she said. 'Thou art my son.'

We were sitting before the hearth, the ashes lay cold upon it; the old shrunken woman grasped my hand so tightly in hers that I could not choose but stay. I looked fixedly at her, striving to read the story of her life from the things among which she was crouching. Had she indeed any life in her? It was a mystery. Yet I saw plainly that once she must have been young and beautiful; fair, with all the charm of simplicity, perfect as some Greek statue, with the brow of a vestal.

'Ah! ah!' I cried, 'now I know thee! Miserable woman, why hast thou prostituted thyself? In the age of thy passions, in the time of thy prosperity, the grace and purity of thy youth were forgotten. Forgetful of thy heroic devotion, thy pure life, thy abundant faith, thou didst resign thy primitive power and thy spiritual supremacy for fleshly power. Thy linen vestments, thy couch of moss, the cell in the rock, bright with rays of the Light Divine, was forsaken; thou hast sparkled with diamonds, and shone with the glitter of luxury and pride. Then, grown bold and insolent, seizing and overturning all things in thy course like a courtesan eager for pleasure in her days of splendour, thou hast steeped thyself in blood like some queen stupefied by empery. Dost thou not remember to have been dull and heavy at times, and the sudden marvellous lucidity of other moments; as when Art emerges from an orgy? Oh! poet, painter, and singer, lover of splendid ceremonies and protector of the arts, was thy friendship for art perchance a caprice, that so thou shouldst sleep beneath magnificent canopies?

Was there not a day when, in thy fantastic pride, though chastity and humility were prescribed to thee, thou hadst brought all things beneath thy feet, and set thy foot on the necks of princes ; when earthly dominion, and wealth, and the mind of man bore thy yoke ? Exulting in the abasement of humanity, joying to witness the uttermost lengths to which man's folly would go, thou hast bidden thy lovers walk on all fours, and required of them their lands and wealth, nay, even their wives if they were worth aught to thee. Thou hast devoured millions of men without a cause ; thou hast flung away lives like sand blown by the wind from West to East. Thou hast come down from the heights of thought to sit among the kings of men. Woman ! instead of comforting men, thou hast tormented and afflicted them ! Knowing that thou couldst ask and have, thou hast demanded—blood ! A little flour surely should have contented thee, accustomed as thou hadst been to live on bread and to mingle water with thy wine. Unlike all others in all things, formerly thou wouldst bid thy lovers fast, and they obeyed. Why should thy fancies have led thee to require things impossible ? Why, like a courtesan spoiled by her lovers, hast thou doted on follies, and left those undeceived who sought to explain and justify all thy errors ? Then came the days of thy later passions, terrible like the love of a woman of forty years, with a fierce cry thou hast sought to clasp the whole universe in one last embrace— and thy universe recoiled from thee !

'Then old men succeeded to thy young lovers ; decrepitude came to thy feet and made thee hideous. Yet, even then, men with the eagle power of vision said to thee in a glance, "Thou shalt perish ingloriously, because thou hast fallen away, because thou hast broken the vows of thy maidenhood. The angel with peace written on her forehead, who should have shed light and joy along her path, has been a Messalina, delighting in the circus, in debauchery, and abuse of power. The days of thy virginity cannot return ; henceforward thou shalt be subject to a master. Thy hour has come ; the hand of death is upon thee. Thy heirs believe that thou art rich ; they will kill thee and find nothing. Yet try at least to fling away this raiment no longer in fashion ; be once more as in the days of old !—Nay, thou art dead, and by thy own deed ! ''

'Is not this thy story ?' so I ended. 'Decrepit, toothless, shivering crone, now forgotten, going thy ways without so much as a glance from passers-by ! Why art thou still alive ? What doest thou in that beggar's garb, uncomely and desired of none ? Where are thy riches ? —for what were they spent ? Where are thy treasures ? —what great deeds hast thou done ?'

At this demand, the shrivelled woman raised her bony form, flung off her rags, and grew tall and radiant, smiling as she broke forth from the dark chrysalid sheath. Then like a butterfly, this diaphanous creature emerged, fair and youthful, clothed in white linen, an Indian from creation issuing her palms. Her golden hair rippled over her shoulders, her eyes glowed, a bright mist clung about her, a ring of gold hovered above her head, she shook the flaming blade of a sword towards the spaces of heaven.

'See and believe !' she cried.

And suddenly I saw, afar off, many thousands of cathedrals like the one that I had just quitted ; but these were covered with pictures and with frescoes, and I heard them echo with entrancing music. Myriads of human creatures flocked to these great buildings, swarming about them like ants on an ant-heap. Some were eager to rescue books from oblivion or to copy manuscripts, others were helping the poor, but nearly all were studying. Up above this countless multitude rose giant statues that they had erected in their midst, and by the gleams of a strange light from some luminary as powerful as the sun, I read the inscriptions on the bases of the statues— Science, History, Literature.

The light died out. Again I faced the young girl. Gradually she slipped into the dreary sheath, into the ragged cere-cloths, and became an aged woman again. Her familiar brought her a little dust, and she stirred it into the ashes of her chafing-dish, for the weather was cold and stormy ; and then he lighted for her, whose palaces had been lit with thousands of wax-tapers, a little cresset, that she might see to read her prayers through the hours of night.

'There is no faith left in the earth ! . . .' she said.

In such a perilous plight did I behold the fairest and the greatest, the truest and most life-giving of all Powers.

'Wake up, sir, the doors are just about to be shut,' said a hoarse voice. I turned and beheld the beadle's ugly countenance ; the man was shaking me by the arm, and the cathedral lay wrapped in shadows as a man is wrapped in his cloak.

'Belief,' I said to myself, 'is Life ! I have just witnessed the funeral of a monarchy, now we must defend the Church.'

Paris, *February* 1831.

MELMOTH RECONCILED

To Monsieur le Général Baron de Pommereul, a token of the friendship between our fathers, which survives in their sons.

De Balzac.

THERE is a special variety of human nature obtained in the Social Kingdom by a process analogous to that of the gardener's craft in the Vegetable Kingdom, to wit, by the forcing-house—a species of hybrid which can be raised neither from seed nor from slips. This product is known as the Cashier, an anthropomorphous growth, watered by religious doctrine, trained up in fear of the guillotine, pruned by vice, to flourish on a third floor with an estimable wife by his side and an uninteresting family. The number of cashiers in Paris must always be a problem for the physiologist. Has any one as yet been able to state correctly the terms of the proportion sum wherein the cashier figures as the unknown x? Where will you find the man who shall live with wealth, like a cat with a caged mouse? This man, for further qualification, shall be capable of sitting boxed in behind an iron grating for seven or eight hours a day during seven-eighths of the year, perched upon a cane-seated chair in a space as narrow as a lieutenant's cabin on board a man-of-war. Such a man must be able to defy anchylosis of the knee and thigh joints; he must have a soul above meanness, in order to live meanly; must lose all relish for money by dint of handling it. Demand this peculiar specimen of any creed, educational system, school, or institution you please, and select Paris, that city of fiery ordeals and branch establishment of hell, as the soil in which to plant the said cashier. So be it. Creeds, schools, institutions, and moral systems, all human rules and regulations, great and small, will, one after another, present much the same face that an intimate friend turns upon you when you ask him to lend you a thousand francs. With a dolorous dropping of the jaw, they indicate the guillotine, much as your friend aforesaid will furnish you with the address of the money-lender, pointing you to one of the hundred gates by which a man comes to the last refuge of the destitute.

Yet nature has her freaks in the making of a man's mind; she indulges herself and makes a few honest folk now and again, and now and then a cashier.

Wherefore, that race of corsairs whom we dignify with the title of bankers, the gentry who take out a license for which they pay a thousand crowns, as the privateer takes out his letters of marque, hold these rare products of the incubations of virtue in such esteem that they confine them in cages in their counting-houses, much as governments procure and maintain specimens of strange beasts at their own charges.

If the cashier is possessed of an imagination or of a fervid temperament; if, as will sometimes happen to the most complete cashier, he loves his wife, and that wife grows tired of her lot, has ambitions, or merely some vanity in her composition, the cashier is undone. Search the chronicles of the counting-house. You will not find a single instance of a cashier attaining *a position*, as it is called. They are sent to the hulks; they go to foreign parts; they vegetate on a second floor in the Rue Saint-Louis among the market gardens of the Marais. Some day, when the cashiers of Paris come to a sense of their real value, a cashier will be hardly obtainable for money. Still, certain it is that there are people who are fit for nothing but to be cashiers, just as the bent of a certain order of mind inevitably makes for rascality. But, oh marvel of our civilisation! Society rewards virtue with an income of a hundred louis in old age, a dwelling on a second floor, bread sufficient, occasional new bandana handkerchiefs, an elderly wife and her offspring.

So much for virtue. But for the opposite course, a little boldness, a faculty for keeping on the windward side of the law, as Turenne outflanked Montecuculli, and Society will sanction the theft of millions, shower ribands upon the thief, cram him with honours, and smother him with consideration.

Government, moreover, works harmoniously with this profoundly illogical reasoner—Society. Government levies a conscription on the young intelligence of the kingdom at the age of seventeen or eighteen, a conscription of precocious power. Great ability is prematurely exhausted by excessive brain-work before it is sent up to be submitted to a process of selection. Nurserymen sort and select seeds in much the same way. To this process the Government brings professional appraisers of talent, men who can assay brains as experts assay gold at the Mint. Five hundred such heads, set afire with hope, are sent up annually by the most progressive portion of the population; and of these the Government takes one-third, puts them in sacks called the Écoles, and shakes them up together for three years. Though every one of these young plants represents vast productive power, they are made, as one may say, into cashiers. They receive appointments; the rank and file of engineers is made up of them; they are employed as captains of artillery; there is no (subaltern) grade to which they may not aspire. Finally, when these men, the pick of the youth of the nation, fattened on mathematics and stuffed with knowledge, have attained the age of fifty years, they have their reward, and receive as the price of their services the third-floor lodging, the wife and family, and all the comforts that sweeten life for mediocrity. If from among this race of dupes there should escape some five or six men of genius who climb the highest heights, is it not miraculous ?

This is an exact statement of the relations between Talent and Probity on the one hand, and Government and Society on the other, in an age that considers itself to be progressive. Without this prefatory explanation a recent occurrence in Paris would seem improbable; but preceded by this summing up of the situation, it will perhaps receive some thoughtful attention from minds capable of recognising the real plague-spots of our civilisation, a civilisation which since 1815 has been moved by the spirit of gain rather than by principles of honour.

About five o'clock, on a dull autumn afternoon, the cashier of one of the largest banks in Paris was still at his desk, working by the light of a lamp that had been lit for some time. In accordance with the use and wont of commerce, the counting-house was in the darkest corner of the low-ceiled and far from spacious mezzanine floor, and at the very end of a passage lighted only by borrowed lights. The office doors along this corridor, each with its label, gave the place the look of a bath-house. At four o'clock the stolid porter had proclaimed, according to his orders, ' The bank is closed.' And by this time the departments were deserted, the letters despatched, the clerks had taken their leave. The wives of the partners in the firm were expecting their lovers; the two bankers dining with their mistresses. Everything was in order.

The place where the strong boxes had been bedded in sheet-iron was just behind the little sanctum, where the cashier was busy. Doubtless he was balancing his books. The open front gave a glimpse of a safe of hammered iron, so enormously heavy (thanks to the science of the

modern inventor) that burglars could not carry it away.
The door only opened at the pleasure of those who knew
its password. The letter-lock was a warden who kept
its own secret and could not be bribed; the mysterious
word was an ingenious realisation of the ' Open sesame!'
in the *Arabian Nights*. But even this was as nothing.
A man might discover the password; but unless he knew
the lock's final secret, the *ultima ratio* of this gold-guarding
dragon of mechanical science, it discharged a blunderbuss
at his head.

The door of the room, the walls of the room, the
shutters of the windows in the room, the whole place, in
fact, was lined with sheet-iron a third of an inch in
thickness, concealed behind the thin wooden panelling.
The shutters had been closed, the door had been shut.
If ever man could feel confident that he was absolutely
alone, and that there was no remote possibility of being
watched by prying eyes, that man was the cashier of
the house of Nucingen and Company, in the Rue Saint-
Lazare.

Accordingly the deepest silence prevailed in that iron
cave. The fire had died out in the stove, but the room
was full of that tepid warmth which produces the dull
heavy-headedness and nauseous queasiness of a morning
after an orgy. The stove is a mesmerist that plays no
small part in the reduction of bank clerks and porters to
a state of idiocy.

A room with a stove in it is a retort in which the
power of strong men is evaporated, where their vitality
is exhausted, and their wills enfeebled. Government
offices are part of a great scheme for the manufacture
of the mediocrity necessary for the maintenance of a
Feudal System on a pecuniary basis—and money is the
foundation of the Social Contract. (See *Les Employés*.)
The mephitic vapours in the atmosphere of a crowded
room contribute in no small degree to bring about a
gradual deterioration of intelligences, the brain that

gives off the largest quantity of nitrogen asphyxiates the others, in the long run.

The cashier was a man of five-and-forty or there-abouts. As he sat at the table, the light from a moderator lamp shining full on his bald head and glistening fringe of iron-grey hair that surrounded it—this baldness and the round outlines of his face made his head look very like a ball. His complexion was brick-red, a few wrinkles had gathered about his eyes, but he had the smooth, plump hands of a stout man. His blue cloth coat, a little rubbed and worn, and the creases and shininess of his trousers, traces of hard wear that the clothes-brush fails to remove, would impress a superficial observer with the idea that here was a thrifty and upright human being, sufficient of the philosopher or of the aristocrat to wear shabby clothes. But, unluckily, it is easy to find penny-wise people who will prove weak, wasteful, or incompetent in the capital things of life.

The cashier wore the ribbon of the Legion of Honour at his button-hole, for he had been a major of dragoons in the time of the Emperor. M. de Nucingen, who had been a contractor before he became a banker, had had reason in those days to know the honourable disposition of his cashier, who then occupied a high position. Reverses of fortune had befallen the major, and the banker out of regard for him paid him five hundred francs a month. The soldier had become a cashier in the year 1813, after his recovery from a wound received at Studzianka during the Retreat from Moscow, followed by six months of enforced idleness at Strasbourg, whither several officers had been transported by order of the Emperor, that they might receive skilled attention. This particular officer, Castanier by name, retired with the honorary grade of colonel, and a pension of two thousand four hundred francs.

In ten years' time the cashier had completely effaced the soldier, and Castanier inspired the banker with such trust in him, that he was associated in the transactions that went on in the private office behind his little counting-house. The baron himself had access to it by means of a secret staircase. There, matters of business were decided. It was the bolting-room where proposals were sifted; the privy council chamber where the reports of the money market were analysed; circular notes issued thence; and finally, the private ledger and the journal which summarised the work of all the departments were kept there.

Castanier had gone himself to shut the door which opened on to a staircase that led to the parlour occupied by the two bankers on the first floor of their hôtel. This done, he had sat down at his desk again, and for a moment he gazed at a little collection of letters of credit drawn on the firm of Watschildine of London. Then he had taken up the pen and imitated the banker's signature upon each. *Nucingen* he wrote, and eyed the forged signatures critically to see which seemed the most perfect copy.

Suddenly he looked up as if a needle had pricked him. 'You are not alone!' a boding voice seemed to cry in his heart; and indeed the forger saw a man standing at the little grated window of the counting-house, a man whose breathing was so noiseless that he did not seem to breathe at all. Castanier looked, and saw that the door at the end of the passage was wide open; the stranger must have entered by that way.

For the first time in his life the old soldier felt a sensation of dread that made him stare open-mouthed and wide-eyed at the man before him; and for that matter, the appearance of the apparition was sufficiently alarming even if unaccompanied by the mysterious circumstances of so sudden an entry. The rounded forehead, the harsh colouring of the long oval face, indicated quite as plainly as the cut of his clothes that the man was an Englishman, reeking of his native isles.

You had only to look at the collar of his overcoat, at the voluminous cravat which smothered the crushed frills of a shirt front so white that it brought out the changeless leaden hue of an impassive face, and the thin red line of the lips that seemed made to suck the blood of corpses; and you could guess at once at the black gaiters buttoned up to the knee, and the half-puritanical costume of a wealthy Englishman dressed for a walking excursion. The intolerable glitter of the stranger's eyes produced a vivid and unpleasant impression, which was only deepened by the rigid outlines of his features. The dried-up, emaciated creature seemed to carry within him some gnawing thought that consumed him and could not be appeased.

He must have digested his food so rapidly that he could doubtless eat continually without bringing any trace of colour into his face or features. A tun of Tokay *vin de succession* would not have caused any faltering in that piercing glance that read men's inmost thoughts, nor dethroned the merciless reasoning faculty that always seemed to go to the bottom of things. There was something of the fell and tranquil majesty of a tiger about him.

'I have come to cash this bill of exchange, sir,' he said. Castanier felt the tones of his voice thrill through every nerve with a violent shock similar to that given by a discharge of electricity.

'The safe is closed,' said Castanier.

'It is open,' said the Englishman, looking round the counting-house. 'To-morrow is Sunday, and I cannot wait. The amount is for five hundred thousand francs. You have the money there, and I must have it.'

'But how did you come in, sir?'

The Englishman smiled. That smile frightened Castanier. No words could have replied more fully nor more peremptorily than that scornful and imperial curl of the stranger's lips. Castanier turned away, took up fifty packets, each containing ten thousand francs in bank-notes, and held them out to the stranger, receiving in exchange for them a bill accepted by the Baron de Nucingen. A sort of convulsive tremor ran through him as he saw a red gleam in the stranger's eyes when they fell on the forged signature on the letter of credit.

'It . . . it wants your signature . . .' stammered Castanier, handing back the bill.

'Hand me your pen,' answered the Englishman.

Castanier handed him the pen with which he had just committed forgery. The stranger wrote *John Melmoth*, then he returned the slip of paper and the pen to the cashier. Castanier looked at the handwriting, noticing that it sloped from right to left in the Eastern fashion, and Melmoth disappeared so noiselessly that when Castanier looked up again an exclamation broke from him, partly because the man was no longer there, partly because he felt a strange painful sensation such as our imagination might take for an effect of poison.

The pen that Melmoth had handled sent the same sickening heat through him that an emetic produces. But it seemed impossible to Castanier that the English-man should have guessed his crime. His inward qualms he attributed to the palpitation of the heart that, according to received ideas, was sure to follow at once on such a 'turn' as the stranger had given him.

'The devil take it; I am very stupid. Providence is watching over me; for if that brute had come round to see my gentlemen to-morrow, my goose would have been cooked!' said Castanier, and he burned the unsuccessful attempts at forgery in the stove.

He put the bill that he meant to take with him in an envelope, and helped himself to five hundred thousand francs in French and English bank-notes from the safe, which he locked. Then he put everything in order, lit a candle, blew out the lamp, took up his hat and umbrella, and went out sedately, as usual, to leave one of the two keys of the strong room with Madame de Nucingen, in the absence of her husband the Baron.

'You are in luck, M. Castanier,' said the banker's wife as he entered her room ; 'we have a holiday on Monday ; you can go into the country, or to Soizy.'

'Madame, will you be so good as to tell your husband that the bill of exchange on Watschildine, which was behind time, has just been presented ? The five hundred thousand francs have been paid ; so I shall not come back till noon on Tuesday.'

'Good-bye, Monsieur ; I hope you will have a pleasant time.'

'The same to you, Madame,' replied the old dragoon as he went out. He glanced as he spoke at a young man well known in fashionable society at that time, a M. de Rastignac, who was regarded as Madame de Nucingen's lover.

'Madame,' remarked this latter, 'the old boy looks to me as if he meant to play you some ill turn.'

'Pshaw ! impossible ; he is too stupid.'

'Piquoizeau,' said the cashier, walking into the porter's room, 'what made you let anybody come up after four o'clock ? '

'I have been smoking a pipe here in the doorway ever since four o'clock,' said the man, 'and nobody has gone into the bank. Nobody has come out either except the gentlemen——'

'Are you quite sure ?'

'Yes, upon my word and honour. Stay, though, at four o'clock M. Werbrust's friend came, a young fellow from Messrs. du Tillet & Co., in the Rue Joubert.'

'All right,' said Castanier, and he hurried away.

The sickening sensation of heat that he had felt when he took back the pen returned in greater intensity. '*Mille diables !* ' thought he, as he threaded his way along the Boulevard de Gand, 'haven't I taken proper precautions ? Let me think ! Two clear days, Sunday and Monday, then a day of uncertainty before they begin to look for me ; altogether, three days and four nights' respite. I have a couple of passports and two different disguises ; is not that enough to throw the cleverest detective off the scent ? On Tuesday morning I shall draw a million francs in London before the slightest suspicion has been aroused. My debts I am leaving behind for the benefit of my creditors, who will put a " P "[1] on the bills, and I shall live comfortably in Italy for the rest of my days as the Conte Ferraro. I was alone with him when he died, poor fellow, in the marsh of Zembin, and I shall slip into his skin. . . . *Mille diables !* the woman who is to follow after me might give them a clue ! Think of an old campaigner like me infatuated enough to tie myself to a petticoat tail ! . . . Why take her ? I must leave her behind. Yes, I could make up my mind to it ; but—I know myself—I should be ass enough to go back for her. Still, nobody knows Aquilina. Shall I take her or leave her ? '

' You will not take her ! ' cried a voice that filled Castanier with sickening dread. He turned sharply, and saw the Englishman.

' The devil is in it ! ' cried the cashier aloud.

Melmoth had passed his victim by this time ; and if Castanier's first impulse had been to fasten a quarrel on a man who read his own thoughts, he was so much torn by opposing feelings that the immediate result was a temporary paralysis. When he resumed his walk he fell once more into that fever of irresolution which besets those who are so carried away by passion that they are ready to commit a crime, but have not sufficient strength of character to keep it to themselves without suffering terribly in the process. So, although Castanier had made up his mind to reap the fruits of a crime which was already half executed, he hesitated to carry out his designs.

[1] Protested.

For him, as for many men of mixed character in whom weakness and strength are equally blended, the least trifling consideration determines whether they shall continue to lead blameless lives or become actively criminal. In the vast masses of men enrolled in Napoleon's armies there were many who, like Castanier, possessed the purely physical courage demanded on the battlefield, yet lacked the moral courage which makes a man as great in crime as he could have been in virtue.

The letter of credit was drafted in such terms that immediately on his arrival he might draw twenty-five thousand pounds on the firm of Watschildine, the London correspondents of the house of Nucingen. The London house had been already advised of the draft about to be made upon them; he had written to them himself. He had instructed an agent (chosen at random) to take his passage in a vessel which was to leave Portsmouth with a wealthy English family on board, who were going to Italy, and the passage-money had been paid in the name of the Conte Ferraro. The smallest details of the scheme had been thought out. He had arranged matters so as to divert the search that would be made for him into Belgium and Switzerland, while he himself was at sea in the English vessel. Then, by the time that Nucingen might flatter himself that he was on the track of his late cashier, the said cashier, as the Conte Ferraro, hoped to be safe in Naples. He had determined to disfigure his face in order to disguise himself the more completely, and by means of an acid to imitate the scars of smallpox. Yet, in spite of all these precautions, which surely seemed as if they must secure him complete immunity, his conscience tormented him; he was afraid. The even and peaceful life that he had led for so long had modified the morality of the camp. His life was stainless as yet; he could not sully it without a pang. So for the last time he abandoned himself to all the influences of the better self that strenuously resisted.

E

' Pshaw ! ' he said at last, at the corner of the Boulevard
and the Rue Montmartre, 'I will take a cab after the
play this evening and go out to Versailles. A post-
chaise will be ready for me at my old quartermaster's
place. He would keep my secret even if a dozen men
were standing ready to shoot him down. The chances
are all in my favour, so far as I see ; so I shall take my
little Naqui with me, and I will go.'

' You will not go ! ' exclaimed the Englishman, and
the strange tones of his voice drove all the cashier's blood
back to his heart.

Melmoth stepped into a tilbury which was waiting for
him, and was whirled away so quickly, that when Castanier
looked up he saw his foe some hundred paces away from
him, and before it even crossed his mind to cut off the
man's retreat the tilbury was far on its way up the
Boulevard Montmartre.

' Well, upon my word, there is something supernatural
about this ! ' said he to himself. ' If I were fool enough
to believe in God, I should think that He had set Saint
Michael on my tracks. Suppose that the devil and the
police should let me go on as I please, so as to nab me
in the nick of time ? Did any one ever see the like !
But there, this is folly. . . .'

Castanier went along the Rue du Faubourg-Mont-
martre, slackening his pace as he neared the Rue Richer.
There, on the second floor of a block of buildings which
looked out upon some gardens, lived the unconscious
cause of Castanier's crime—a young woman known in
the quarter as Mme. de la Garde. A concise history
of certain events in the cashier's past life must be given
in order to explain these facts, and to give a complete
presentment of the crisis when he yielded to temptation.

Mme. de la Garde said that she was a Piedmontese.
No one, not even Castanier, knew her real name. She
was one of those young girls who are driven by dire
misery, by inability to earn a living, or by fear of starva-

tion, to have recourse to a trade which most of them loathe, many regard with indifference, and some few follow in obedience to the laws of their constitution. But on the brink of the gulf of prostitution in Paris, the young girl of sixteen, beautiful and pure as the Madonna, had met with Castanier. The old dragoon was too rough and homely to make his way in society, and he was tired of tramping the boulevard at night and of the kind of conquests made there by gold. For some time past he had desired to bring a certain regularity into an irregular life. He was struck by the beauty of the poor child who had drifted by chance into his arms, and his determination to rescue her from the life of the streets was half benevolent, half selfish, as some of the thoughts of the best of men are apt to be. Social conditions mingle elements of evil with the promptings of natural goodness of heart, and the mixture of motives underlying a man's intentions should be leniently judged. Castanier had just cleverness enough to be very shrewd where his own interests were concerned. So he concluded to be a philanthropist on either count, and at first made her his mistress.

'Hey! hey!' he said to himself, in his soldierly fashion, 'I am an old wolf, and a sheep shall not make a fool of me. Castanier, old man, before you set up housekeeping, reconnoitre the girl's character for a bit, and see if she is a steady sort.'

This irregular union gave the Piedmontese a status the most nearly approaching respectability among those which the world declines to recognise. During the first year she took the *nom de guerre* of Aquilina, one of the characters in *Venice Preserved* which she had chanced to read. She fancied that she resembled the courtesan in face and general appearance, and in a certain precocity of heart and brain of which she was conscious. When Castanier found that her life was as well regulated and virtuous as was possible for a social outlaw, he manifested a desire that they should live as husband and wife. So she took the name of Mme. de la Garde, in order to approach, as closely as Parisian usages permit, the conditions of a real marriage. As a matter of fact, many of these unfortunate girls have one fixed idea, to be looked upon as respectable middle-class women, who lead humdrum lives of faithfulness to their husbands; women who would make excellent mothers, keepers of household accounts, and menders of household linen. This longing springs from a sentiment so laudable, that society should take it into consideration. But society, incorrigible as ever, will assuredly persist in regarding the married woman as a corvette duly authorised by her flag and papers to go on her own course, while the woman who is a wife in all but name is a pirate and an outlaw for lack of a document. A day came when Mme. de la Garde would fain have signed herself 'Mme. Castanier.' The cashier was put out by this.

'So you do not love me well enough to marry me?' she said.

Castanier did not answer; he was absorbed by his thoughts. The poor girl resigned herself to her fate. The ex-dragoon was in despair. Naqui's heart softened towards him at the sight of his trouble; she tried to soothe him, but what could she do when she did not know what ailed him? When Naqui made up her mind to know the secret, although she never asked him a question, the cashier dolefully confessed to the existence of a Mme. Castanier. This lawful wife, a thousand times accursed, was living in a humble way in Strasbourg on a small property there; he wrote to her twice a year, and kept the secret of her existence so well, that no one suspected that he was married. The reason of this reticence? If it is familiar to many military men who may chance to be in a like predicament, it is perhaps worth while to give the story.

Your genuine trooper (if it is allowable here to

employ the word which in the army signifies a man who
is destined to die as a captain) is a sort of serf, a part
and parcel of his regiment, an essentially simple creature,
and Castanier was marked out by nature as a victim to
the wiles of mothers with grown-up daughters left too
long on their hands. It was at Nancy, during one of
those brief intervals of repose when the Imperial armies
were not on active service abroad, that Castanier was so
unlucky as to pay some attention to a young lady with
whom he danced at a *ridotto*, the provincial name for the
entertainments often given by the military to the townsfolk, or *vice versâ*, in garrison towns. A scheme for
inveigling the gallant captain into matrimony was immediately set on foot, one of those schemes by which
mothers secure accomplices in a human heart by touching
all its motive springs, while they convert all their friends
into fellow-conspirators. Like all people possessed by
one idea, these ladies press everything into the service
of their great project, slowly elaborating their toils,
much as the ant-lion excavates its funnel in the sand and
lies in wait at the bottom for its victim. Suppose that
no one strays, after all, into that carefully constructed
labyrinth? Suppose that the ant-lion dies of hunger and
thirst in her pit? Such things may be, but if any heedless creature once enters in, it never comes out. All
the wires which could be pulled to induce action on the
captain's part were tried; appeals were made to the secret
interested motives that always come into play in such cases;
they worked on Castanier's hopes and on the weaknesses and
vanity of human nature. Unluckily, he had praised the
daughter to her mother when he brought her back after
a waltz, a little chat followed, and then an invitation in
the most natural way in the world. Once introduced
into the house, the dragoon was dazzled by the hospitality
of a family who appeared to conceal their real wealth
beneath a show of careful economy. He was skilfully
flattered on all sides, and every one extolled for his benefit

the various treasures there displayed. A neatly timed
dinner, served on plate lent by an uncle, the attention
shown to him by the only daughter of the house, the
gossip of the town, a well-to-do sub-lieutenant who
seemed likely to cut the ground from under his feet—
all the innumerable snares, in short, of the provincial
ant-lion were set for him, and to such good purpose, that
Castanier said five years later, 'To this day I do not
know how it came about !'

The dragoon received fifteen thousand francs with the
lady, who, after two years of marriage, became the
ugliest and consequently the most peevish woman on
earth. Luckily they had no children. The fair complexion (maintained by a Spartan regimen), the fresh,
bright colour in her face, which spoke of an engaging
modesty, became overspread with blotches and pimples ;
her figure, which had seemed so straight, grew crooked,
the angel became a suspicious and shrewish creature who
drove Castanier frantic. Then the fortune took to itself
wings. At length the dragoon, no longer recognising
the woman whom he had wedded, left her to live on a
little property at Strasbourg, until the time when it
should please God to remove her to adorn Paradise. She
was one of those virtuous women who, for want of other
occupation, would weary the life out of an angel with
complainings, who pray till (if their prayers are heard in
heaven) they must exhaust the patience of the Almighty,
and say everything that is bad of their husbands in dove-
like murmurs over a game of boston with their neighbours. When Aquilina learned all these troubles she
clung still more affectionately to Castanier, and made
him so happy, varying with woman's ingenuity the
pleasures with which she filled his life, that all unwittingly she was the cause of the cashier's downfall.

Like many women who seem by nature destined to
sound all the depths of love, Mme. de la Garde was
disinterested. She asked neither for gold nor for jewel-

lery, gave no thought to the future, lived entirely for the
present and for the pleasures of the present. She accepted
expensive ornaments and dresses, the carriage so eagerly
coveted by women of her class, as one harmony the more
in the picture of life. There was absolutely no vanity in
her desire not to appear at a better advantage but to look
the fairer, and, moreover, no woman could live without luxuries more cheerfully. When a man of generous
nature (and military men are mostly of this stamp) meets
with such a woman, he feels a sort of exasperation at
finding himself her debtor in generosity. He feels that
he could stop a mail coach to obtain money for her if he
has not sufficient for her whims. He will commit a
crime if so he may be great and noble in the eyes of
some woman or of his special public ; such is the nature
of the man. Such a lover is like a gambler who would be
dishonoured in his own eyes if he did not repay the sum
he borrowed from a waiter in a gaming-house ; but will
shrink from no crime, will leave his wife and children
without a penny, and rob and murder, if so he may come
to the gaming table with a full purse, and his honour
remain untarnished among the frequenters of that fatal
abode. So it was with Castanier.

He had begun by installing Aquilina in a modest
fourth-floor dwelling, the furniture being of the simplest
kind. But when he saw the girl's beauty and great
qualities, when he had known inexpressible and unlooked-
for happiness with her, he began to dote upon her, and
longed to adorn his idol. Then Aquilina's toilette was
so comically out of keeping with her poor abode, that for
both their sakes it was clearly incumbent on him to
move. The change swallowed up almost all Castanier's
savings, for he furnished his domestic paradise with all
the prodigality that is lavished on a kept mistress. A
pretty woman must have everything pretty about her ;
the unity of charm in the woman and her surroundings singles her out from among her sex. This senti-

ment of homogeneity indeed, though it has frequently escaped the attention of observers, is instinctive in human nature; and the same prompting leads elderly spinsters to surround themselves with dreary relics of the past. But the lovely Piedmontese must have the newest and latest fashions, and all that was daintiest and prettiest in stuffs for hangings, in silks or jewellery, in fine china and other brittle and fragile wares. She asked for nothing; but when she was called upon to make a choice, when Castanier asked her, 'Which do you like?' she would answer, 'Why, this is the nicest!' Love never counts the cost, and Castanier therefore always took the 'nicest.'

When once the standard had been set up, there was nothing for it but everything in the household must be in conformity, from the linen plate and crystal through a thousand and one items of expenditure down to the pots and pans in the kitchen. Castanier had meant to 'do things simply,' as the saying goes, but he gradually found himself more and more in debt. One expense entailed another. The clock called for candle sconces. Fires must be lighted in the ornamental grates, but the curtains and hangings were too fresh and delicate to be soiled by smuts, so they must be replaced by patent and elaborate fireplaces, warranted to give out no smoke, recent inventions of the people who are clever at drawing up a prospectus. Then Aquilina found it so nice to run about barefooted on the carpet in her room, that Castanier must have soft carpets laid everywhere for the pleasure of playing with Naqui. A bathroom, too, was built for her, everything to the end that she might be more comfortable.

Shopkeepers, workmen, and manufacturers in Paris have a mysterious knack of enlarging a hole in a man's purse. They cannot give the price of anything upon inquiry; and as the paroxysm of longing cannot abide delay, orders are given by the feeble light of an approximate estimate of cost. The same people never send in the bills at once, but ply the purchaser with furniture till his head spins. Everything is so pretty, so charming; and every one is satisfied.

A few months later the obliging furniture dealers are metamorphosed, and reappear in the shape of alarming totals on invoices that fill the soul with their horrid clamour; they are in urgent want of the money; they are, as you may say, on the brink of bankruptcy, their tears flow, it is heartrending to hear them! And then ——the gulf yawns, and gives up serried columns of figures marching four deep, when as a matter of fact they should have issued innocently three by three.

Before Castanier had any idea of how much he had spent, he had arranged for Aquilina to have a carriage from a livery stable when she went out, instead of a cab. Castanier was a gourmand; he engaged an excellent cook; and Aquilina, to please him, had herself made the purchases of early fruit and vegetables, rare delicacies, and exquisite wines. But, as Aquilina had nothing of her own, these gifts of hers, so precious by reason of the thought and tact and graciousness that prompted them, were no less a drain upon Castanier's purse; he did not like his Naqui to be without money, and Naqui could not keep money in her pocket. So the table was a heavy item of expenditure for a man with Castanier's income. The ex-dragoon was compelled to resort to various shifts for obtaining money, for he could not bring himself to renounce this delightful life. He loved the woman too well to cross the freaks of the mistress. He was one of those men who, through self-love or through weakness of character, can refuse nothing to a woman; false shame overpowers them, and they rather face ruin than make the admissions: 'I cannot——' 'My means will not permit——' 'I cannot afford——'

When, therefore, Castanier saw that if he meant to emerge from the abyss of debt into which he had

plunged, he must part with Aquilina and live upon
bread and water, he was so unable to do without her or
to change his habits of life, that daily he put off his plans
of reform until the morrow. The debts were pressing,
and he began by borrowing money. His position and
previous character inspired confidence, and of this he
took advantage to devise a system of borrowing money
as he required it. Then, as the total amount of debt
rapidly increased, he had recourse to those commercial
inventions known as *accommodation bills.* This form of
bill does not represent goods or other value received, and
the first endorser pays the amount named for the obliging
person who accepts it. This species of fraud is tolerated
because it is impossible to detect it, and, moreover, it is
an imaginary fraud which only becomes real if payment
is ultimately refused.

When at length it was evidently impossible to borrow
any longer, whether because the amount of the debt was
now so greatly increased, or because Castanier was unable
to pay the large amount of interest on the aforesaid sums
of money, the cashier saw bankruptcy before him. On
making this discovery, he decided for a fraudulent bankruptcy rather than an ordinary failure, and preferred a
crime to a misdemeanour. He determined, after the
fashion of the celebrated cashier of the Royal Treasury,
to abuse the trust deservedly won, and to increase the
number of his creditors by making a final loan of the
sum sufficient to keep him in comfort in a foreign
country for the rest of his days. All this, as has been
seen, he had prepared to do.

Aquilina knew nothing of the irksome cares of this
life ; she enjoyed her existence, as many a woman does,
making no inquiry as to where the money came from,
even as sundry other folk will eat their buttered rolls
untroubled by any restless spirit of curiosity as to the
culture and growth of wheat ; but as the labour and mis-
calculations of agriculture lie on the other side of the

baker's oven, so, beneath the unappreciated luxury of many a Parisian household lie intolerable anxieties and exorbitant toil.

While Castanier was enduring the torture of the strain, and his thoughts were full of the deed that should change his whole life, Aquilina was lying luxuriously back in a great armchair by the fireside, beguiling the time by chatting with her waiting-maid. As frequently happens in such cases, the maid had become the mistress's confidante, Jenny having first assured herself that her mistress's ascendency over Castanier was complete.

'What are we to do this evening? Léon seems determined to come,' Mme. de la Garde was saying, as she read a passionate epistle indited upon a faint grey notepaper.

'Here is the master!' said Jenny.

Castanier came in. Aquilina, nowise disconcerted, crumpled up the letter, took it with the tongs, and held it in the flames.

'So that is what you do with your love-letters, is it?' asked Castanier.

'Oh goodness, yes,' said Aquilina; 'is it not the best way of keeping them safe? Besides, fire should go to the fire, as water makes for the river.'

'You are talking as if it were a real love-letter, Naqui——'

'Well, am I not handsome enough to receive them?' she said, holding up her forehead for a kiss. There was a carelessness in her manner that would have told any man less blind than Castanier that it was only a piece of conjugal duty, as it were, to give this joy to the cashier; but use and wont had brought Castanier to the point where clear-sightedness is no longer possible for love.

'I have taken a box at the Gymnase this evening,' he said; 'let us have dinner early, and then we need not dine in a hurry.'

'Go and take Jenny. I am tired of plays. I do not know what is the matter with me this evening; I would rather stay here by the fire.'

'Come, all the same though, Naqui; I shall not be here to bore you much longer. Yes, Quiqui, I am going to start to-night, and it will be some time before I come back again. I am leaving everything in your charge. Will you keep your heart for me too?'

'Neither my heart nor anything else,' she said; 'but when you come back again, Naqui will still be Naqui for you.'

'Well, this is frankness. So you would not follow me?'

'No.'

'Why not?'

'Eh! why, how can I leave the lover who writes me such sweet little notes?' she asked, pointing to the blackened scrap of paper with a mocking smile.

'Is there any truth in it?' asked Castanier. 'Have you really a lover?'

'Really!' cried Aquilina; 'and have you never given it a serious thought, dear? To begin with, you are fifty years old. Then you have just the sort of face to put on a fruit stall; if the woman tried to sell you for a pumpkin, no one would contradict her. You puff and blow like a seal when you come upstairs; your paunch rises and falls like the diamond on a woman's forehead! It is pretty plain that you served in the dragoons; you are a very ugly-looking old man. Fiddle-de-dee. If you have any mind to keep my respect, I recommend you not to add imbecility to these qualities by imagining that such a girl as I am will be content with your asthmatic love, and not look for youth and good looks and pleasure by way of a variety——'

'Aquilina! you are laughing, of course?'

'Oh, very well; and are you not laughing too? Do you take me for a fool, telling me that you are going away ? "I am going to start to-night!" she said, mimicking his tones. Stuff and nonsense! Would you talk like that if you were really going away from your Naqui? You would cry, like the booby that you are!'

'After all, if I go, will you follow?' he asked.

'Tell me first whether this journey of yours is a bad joke or not.'

'Yes, seriously, I am going.'

'Well, then, seriously, I shall stay. A pleasant journey to you, my boy! I will wait till you come back. I would sooner take leave of life than take leave of my dear, cosy Paris——'

'Will you not come to Italy, to Naples, and lead a pleasant life there—a delicious, luxurious life, with this stout old fogey of yours, who puffs and blows like a seal?'

'No.'

'Ungrateful girl!'

'Ungrateful?' she cried, rising to her feet. 'I might leave this house this moment and take nothing out of it but myself. I shall have given you all the treasures a young girl can give, and something that not every drop in your veins and mine can ever give me back. If, by any means whatever, by selling my hopes of eternity, for instance, I could recover my past self, body as soul (for I have, perhaps, redeemed my soul), and be pure as a lily for my lover, I would not hesitate a moment! What sort of devotion has rewarded mine? You have housed and fed me, just as you give a dog food and a kennel because he is a protection to the house, and he may take kicks when we are out of humour, and lick our hands as soon as we are pleased to call to him. And which of us two will have been the more generous?'

'Oh! dear child, do you not see that I am joking?' returned Castanier. 'I am going on a short journey; I shall not be away for very long. But come with me to the Gymnase; I shall start just before midnight, after I have had time to say good-bye to you.'

'Poor pet! so you are really going, are you?' she said. She put her arms round his neck, and drew down his head against her bodice.

'You are smothering me!' cried Castanier, with his face buried in Aquilina's breast. That damsel turned to say in Jenny's ear, 'Go to Léon, and tell him not to come till one o'clock. If you do not find him, and he comes here during the leave-taking, keep him in your room.—Well,' she went on, setting free Castanier, and giving a tweak to the tip of his nose, 'never mind, handsomest of seals that you are. I will go to the theatre with you this evening. But all in good time; let us have dinner! There is a nice little dinner for you —just what you like.'

'It is very hard to part from such a woman as you!' exclaimed Castanier.

'Very well then, why do you go?' asked she.

'Ah! why? why? If I were to begin to explain the reasons why, I must tell you things that would prove to you that I love you almost to madness. Ah! if you have sacrificed your honour for me, I have sold mine for you; we are quits. Is that love?'

'What is all this about?' said she. 'Come, now, promise me that if I had a lover you would still love me as a father; that would be love! Come, now, promise it at once, and give us your fist upon it.'

'I should kill you,' and Castanier smiled as he spoke.

They sat down to the dinner table, and went thence to the Gymnase. When the first part of the performance was over, it occurred to Castanier to show himself to some of his acquaintances in the house, so as to turn away any suspicion of his departure. He left Mme. de la Garde in the corner box where she was seated, according to her modest wont, and went to walk up and down in the lobby. He had not gone many paces before he saw the Englishman, and with a sudden return of the sickening sensation of heat that once before had vibrated through him, and of the terror that he had felt already, he stood face to face with Melmoth.

'Forger!'

At the word, Castanier glanced round at the people who were moving about them. He fancied that he could see astonishment and curiosity in their eyes, and wishing to be rid of this Englishman at once, he raised his hand to strike him—and felt his arm paralysed by some invisible power that sapped his strength and nailed him to the spot. He allowed the stranger to take him by the arm, and they walked together to the green-room like two friends.

'Who is strong enough to resist me?' said the Englishman, addressing him. 'Do you not know that everything here on earth must obey me, that it is in my power to do everything. I read men's thoughts, I see the future, and I know the past. I am here, and I can be elsewhere also. Time and space and distance are nothing to me. The whole world is at my beck and call. I have the power of continual enjoyment and of giving joy. I can see through walls, discover hidden treasures, and fill my hands with them. Palaces arise at my nod, and my architect makes no mistakes. I can make all lands break forth into blossom, heap up their gold and precious stones, and surround myself with fair women and ever new faces; everything is yielded up to my will. I could gamble on the Stock Exchange, and my speculations would be infallible; but a man who can find the hoards that misers have hidden in the earth need not trouble himself about stocks. Feel the strength of the hand that grasps you; poor wretch, doomed to shame! Try to bend the arm of iron! try to soften the adamantine heart! Fly from me if you dare! You would hear my voice in the depths of the caves that lie under the Seine; you might hide in the Catacombs, but would you not see me there?

My voice could be heard through the sound of the thunder, my eyes shine as brightly as the sun, for I am the peer of Lucifer !'

Castanier heard the terrible words, and felt no protest nor contradiction within himself. He walked side by side with the Englishman, and had no power to leave him.

'You are mine; you have just committed a crime. I have found at last the mate whom I have sought. Have you a mind to learn your destiny? Aha! you came here to see a play, and you shall see a play—nay, two. Come. Present me to Mme. de la Garde as one of your best friends. Am I not your last hope of escape?'

Castanier, followed by the stranger, returned to his box; and in accordance with the order he had just received, he hastened to introduce Melmoth to Mme. de la Garde. Aquilina seemed to be not in the least surprised. The Englishman declined to take a seat in front, and Castanier was once more beside his mistress; the man's slightest wish must be obeyed. The last piece was about to begin, for, at that time, small theatres only gave three pieces. One of the actors had made the Gymnase the fashion, and that evening Perlet (the actor in question) was to play in a vaudeville called the *Le Comédien d'Étampes*, in which he filled four different parts.

When the curtain rose, the stranger stretched out his hand over the crowded house. Castanier's cry of terror died away, for the walls of his throat seemed glued together as Melmoth pointed to the stage, and the cashier knew that the play had been changed at the Englishman's desire.

He saw the strong-room at the bank; he saw the Baron de Nucingen in conference with a police-officer from the Prefecture, who was informing him of Castanier's conduct, explaining that the cashier had absconded with money taken from the safe, giving the history of the forged signature. The information was put in writing; the document signed and duly despatched to the Public Prosecutor.

'Are we in time, do you think?' asked Nucingen.

'Yes,' said the agent of police; 'he is at the Gymnase, and has no suspicion of anything.'

Castanier fidgeted on his chair, and made as if he would leave the theatre, but Melmoth's hand lay on his shoulder, and he was obliged to sit and watch; the hideous power of the man produced an effect like that of nightmare, and he could not move a limb. Nay, the man himself was the nightmare; his presence weighed heavily on his victim like a poisoned atmosphere. When the wretched cashier turned to implore the Englishman's mercy, he met those blazing eyes that discharged electric currents, which pierced through him and transfixed him like darts of steel.

'What have I done to you?' he said, in his prostrate helplessness, and he breathed hard like a stag at the water's edge. 'What do you want of me?'

'Look!' cried Melmoth.

Castanier looked at the stage. The scene had been changed. The play seemed to be over, and Castanier beheld himself stepping from the carriage with Aquilina; but as he entered the courtyard of the house in the Rue Richer, the scene again was suddenly changed, and he saw his own house. Jenny was chatting by the fire in her mistress's room with a subaltern officer of a line regiment then stationed at Paris.

'He is going, is he?' said the sergeant, who seemed to belong to a family in easy circumstances; 'I can be happy at my ease! I love Aquilina too well to allow her to belong to that old toad! I, myself, am going to marry Mme. de la Garde!' cried the sergeant.

'Old toad!' Castanier murmured piteously.

'Here come the master and mistress; hide yourself!

F

Stay, get in here, Monsieur Léon,' said Jenny. 'The master won't stay here for very long.'

Castanier watched the sergeant hide himself among Aquilina's gowns in her dressing-room. Almost immediately he himself appeared upon the scene, and took leave of his mistress, who made fun of him in 'asides' to Jenny, while she uttered the sweetest and tenderest words in his ears. She wept with one side of her face, and laughed with the other. The audience called for an encore.

'Accursed creature!' cried Castanier from his box.

Aquilina was laughing till the tears came into her eyes.

'Goodness!' she cried, 'how funny Perlet is as the Englishwoman! . . . Why don't you laugh? Every one else in the house is laughing. Laugh, dear!' she said to Castanier.

Melmoth burst out laughing, and the unhappy cashier shuddered. The Englishman's laughter wrung his heart and tortured his brain; it was as if a surgeon had bored his skull with a red-hot iron.

'Laughing! are they laughing!' stammered Castanier.

He did not see the prim English lady whom Perlet was acting with such ludicrous effect, nor hear the English-French that had filled the house with roars of laughter; instead of all this, he beheld himself hurrying from the Rue Richer, hailing a cab on the Boulevard, bargaining with the man to take him to Versailles. Then once more the scene changed. He recognised the sorry inn at the corner of the Rue de l'Orangerie and the Rue des Récollets, which was kept by his old quartermaster. It was two o'clock in the morning, the most perfect stillness prevailed, no one was there to watch his movements. The post-horses were put into the carriage (it came from a house in the Avenue de Paris in which an Englishman lived, and had been ordered in the foreigner's name to avoid raising suspicion). Castanier saw that he had his bills and his passports, stepped into the carriage, and set out. But at the barrier he saw two gendarmes lying in wait for the carriage. A cry of horror burst from him, but Melmoth gave him a glance, and again the sound died in his throat.

'Keep your eyes on the stage, and be quiet!' said the Englishman.

In another moment Castanier saw himself flung into prison at the Conciergerie; and in the fifth act of the drama, entitled *The Cashier*, he saw himself, in three months' time, condemned to twenty years of penal servitude. Again a cry broke from him. He was exposed upon the Place du Palais-de-Justice, and the executioner branded him with a red-hot iron. Then came the last scene of all; among some sixty convicts in the prison yard of the Bicêtre, he was awaiting his turn to have the irons riveted on his limbs.

'Dear me! I cannot laugh any more! . . .' said Aquilina. 'You are very solemn, dear boy; what can be the matter? The gentleman has gone.'

'A word with you, Castanier,' said Melmoth when the piece was at an end, and the attendant was fastening Mme. de la Garde's cloak.

The corridor was crowded, and escape impossible.

'Very well, what is it?'

'No human power can hinder you from taking Aquilina home, and going next to Versailles, there to be arrested.'

'How so?'

'Because you are in a hand that will never relax its grasp,' returned the Englishman.

Castanier longed for the power to utter some word that should blot him out from among living men and hide him in the lowest depths of hell.

'Suppose that the Devil were to make a bid for your soul, would you not give it to him now in exchange for the power of God? One single word, and those five hundred thousand francs shall be back in the Baron de Nucingen's safe; then you can tear up your letter of credit, and all traces of your crime will be obliterated. Moreover, you would have gold in torrents. You hardly believe in anything perhaps? Well, if all this comes to pass, you will believe at least in the Devil.'

'If it were only possible!' said Castanier joyfully.

'The man who can do it all gives you his word that it is possible,' answered the Englishman.

Melmoth, Castanier, and Mme. de la Garde were standing out in the Boulevard when Melmoth raised his arm. A drizzling rain was falling, the streets were muddy, the air was close, there was thick darkness overhead; but in a moment, as the arm was outstretched, Paris was filled with sunlight; it was high noon on a bright July day. The trees were covered with leaves; a double stream of joyous holiday makers strolled beneath them. Sellers of liquorice water shouted their cool drinks. Splendid carriages rolled past along the streets. A cry of terror broke from the cashier, and at that cry rain and darkness once more settled down upon the Boulevard.

Mme. de la Garde had stepped into the carriage. 'Do be quick, dear!' she cried; 'either come in or stay out. Really, you are as dull as ditch-water this evening——'

'What must I do?' Castanier asked of Melmoth.

'Would you like to take my place?' inquired the Englishman.

'Yes.'

'Very well, then; I will be at your house in a few moments.'

'By the by, Castanier, you are rather off your balance,' Aquilina remarked. 'There is some mischief brewing; you were quite melancholy and thoughtful all through the play. Do you want anything that I can give you, dear? Tell me.'

'I am waiting till we are at home to know whether you love me.'

'You need not wait till then,' she said, throwing her arms round his neck. 'There!' she said, as she embraced him, passionately to all appearance, and plied him with the coaxing caresses that are part of the business of such a life as hers, like stage action for an actress.

'Where is the music?' asked Castanier.

'What next? Only think of your hearing music now!'

'Heavenly music!' he went on. 'The sounds seem to come from above.'

'What? You have always refused to give me a box at the Italiens because you could not abide music, and are you turning music-mad at this time of day? Mad— that ·you are! The music is inside your own noddle, old addle-pate!' she went on, as she took his head in her hands and rocked it to and fro on her shoulder. 'Tell me now, old man; isn't it the creaking of the wheels that sings in your ears?'

'Just listen, Naqui! If the angels make music for God Almighty, it must be such music as this that I am drinking in at every pore, rather than hearing. I do not know how to tell you about it; it is as sweet as honey-water!'

'Why, of course, they have music in heaven, for the angels in all the pictures have harps in their hands. He is mad, upon my word!' she said to herself, as she saw Castanier's attitude; he looked like an opium-eater in a blissful trance.

They reached the house. Castanier, absorbed by the thought of all that he had just heard and seen, knew not whether to believe it or no; he was like a drunken man, and utterly unable to think connectedly. He came to himself in Aquilina's room, whither he had been supported by the united efforts of his mistress, the porter, and Jenny; for he had fainted as he stepped from the carriage.

'*He* will be here directly! Oh, my friends, my

friends!' he cried, and he flung himself despairingly into the depths of a low chair beside the fire.

Jenny heard the bell as he spoke, and admitted the Englishman. She announced that 'a gentleman had come who had made an appointment with the master,' when Melmoth suddenly appeared, and deep silence followed. He looked at the porter—the porter went; he looked at Jenny—and Jenny went likewise.

'Madame,' said Melmoth, turning to Aquilina, 'with your permission, we will conclude a piece of urgent business.'

He took Castanier's hand, and Castanier rose, and the two men went into the drawing-room. There was no light in the room, but Melmoth's eyes lit up the thickest darkness. The gaze of those strange eyes had left Aquilina like one spellbound; she was helpless, unable to take any thought for her lover; moreover, she believed him to be safe in Jenny's room, whereas their early return had taken the waiting-woman by surprise, and she had hidden the officer in the dressing-room. It had all happened exactly as in the drama that Melmoth had displayed for his victim. Presently the house-door was slammed violently, and Castanier reappeared.

'What ails you?' cried the horror-struck Aquilina.

There was a change in the cashier's appearance. A strange pallor overspread his once rubicund countenance; it wore the peculiarly sinister and stony look of the mysterious visitor. The sullen glare of his eyes was intolerable, the fierce light in them seemed to scorch. The man who had looked so good-humoured and good-natured had suddenly grown tyrannical and proud. The courtesan thought that Castanier had grown thinner; there was a terrible majesty in his brow; it was as if a dragon breathed forth a malignant influence that weighed upon the others like a close, heavy atmosphere. For a moment Aquilina knew not what to do.

'What passed between you and that diabolical-looking man in those few minutes?' she asked at length.

'I have sold my soul to him. I feel it; I am no longer the same. He has taken my *self*, and given me his soul in exchange.'

'What?'

'You would not understand it at all. . . . Ah! he was right,' Castanier went on, 'the fiend was right! I see everything and know all things.—You have been deceiving me!'

Aquilina turned cold with terror. Castanier lighted a candle and went into the dressing-room. The unhappy girl followed him in dazed bewilderment, and great was her astonishment when Castanier drew the dresses that hung there aside and disclosed the sergeant.

'Come out, my boy,' said the cashier; and, taking Léon by a button of his overcoat, he drew the officer into his room.

The Piedmontese, haggard and desperate, had flung herself into her easy-chair. Castanier seated himself on a sofa by the fire, and left Aquilina's lover in a standing position.

'You have been in the army,' said Léon; 'I am ready to give you satisfaction.'

'You are a fool,' said Castanier drily. 'I have no occasion to fight. I could kill you by a look if I had any mind to do it. I will tell you what it is, youngster; why should I kill you? I can see a red line round your neck—the guillotine is waiting for you. Yes, you will end in the Place de Grève. You are the headsman's property! there is no escape for you. You belong to a *vendita* of the Carbonari. You are plotting against the Government.'

'You did not tell me that,' cried the Piedmontese, turning to Léon.

'So you do not know that the Minister decided this morning to put down your Society?' the cashier continued. The Procureur-Général has a list of your names.

You have been betrayed. They are busy drawing up the indictment at this moment.'

'Then was it you who betrayed him ?' cried Aquilina, and with a hoarse sound in her throat like the growl of a tigress she rose to her feet; she seemed as if she would tear Castanier in pieces.

'You know me too well to believe it,' Castanier retorted. Aquilina was benumbed by his coolness.

'Then how did you know it ?' she murmured.

'I did not know it until I went into the drawing-room; now I know it—now I see and know all things, and can do all things.'

The sergeant was overcome with amazement.

'Very well then, save him, save him, dear !' cried the girl, flinging herself at Castanier's feet. 'If nothing is impossible to you, save him ! I will love you, I will adore you, I will be your slave and not your mistress. I will obey your wildest whims; you shall do as you will with me. Yes, yes, I will give you more than love; you shall have a daughter's devotion as well as . . . Rodolphe ! why will you not understand ! After all, however violent my passions may be, I shall be yours for ever ! What should I say to persuade you ? I will invent pleasures . . . I . . . Great heavens ! one moment ! whatever you shall ask of me   to fling myself from the window, for instance—you will need to say but one word, "Léon !" and I will plunge down into hell. I would bear any torture, any pain of body or soul, anything you might inflict upon me !'

Castanier heard her with indifference. For all answer, he indicated Léon to her with a fiendish laugh.

'The guillotine is waiting for him,' he repeated.

'No, no, no ! He shall not leave this house. I will save him !' she cried. 'Yes; I will kill any one who lays a finger upon him ! Why will you not save him ?' she shrieked aloud; her eyes were blazing, her hair unbound. 'Can you save him ?'

'I can do everything.'

'Why do you not save him?'

'Why?' shouted Castanier, and his voice made the ceiling ring.—'Eh! it is my revenge! Doing evil is my trade!'

'Die?' said Aquilina; 'must he die, my lover? Is it possible?'

She sprang up and snatched a stiletto from a basket that stood on the chest of drawers and went to Castanier, who began to laugh.

'You know very well that steel cannot hurt me now——'

Aquilina's arm suddenly dropped like a snapped harp string.

'Out with you, my good friend,' said the cashier, turning to the sergeant, 'and go about your business.'

He held out his hand; the other felt Castanier's superior power, and could not choose but obey.

'This house is mine; I could send for the commissary of police if I chose, and give you up as a man who has hidden himself on my premises, but I would rather let you go; I am a fiend, I am not a spy.'

'I shall follow him!' said Aquilina.

'Then follow him,' returned Castanier.—'Here, Jenny——'

Jenny appeared.

'Tell the porter to hail a cab for them.—Here, Naqui,' said Castanier, drawing a bundle of bank-notes from his pocket; 'you shall not go away like a pauper from a man who loves you still.'

He held out three hundred thousand francs. Aquilina took the notes, flung them on the floor, spat on them, and trampled upon them in a frenzy of despair.

'We will leave this house on foot,' she cried, 'without a farthing of your money.—Jenny, stay where you are.'

'Good evening!' answered the cashier, as he gathered

up the notes again. 'I have come back from my
journey.—Jenny,' he added, looking at the bewildered
waiting-maid, 'you seem to me to be a good sort of
girl. You have no mistress now. Come here. This
evening you shall have a master.'

Aquilina, who felt safe nowhere, went at once with
the sergeant to the house of one of her friends. But all
Léon's movements were suspiciously watched by the
police, and after a time he and three of his friends were
arrested. The whole story may be found in the news-
papers of that day.

Castanier felt that he had undergone a mental as well
as a physical transformation. The Castanier of old no
longer existed—the boy, the young Lothario, the
soldier who had proved his courage, who had been
tricked into a marriage and disillusioned, the cashier,
the passionate lover who had committed a crime for
Aquilina's sake. His inmost nature had suddenly asserted
itself. His brain had expanded, his senses had developed.
His thoughts comprehended the whole world; he saw all
the things of earth as if he had been raised to some high
pinnacle above the world.

Until that evening at the play he had loved Aquilina
to distraction. Rather than give her up he would have
shut his eyes to her infidelities; and now all that blind
passion had passed away as a cloud vanishes in the sunlight.

Jenny was delighted to succeed to her mistress's
position and fortune, and did the cashier's will in all
things; but Castanier, who could read the inmost
thoughts of the soul, discovered the real motive underlying this purely physical devotion. He amused himself
with her, however, like a mischievous child who greedily
sucks the juice of the cherry and flings away the stone.
The next morning at breakfast-time, when she was fully
convinced that she was a lady and the mistress of the

house, Castanier uttered one by one the thoughts that filled her mind as she drank her coffee.

'Do you know what you are thinking, child?' he said, smiling. 'I will tell you: "So all that lovely rosewood furniture that I coveted so much, and the pretty dresses that I used to try on, are mine now! All on easy terms that Madame refused, I do not know why. My word! if I might drive about in a carriage, have jewels and pretty things, a box at the theatre, and put something by! with me he should lead a life of pleasure fit to kill him if he were not as strong as a Turk! I never saw such a man!"—Was not that just what you were thinking,' he went on, and something in his voice made Jenny turn pale. 'Well, yes, child; you could not stand it, and I am sending you away for your own good; you would perish in the attempt. Come, let us part good friends,' and he coolly dismissed her with a very small sum of money.

The first use that Castanier had promised himself that he would make of the terrible power bought at the price of his eternal happiness, was the full and complete indulgence of all his tastes.

He first put his affairs in order, readily settled his account with M. de Nucingen, who found a worthy German to succeed him, and then determined on a carouse worthy of the palmiest days of the Roman Empire. He plunged into dissipation as recklessly as Belshazzar of old went to that last feast in Babylon. Like Belshazzar, he saw clearly through his revels a gleaming hand that traced his doom in letters of flame, not on the narrow walls of the banqueting-chamber, but over the vast spaces of heaven that the rainbow spans. His feast was not, indeed, an orgy confined within the limits of a banquet, for he squandered all the powers of soul and body in exhausting all the pleasures of earth. The table was in some sort earth itself, the earth that trembled beneath his feet. His was the last festival of

the reckless spendthrift who has thrown all prudence to
the winds. The devil had given him the key of the
storehouse of human pleasures ; he had filled and refilled
his hands, and he was fast nearing the bottom. In a
moment he had felt all that that enormous power could
accomplish ; in a moment he had exercised it, proved it,
wearied of it. What had hitherto been the sum of
human desires became as nothing. So often it happens
that with possession the vast poetry of desire must end,
and the thing possessed is seldom the thing that we
dreamed of.

Beneath Melmoth's omnipotence lurked this tragical
anti-climax of so many a passion, and now the inanity of
human nature was revealed to his successor, to whom
infinite power brought Nothingness as a dowry.

To come to a clear understanding of Castanier's
strange position, it must be borne in mind how suddenly these revolutions of thought and feeling had been
wrought ; how quickly they had succeeded each other ;
and of these things it is hard to give any idea to those
who have never broken the prison bonds of time, and
space, and distance. His relation to the world without
had been entirely changed with the expansion of his
faculties.

Like Melmoth himself, Castanier could travel in a
few moments over the fertile plains of India, could soar
on the wings of demons above African desert spaces, or
skim the surface of the seas. The same insight that
could read the inmost thoughts of others, could apprehend
at a glance the nature of any material object, just as he
caught as it were all flavours at once upon his tongue.
He took his pleasure like a despot ; a blow of the axe
felled the tree that he might eat its fruits. The trans-
itions, the alternations that measure joy and pain, and
diversify human happiness, no longer existed for him.
He had so completely glutted his appetites that pleasure
must overpass the limits of pleasure to tickle a palate

cloyed with satiety, and suddenly grown fastidious beyond all measure, so that ordinary pleasures became distasteful. Conscious that at will he was the master of all the women that he could desire, knowing that his power was irresistible, he did not care to exercise it ; they were pliant to his unexpressed wishes, to his most extravagant caprices, until he felt a horrible thirst for love, and would have love beyond their power to give.

The world refused him nothing save faith and prayer, the soothing and consoling love that is not of this world.   He was obeyed—it was a horrible position.

The torrents of pain, and pleasure, and thought that shook his soul and his bodily frame would have over-whelmed the strongest human being ; but in him there was a power of vitality proportioned to the power of the sensations that assailed him.   He felt within him a vague immensity of longing that earth could not satisfy.   He spent his days on outspread wings, longing to traverse the luminous fields of space to other spheres that he knew afar by intuitive perception, a clear and hopeless knowledge.   His soul dried up within him, for he hungered and thirsted after things that can neither be drunk nor eaten, but for which he could not choose but crave.   His lips, like Melmoth's, burned with desire ; he panted for the unknown, for he knew all things.

The mechanism and the scheme of the world was apparent to him, and its working interested him no longer; he did not long disguise the profound scorn that makes of a man of extraordinary powers a sphinx who knows everything and says nothing, and sees all things with an unmoved countenance.   He felt not the slightest wish to communicate his know-ledge to other men.   He was rich with all the wealth of the world, with one effort he could make the circle of the globe, and riches and power were meaning-less for him.   He felt the awful melancholy of omnipo-tence, a melancholy which Satan and God relieve by

the exercise of infinite power in mysterious ways known
to them alone.   Castanier had not, like his Master, the
inextinguishable energy of hate and malice ; he felt that
he was a devil, but a devil whose time was not yet
come, while Satan is a devil through all eternity, and
being damned beyond redemption, delights to stir up the
world, like a dung heap, with his triple fork and to thwart
therein the designs of God.   But Castanier, for his misfortune, had one hope left.

If in a moment he could move from one pole to the
other as a bird springs restlessly from side to side in its
cage, when, like the bird, he had crossed his prison, he
saw the vast immensity of space beyond it.   That vision
of the Infinite left him for ever unable to see humanity
and its affairs as other men saw them.   The insensate
fools who long for the power of the Devil gauge its
desirability from a human standpoint ; they do not see
that with the Devil's power they will likewise assume his
thoughts, and that they will be doomed to remain as
men among creatures who will no longer understand
them.   The Nero unknown to history who dreams of
setting Paris on fire for his private entertainment, like an
exhibition of a burning house on the boards of a theatre,
does not suspect that if he had that power, Paris would
become for him as little interesting as an ant-heap by
the roadside to a hurrying passer-by.   The circle of the
sciences was for Castanier something like a logogriph
for a man who does not know the key to it.   Kings and
Governments were despicable in his eyes.   His great
debauch had been in some sort a deplorable farewell
to his life as a man.   The earth had grown too
narrow for him, for the infernal gifts laid bare for him
the secrets of creation—he saw the cause and foresaw its
end.   He was shut out from all that men call 'heaven'
in all languages under the sun ; he could no longer think
of heaven.

Then he came to understand the look on his predecessor's face and the drying up of the life within ; then he knew all that was meant by the baffled hope that gleamed in Melmoth's eyes ; he, too, knew the thirst that burned those red lips, and the agony of a continual struggle between two natures grown to giant size. Even yet he might be an angel, and he knew himself to be a fiend. His was the fate of a sweet and gentle creature that a wizard's malice has imprisoned in a mis-shapen form, entrapping it by a pact, so that another's will must set it free from its detested envelope.

As a deception only increases the ardour with which a man of really great nature explores the infinite of senti-ment in a woman's heart, so Castanier awoke to find that one idea lay like a weight upon his soul, an idea which was perhaps the key to loftier spheres. The very fact that he had bartered away his eternal happiness led him to dwell in thought upon the future of those who pray and believe. On the morrow of his debauch, when he entered into the sober possession of his power, this idea made him feel himself a prisoner ; he knew the burden of the woe that poets, and prophets, and great oracles of faith have set forth for us in such mighty words ; he felt the point of the Flaming Sword plunged into his side, and hurried in search of Melmoth. What had become of his predecessor ?

The Englishman was living in a mansion in the Rue Férou, near Saint-Sulpice—a gloomy, dark, damp, and cold abode. The Rue Férou itself is one of the most dismal streets in Paris ; it has a north aspect like all the streets that lie at right angles to the left bank of the Seine, and the houses are in keeping with the site. As Castanier stood on the threshold he found that the door itself, like the vaulted roof, was hung with black ; rows of lighted tapers shone brilliantly as though some king were lying in state ; and a priest stood on either side of a catafalque that had been raised there.

'There is no need to ask why you have come, sir,' the

old hall porter said to Castanier ; 'you are so like our poor
dear master that is gone.   But if you are his brother, you
have come too late to bid him good-bye.   The good gentleman died the night before last.'

'How did he die ?' Castanier asked of one of the
priests.

'Set your mind at rest,' said an old priest ; he partly
raised as he spoke the black pall that covered the catafalque.

Castanier, looking at him, saw one of those faces that
faith has made sublime ; the soul seemed to shine forth
from every line of it, bringing light and warmth for
other men, kindled by the unfailing charity within.
This was Sir John Melmoth's confessor.

'Your brother made an end that men may envy, and
that must rejoice the angels.   Do you know what joy
there is in heaven over a sinner that repents ?   His tears
of penitence, excited by grace, flowed without ceasing ;
death alone checked them.   The Holy Spirit dwelt in
him.   His burning words, full of lively faith, were
worthy of the Prophet-King.   If, in the course of my
life, I have never heard a more dreadful confession than
from the lips of this Irish gentleman, I have likewise
never heard such fervent and passionate prayers.   However great the measures of his sins may have been, his
repentance has filled the abyss to overflowing.   The
hand of God was visibly stretched out above him, for he
was completely changed, there was such heavenly
beauty in his face.   The hard eyes were softened by
tears ; the resonant voice that struck terror into those
who heard it took the tender and compassionate tones of
those who themselves have passed through deep humilia-
tion.   He so edified those who heard his words, that
some who had felt drawn to see the spectacle of a
Christian's death fell on their knees as he spoke of
heavenly things, and of the infinite glory of God, and gave
thanks and praise to Him.   If he is leaving no worldly
wealth to his family, no family can possess a greater

blessing than this that he surely gained for them, a soul among the blessed, who will watch over you all and direct you in the path to heaven.'

These words made such a vivid impression upon Castanier that he instantly hurried from the house to the Church of Saint-Sulpice, obeying what might be called a decree of fate. Melmoth's repentance had stupefied him.

At that time, on certain mornings in the week, a preacher, famed for his eloquence, was wont to hold conferences, in the course of which he demonstrated the truths of the Catholic faith for the youth of a generation proclaimed to be indifferent in matters of belief by another voice no less eloquent than his own. The conference had been put off to a later hour on account of Melmoth's funeral, so Castanier arrived just as the great preacher was epitomising the proofs of a future existence of happiness with all the charm of eloquence and force of expression which have made him famous. The seeds of divine doctrine fell into a soil prepared for them in the old dragoon, into whom the Devil had glided. Indeed, if there is a phenomenon well attested by experience, is it not the spiritual phenomenon commonly called 'the faith of the peasant'? The strength of belief varies inversely with the amount of use that a man has made of his reasoning faculties. Simple people and soldiers belong to the unreasoning class. Those who have marched through life beneath the banner of instinct are far more ready to receive the light than minds and hearts overwearied with the world's sophistries.

Castanier had the southern temperament; he had joined the army as a lad of sixteen, and had followed the French flag till he was nearly forty years old. As a common trooper, he had fought day and night, and day after day, and, as in duty bound, had thought of his horse first, and of himself afterwards. While he served his military apprenticeship, therefore, he had but little leisure

in which to reflect on the destiny of man, and when he
became an officer he had his men to think of. He had
been swept from battlefield to battlefield, but he had
never thought of what comes after death. A soldier's
life does not demand much thinking. Those who
cannot understand the lofty political ends involved and the
interests of nation and nation ; who cannot grasp political
schemes as well as plans of campaign, and combine the
science of the tactician with that of the administrator,
are bound to live in a state of ignorance ; the most boorish
peasant in the most backward district in France is scarcely
in a worse case. Such men as these bear the brunt of
war, yield passive obedience to the brain that directs
them, and strike down the men opposed to them as the
woodcutter fells timber in the forest. Violent physical
exertion is succeeded by times of inertia, when they
repair the waste. They fight and drink, fight and eat,
fight and sleep, that they may the better deal hard
blows ; the powers of the mind are not greatly exercised
in this turbulent round of existence, and the character is
as simple as heretofore.

When the men who have shown such energy on the
battlefield return to ordinary civilisation, most of those
who have not risen to high rank seem to have acquired
no ideas, and to have no aptitude, no capacity, for grasping
new ideas. To the utter amazement of a younger
generation, those who made our armies so glorious and
so terrible are as simple as children, and as slow-witted
as a clerk at his worst, and the captain of a thunder-
ing squadron is scarcely fit to keep a merchant's
day-book. Old soldiers of this stamp, therefore, being
innocent of any attempt to use their reasoning faculties,
act upon their strongest impulses. Castanier's crime
was one of those matters that raise so many questions,
that, in order to debate about it, a moralist might call for
its 'discussion by clauses,' to make use of a parliamentary
expression.

Passion had counselled the crime; the cruelly irresistible power of feminine witchery had driven him to commit it; no man can say of himself, 'I will never do that,' when a siren joins in the combat and throws her spells over him.

So the word of life fell upon a conscience newly awakened to the truths of religion which the French Revolution and a soldier's career had forced Castanier to neglect. The solemn words, 'You will be happy or miserable for all eternity!' made but the more terrible impression upon him, because he had exhausted earth and shaken it like a barren tree; because his desires could effect all things, so that it was enough that any spot in earth or heaven should be forbidden him, and he forthwith thought of nothing else. If it were allowable to compare such great things with social follies, Castanier's position was not unlike that of a banker who, finding that his all-powerful millions cannot obtain for him an entrance into the society of the noblesse, must set his heart upon entering that circle, and all the social privileges that he has already acquired are as nothing in his eyes from the moment when he discovers that a single one is lacking.

Here was a man more powerful than all the kings on earth put together; a man who, like Satan, could wrestle with God Himself; leaning against one of the pillars in the Church of Saint-Sulpice, weighed down by the feelings and thoughts that oppressed him, and absorbed in the thought of a Future, the same thought that had engulfed Melmoth.

'He was very happy, was Melmoth!' cried Castanier. 'He died in the certain knowledge that he would go to heaven.'

In a moment the greatest possible change had been wrought in the cashier's ideas. For several days he had been a devil, now he was nothing but a man; an image of the fallen Adam, of the sacred tradition embodied in all cosmogonies.   But while he had thus shrunk to man's he retained a germ of greatness, he had been steeped in the Infinite.   The power of hell had revealed the divine power.   He thirsted for heaven as he had never thirsted after the pleasures of earth, that are so soon exhausted.   The enjoyments which the fiend promises are but the enjoyments of earth on a larger scale, but to the joys of heaven there is no limit.   He believed in God, and the spell that gave him the treasures of the world was as nothing to him now ; the treasures themselves seemed to him as contemptible as pebbles to an admirer of diamonds ; they were but gewgaws compared with the eternal glories of the other life.   A curse lay, he thought, on all things that came to him from this source. He sounded dark depths of painful thought as he listened to the service performed for Melmoth.   The *Dies iræ* filled him with awe ; he felt all the grandeur of that cry of a repentant soul trembling before the Throne of God. The Holy Spirit, like a devouring flame, passed through him as fire consumes straw.

The tears were falling from his eyes when—'Are you a relation of the dead?' the beadle asked him.

'I am his heir,' Castanier answered.

'Give something for the expenses of the services!' cried the man.

'No,' said the cashier.   (The Devil's money should not go to the Church.)

'For the poor!'

'No.'

'For repairing the Church!'

'No.'

'The Lady Chapel!'

'No.'

'For the schools!'

'No.'

Castanier went, not caring to expose himself to the sour looks that the irritated functionaries gave him.

Outside, in the street, he looked up at the Church of Saint-Sulpice. 'What made people build the giant cathedrals I have seen in every country?' he asked himself. 'The feeling shared so widely throughout all time must surely be based upon something.'

'Something! Do you call God *something*?' cried his conscience. 'God! God! God! . . .'

The word was echoed and re-echoed by an inner voice, till it overwhelmed him; but his feeling of terror subsided as he heard sweet distant sounds of music that he had caught faintly before. They were singing in the church, he thought, and his eyes scanned the great doorway. But as he listened more closely, the sounds poured upon him from all sides; he looked round the square, but there was no sign of any musicians. The melody brought visions of a distant heaven and far-off gleams of hope; but it also quickened the remorse that had set the lost soul in a ferment. He went on his way through Paris, walking as men walk who are crushed beneath the burden of their sorrow, seeing everything with unseeing eyes, loitering like an idler, stopping without cause, muttering to himself, careless of the traffic, making no effort to avoid a blow from a plank of timber.

Imperceptibly repentance brought him under the influence of the divine grace that soothes while it bruises the heart so terribly. His face came to wear a look of Melmoth, something great, with a trace of madness in the greatness. A look of dull and hopeless distress, mingled with the excited eagerness of hope, and, beneath it all, a gnawing sense of loathing for all that the world can give. The humblest of prayers lurked in the eyes that saw with such dreadful clearness. His power was the measure of his anguish. His body was bowed down by the fearful storm that shook his soul, as the tall pines bend before the blast. Like his predecessor, he could not refuse to bear the burden of life; he was afraid to die while he

bore the yoke of hell.   The torment grew intolerable.

At last, one morning, he bethought himself how that
Melmoth (now among the blessed) had made the proposal
of an exchange, and how that he had accepted it; others,
doubtless, would follow his example; for in an age
proclaimed, by the inheritors of the eloquence of the
Fathers of the Church, to be fatally indifferent to
religion, it should be easy to find a man who would
accept the conditions of the contract in order to prove
its advantages.

' There is one place where you can learn what kings
will fetch in the market; where nations are weighed in
the balance and systems appraised; where the value of a
government is stated in terms of the five-franc piece;
where ideas and beliefs have their price, and everything
is discounted; where God Himself, in a manner, borrows
on the security of His revenue of souls, for the Pope has
a running account there.   Is it not there that I should
go to traffick in souls?'

Castanier went quite joyously on 'Change, thinking
that it would be as easy to buy a soul as to invest money
in the Funds.   Any ordinary person would have feared
ridicule, but Castanier knew by experience that a desperate man takes everything seriously.   A prisoner lying
under sentence of death would listen to the madman who
should tell him that by pronouncing some gibberish he
could escape through the keyhole; for suffering is credulous, and clings to an idea until it fails, as the swimmer
borne along by the current clings to the branch that
snaps in his hand.

Towards four o'clock that afternoon Castanier appeared
among the little knots of men who were transacting
private business after 'Change.   He was personally known
to some of the brokers; and while affecting to be in search
of an acquaintance, he managed to pick up the current
gossip and rumours of failure.

'Catch me negotiating bills for Claparon & Co., my boy. The bank collector went round to return their acceptances to them this morning,' said a fat banker in his outspoken way. 'If you have any of their paper, look out.'

Claparon was in the building, in deep consultation with a man well known for the ruinous rate at which he lent money. Castanier went forthwith in search of the said Claparon, a merchant who had a reputation for taking heavy risks that meant wealth or utter ruin. The money-lender walked away as Castanier came up. A gesture betrayed the speculator's despair.

'Well, Claparon, the Bank wants a hundred thousand francs of you, and it is four o'clock; the thing is known, and it is too late to arrange your little failure comfortably,' said Castanier.

'Sir!'

'Speak lower,' the cashier went on. 'How if I were to propose a piece of business that would bring you in as much money as you require?'

'It would not discharge my liabilities; every business that I ever heard of wants a little time to simmer in.'

'I know of something that will set you straight in a moment,' answered Castanier; 'but first you would have to——'

'Do what?'

'Sell your share of paradise. It is a matter of business like anything else, isn't it? We all hold shares in the great Speculation of Eternity.'

'I tell you this,' said Claparon angrily, 'that I am just the man to lend you a slap in the face. When a man is in trouble, it is no time to play silly jokes on him.'

'I am talking seriously,' said Castanier, and he drew a bundle of notes from his pocket.

'In the first place,' said Claparon, 'I am not going to sell my soul to the Devil for a trifle. I want five hundred thousand francs before I strike——'

'Who talks of stinting you?' asked Castanier, cutting him short. 'You should have more gold than you could stow in the cellars of the Bank of France.'

He held out a handful of notes. That decided Claparon.

'Done,' he cried; 'but how is the bargain to be made?'

'Let us go over yonder, no one is standing there,' said Castanier, pointing to a corner of the court.

Claparon and his tempter exchanged a few words, with their faces turned to the wall. None of the onlookers guessed the nature of this by-play, though their curiosity was keenly excited by the strange gestures of the two contracting parties. When Castanier returned, there was a sudden outburst of amazed exclamation. As in the Assembly where the least event immediately attracts attention, all faces were turned to the two men who had caused the sensation, and a shiver passed through all beholders at the change that had taken place in them.

The men who form the moving crowd that fills the Stock Exchange are soon known to each other by sight. They watch each other like players round a card-table. Some shrewd observers can tell how a man will play and the condition of his exchequer from a survey of his face; and the Stock Exchange is simply a vast card-table. Every one, therefore, had noticed Claparon and Castanier. The latter (like the Irishman before him) had been muscular and powerful, his eyes were full of light, his colour high. The dignity and power in his face had struck awe into them all; they wondered how old Castanier had come by it; and now they beheld Castanier divested of his power, shrunken, wrinkled, aged, and feeble. He had drawn Claparon out of the crowd with the energy of a sick man in a fever fit; he had looked like an opium-eater during the brief period of excitement that the drug can give; now, on his return, he seemed to be in the condition of utter exhaustion in which the patient dies after the fever departs, or to be suffering from the horrible prostration that follows on excessive indulgence in the delights of narcotics. The infernal power that had upheld him through his debauches had left him, and the body was left unaided and alone to endure the agony of remorse and the heavy burden of sincere repentance. Claparon's troubles every one could guess; but Claparon reappeared, on the other hand, with sparkling eyes, holding his head high with the pride of Lucifer. The crisis had passed from the one man to the other.

'Now you can drop off with an easy mind, old man,' said Claparon to Castanier.

'For pity's sake, send for a cab and for a priest; send for the curate of Saint-Sulpice!' answered the old dragoon, sinking down upon the kerbstone.

The words 'a priest' reached the ears of several people, and produced uproarious jeering among the stockbrokers, for faith with these gentlemen means a belief that a scrap of paper called a mortgage represents an estate, and the List of Fundholders is their Bible.

'Shall I have time to repent?' said Castanier to himself, in a piteous voice, that impressed Claparon.

A cab carried away the dying man; the speculator went to the bank at once to meet his bills; and the momentary sensation produced upon the throng of business men by the sudden change on the two faces, vanished like the furrow cut by a ship's keel in the sea. News of the greatest importance kept the attention of the world of commerce on the alert; and when commercial interests are at stake, Moses might appear with his two luminous horns, and his coming would scarcely receive the honours of a pun; the gentlemen whose business it is to write the Market Reports would ignore his existence.

When Claparon had made his payments, fear seized upon him. There was no mistake about his power. He went on 'Change again, and offered his bargain to other men in embarrassed circumstances. The Devil's bond,

'together with the rights, easements, and privileges apper-
taining thereunto,'—to use the expression of the notary
who succeeded Claparon, changed hands for the sum of
seven hundred thousand francs.   The notary in his turn
parted with the agreement with the Devil for five hundred
thousand francs to a building contractor in difficulties,
who likewise was rid of it to an iron merchant in consideration of a hundred thousand crowns.   In fact, by
five o'clock people had ceased to believe in the strange
contract, and purchasers were lacking for want of confidence.

At half-past five the holder of the bond was a house-
painter, who was lounging by the door of the building in
the Rue Feydeau, where at that time stockbrokers tem-
porarily congregated.   The house-painter, simple fellow,
could not think what was the matter with him.   He
'felt all anyhow'; so he told his wife when he went
home.

The Rue Feydeau, as idlers about town are aware, is
a place of pilgrimage for youths who for lack of a mistress
bestow their ardent affection upon the whole sex.   On
the first floor of the most rigidly respectable domicile
therein dwelt one of those exquisite creatures whom it has
pleased heaven to endow with the rarest and most sur-
passing beauty.   As it is impossible that they should all
be duchesses or queens (since there are many more pretty
women in the world than titles and thrones for them to
adorn), they are content to make a stockbroker or a
banker happy at a fixed price.   To this good-natured
beauty, Euphrasia by name, an unbounded ambition had
led a notary's clerk to aspire.   In short, the second clerk
in the office of Maître Crottat, notary, had fallen in love
with her, as youth at two-and-twenty can fall in love.
The scrivener would have murdered the Pope and
run amuck through the whole sacred college to procure
the miserable sum of a hundred louis to pay for a shawl
which had turned Euphrasia's head, at which price her

waiting-woman had promised that Euphrasia should be his. The infatuated youth walked to and fro under Madam Euphrasia's windows, like the polar bears in their cage at the Jardin des Plantes, with his right hand thrust beneath his waistcoat in the region of the heart, which he was fit to tear from his bosom, but as yet he had only wrenched at the elastic of his braces.

'What can one do to raise ten thousand francs?' he asked himself. 'Shall I make off with the money that I must pay on the registration of that conveyance? Good heavens! my loan would not ruin the purchaser, a man with seven millions! And then next day I would fling myself at his feet and say, "I have taken ten thousand francs belonging to you, sir; I am twenty-two years of age, and I am in love with Euphrasia—that is my story. My father is rich, he will pay you back; do not ruin me! Have not you yourself been twenty-two years old and madly in love?" But these beggarly landowners have no souls! He would be quite likely to give me up to the public prosecutor, instead of taking pity upon me. Good God! if it were only possible to sell your soul to the Devil! But there is neither a God nor a Devil; it is all nonsense out of nursery tales and old wives' talk. What shall I do?'

'If you have a mind to sell your soul to the Devil, sir,' said the house-painter, who had overheard something that the clerk let fall, 'you can have the ten thousand francs.'

'And Euphrasia!' cried the clerk, as he struck a bargain with the devil that inhabited the house-painter.

The pact concluded, the frantic clerk went to find the shawl, and mounted Madam Euphrasia's staircase; and as (literally) the devil was in him, he did not come down for twelve days, drowning the thought of hell and of his privileges in twelve days of love and riot and forgetfulness, for which he had bartered away all his hopes of a paradise to come.

And in this way the secret of the vast power discovered and acquired by the Irishman, the offspring of Mathurin's brain, was lost to mankind; and the various Orientalists, Mystics, and Archæologists who take an interest in these matters were unable to hand down to posterity the proper method of invoking the Devil, for the following sufficient reasons :—

On the thirteenth day after these frenzied nuptials the wretched clerk lay on a pallet bed in a garret in his master's house in the Rue Saint-Honoré. Shame, the stupid goddess who dares not behold herself, had taken possession of the young man. He had fallen ill; he would nurse himself; misjudged the quantity of a remedy devised by the skill of a practitioner well known on the walls of Paris, and succumbed to the effects of an overdose of mercury. His corpse was as black as a mole's back. A devil had left unmistakable traces of its passage there; could it have been Ashtaroth?

'The estimable youth to whom you refer has been carried away to the planet Mercury,' said the head clerk to a German demonologist who came to investigate the matter at first hand.

'I am quite prepared to believe it,' answered the Teuton.

'Oh!'

'Yes, sir,' returned the other. 'The opinion you advance coincides with the very words of Jacob Boehme. In the forty-eighth proposition of *The Threefold Life of Man* he says that "if God hath brought all things to pass with a LET THERE BE, the FIAT is the secret matrix which comprehends and apprehends the nature which is formed by the spirit born of Mercury and of God."'

'What do you say, sir?'

The German delivered his quotation afresh.

'We do not know it,' said the clerks.

'*Fiat?* . . .' said a clerk. '*Fiat lux!*'

'You can verify the citation for yourselves,' said the German. 'You will find the passage in the *Treatise of the Threefold Life of Man*, page 75; the edition was published by M. Migneret in 1809. It was translated into French by a philosopher who had a great admiration for the famous shoemaker.'

'Oh! he was a shoemaker, was he?' said the head clerk.

'In Prussia,' said the German.

'Did he work for the King of Prussia?' inquired a Bœotian of a second clerk.

'He must have vamped up his prose,' said a third.

'That man is colossal!' cried the fourth, pointing to the Teuton.

That gentleman, though a demonologist of the first rank, did not know the amount of devilry to be found in a notary's clerk. He went away without the least idea that they were making game of him, and fully under the impression that the young fellows regarded Boehme as a colossal genius.

'Education is making strides in France,' said he to himself.

PARIS, *May* 6, 1835.

THE MARANAS

To Madame la Comtesse Merlin

IN spite of the discipline enforced by Marshal Suchet in the division he commanded in the Peninsular War, all his efforts could not restrain an outbreak of license and tumult at the taking of Taragona. Indeed, according to trustworthy military authorities, the intoxication of victory resulted in something very like a sack of the town. Pillage was promptly put down by the Marshal; and as soon as order was restored, a commandant appointed, the military administrators appeared upon the scene, and the town began to wear a nondescript aspect —the organisation was French, but the Spanish population was left free to follow *in petto* its own national customs. It would be a task of no little difficulty to determine the exact duration of the pillage, but its cause (like that of most sublunary events) is sufficiently easy to discover.

In the Marshal's division of the army there was a regiment composed almost entirely of Italians, commanded by a certain Colonel Eugène, a man of extraordinary valour, a second Murat, who, having come to the trade of war too late, had gained no Grand Duchy of Berg, no Kingdom of Naples, nor a ball through the heart at Pizzo. But if he had received no crown, his chances of receiving bullets were admirably good; and it would have been in no wise astonishing if he had had more than one of them. This regiment was made up from the

110

wrecks of the Italian Legion, which is in Italy very
much what the colonial battalions are in France.
Stationed in the isle of Elba, it had provided an honourable way out of the difficulty experienced by families
with regard to the future of unmanageable sons, as well
as a career for those great men spoiled in the making,
whom society is too ready to brand as *mauvais sujets*.
All of them were men misunderstood, for the most part—
men who may become heroes if a woman's smile raises
them out of the beaten track of glory ; or terrible after
an orgy, when some ugly suggestion, dropped by a boon
companion, has gained possession of their minds.

Napoleon had enrolled these men of energy in the Sixth
Regiment of the line, hoping to metamorphose them into
generals, with due allowance for the gaps to be made in
their ranks by bullets ; but the Emperor's estimate of the
ravages of death proved more correct than the rest of his
calculations.   It was often decimated, but its character
remained the same ; and the Sixth acquired a name for
splendid bravery in the field, and the very worst reputation
in private life.

These Italians had lost their captain during the siege
of Taragona.   He was the famous Bianchi who laid a
wager during the campaign that he would eat a Spanish
sentinel's heart—and won his bet.   The story of this
pleasantry of the camp is told elsewhere in the *Scènes de la
Vie Parisienne*; therein will be found certain details which
corroborate what has been said here concerning the
legion.   Bianchi, the prince of those fiends incarnate who
had earned the double reputation of the regiment, possessed the chivalrous sense of honour which, in the army,
covers a multitude of the wildest excesses.   In a word,
had he lived a few centuries earlier, he would have made a
gallant buccaneer.   Only a few days before he fell, he
had distinguished himself by such conspicuous courage in
action, that the Marshal sought to recognise it.   Bianchi
had refused promotion, pension, or a fresh decoration,

and asked as a favour to be allowed to mount the first scaling-ladder at the assault of Taragona as his sole reward. The Marshal granted the request, and forgot his promise; but Bianchi himself put him in mind of it and of Bianchi, for the berserker Captain was the first to plant the flag of France upon the wall; and there he fell, killed by a monk.

This historical digression is necessary to explain how it came to pass that the Sixth Regiment of the line was the first to enter Taragona, and how the tumult, sufficiently natural after a town has been carried by storm, degenerated so quickly into an attempt to sack it. Moreover, among these men of iron, there were two officers, otherwise but little remarkable, who were destined by force of circumstances to play an important part in this story.

The first of these, a captain on the clothing establishment—half-civilian, half-officer—was generally said, in soldierly language, to 'take good care of number one.'

Outside his regiment he was wont to swagger and brag of his connection with it; he would curl his moustache and look a terrible fellow, but his mess had no great opinion of him. His money was the secret of his valorous discretion. For a double reason, moreover, he had been nicknamed *Captain of the Ravens*; because, in the first place, he scented the powder a league away; and, in the second, scurried out of range like a bird on the wing; the nickname was likewise a harmless soldier's joke, a personality of which another might have been proud. Captain Montefiore, of the illustrious family of the Montefiori of Milan (though by the law of the kingdom of Italy he might not bear his title), was one of the prettiest fellows in the army. Possibly his beauty may secretly have been an additional cause of his prudence on the field of battle. A wound in the face by spoiling his profile, scarring his forehead, or seaming his cheeks, would have spoiled one of the finest heads in Italy, and destroyed the delicate proportions of a countenance such as no woman ever pictured in dreams. In Girodet's picture of the *Revolt of Cairo* there is a young dying Turk who has the same type of face, the same melancholy expression, of which women are nearly always the dupes. The Marchese di Montefiore had property of his own, but it was entailed, and he had anticipated his income for several years in order to pay for escapades peculiarly Italian and inconceivable in Paris. He had ruined himself by running a theatre in Milan for the special purpose of foisting upon the public a *cantatrice* who could not sing, but who loved him (so he said) to distraction.

So Montefiore the captain had good prospects, and was in no hurry to risk them for a paltry scrap of red ribbon. If he was no hero, he was at any rate a philosopher; besides, precedents (if it is allowable to make use of parliamentary expressions in this connection), precedents are forthcoming. Did not Philip II. swear during the battle of Saint-Quentin that he would never go under fire again, nor near it, save the faggots of the Inquisition? Did not the Duke of Alva approve the notion that the involuntary exchange of a crown for a cannon-ball was the worst kind of trade in the world? Montefiore, therefore, as a Marquis, was of Philip II.'s way of thinking; he was a Philippist in his quality of gay young bachelor, and in other respects quite as astute a politician as Philip II. himself. He comforted himself for his nickname, and for the slight esteem in which he was held by his regiment, with the thought that his comrades were sorry scamps; and even if they should survive this war of extermination, their opinion of him was not likely to gain much credence hereafter. Was not his face as good as a certificate of merit? He saw himself a colonel through some accident of feminine favour; or, by a skilfully effected transition, the captain on the clothing establishment would become an orderly, and the orderly would in turn

H

become the aide-de-camp of some good-natured marshal.
The bravery of the uniform and the bravery of the man
were all as one to the captain on the clothing establishment. So some broad sheet or other would one day call
him 'the brave Colonel Montefiore,' and so forth.
Then he would have a hundred thousand scudi a year,
he would marry the daughter of a noble house, and no
one would dare to breathe a word against his courage
nor to seek to verify his wounds. Finally, it should be
stated that Captain Montefiore had a friend in the person
of the quartermaster, a Provençal, born in the Nice
district, Diard by name.

A friend, be it in the convict's prison or in an artist's
garret, is a compensation for many troubles ; and Montefiore and Diard, being a pair of philosophers, found com-
pensations for their hard life in companionship in vice,
much as two artists will lull the consciousness of their
hardships to sleep by hopes of future fame. Both looked
at war as a means to an end, and not as an end in itself,
and frankly called those who fell, fools for their pains.
Chance had made soldiers of both, when they should
have been by rights deliberating in a congress round a
table covered with a green cloth. Nature had cast
Montefiore in the mould of Rizzio, and Diard in the
crucible whence she turns out diplomatists. Both possessed
the excitable, nervous, half-feminine temperament, which
is always energetic, be it in good or evil ; always at the
mercy of the caprices of the moment, and swayed by an
impulse equally unaccountable to commit a crime or to
do a generous deed, to act as a hero or as a craven
coward. The fate of such natures as these depends at
every moment of their lives upon the intensity of the
impressions produced upon the nervous system by vehement and short-lived passions.

Diard was a very fair accountant, but not one of the
men would have trusted him with his purse, or made
him his executor, possibly by reason of the suspicion

that the soldier feels of officialdom. The quarter-master's character was not wanting in dash, nor in a certain boyish enthusiasm, which is apt to wear off as a man grows older and reasons and makes forecasts. And for the rest, his humour was variable as the beauty of a blonde can sometimes be. He was a great talker on every subject. He called himself an artist ; and, in imitation of two celebrated generals, collected works of art, simply, he asserted, to secure them for posterity. His comrades would have been hard put to it to say what they really thought of him. Many of them, who were wont to borrow of him at need, fancied that he was rich ; but he was a gambler, and a gambler's property cannot be called his own. He played heavily, so did Montefiore, and all the officers played with them ; for to man's shame, be it said, plenty of men will meet on terms of equality round a gaming table with others whom they do not respect and will not recognise if they meet them elsewhere. It was Montefiore who had made that bet with Bianchi about the Spaniard's heart.

Montefiore and Diard were among the last to advance to the assault of the place, but they were the first to go forward into the town itself when it was taken. Such things happen in a *mêlée*, and the two friends were old hands. Mutually supported, therefore, they plunged boldly into a labyrinth of narrow dark little streets, each bent upon his own private affairs ; the one in search of Madonnas on canvas, and the other of living originals.

In some quarter of Taragona, Diard espied a piece of ecclesiastical architecture, saw that it was the porch of a convent, and that the doors had been forced, and rushed in to restrain the fury of the soldiery. He was not a moment too soon. Two Parisians were about to riddle one of Albani's Virgins with shot, and of these light infantrymen he bought the picture, undismayed by the moustaches with which the zealous iconoclasts had adorned it.

Montefiore, left outside, contemplated the front of a cloth merchant's house opposite the convent. He was looking it up and down, when a corner of a blind was raised, a girl's head peered forth, a glance like a lightning flash answered his, and—a shot was fired at him from the building. Taragona carried by assault, Taragona roused to fury, firing from every window, Taragona outraged, dishevelled, and half-naked, with French soldiers pouring through her blazing streets, slaying there and being slain, was surely worth a glance from fearless Spanish eyes. What was it but a bull-fight on a grander scale? Montefiore forgot the pillaging soldiers, and for a moment heard neither the shrieks, nor the rattle of musketry, nor the dull thunder of the cannon. He, the Italian libertine, tired of Italian beauties, weary of all women, dreaming of an impossible woman because the possible had ceased to have any attraction for him, had never beheld so exquisitely lovely a profile as that of this Spanish girl. The jaded voluptuary, who had squandered his fortune on follies innumerable and on the gratification of a young man's endless desires; the most abominable monstrosity that our society can produce, could still tremble. The bright idea of setting fire to the house instantly flashed through his mind, suggested, doubtless, by the shot from the patriotic cloth merchant's window; but he was alone, and the means of doing it were to seek, fighting was going forward in the market-place, where a few desperate men still defended themselves.

He thought better of it. Diard came out of the convent, Montefiore kept his discovery to himself, and the pair made several excursions through the town together; but on the morrow the Italian was quartered in the cloth merchant's house, a very appropriate arrangement for a captain on the clothing establishment.

The first floor of the worthy Spaniard's abode consisted of a vast dimly-lighted shop; protected in front, as the old houses in the Rue des Lombards in Paris used to be, by heavy iron bars. Behind the shop lay the parlour, lighted by windows that looked out into an inner yard. It was a large room, redolent of the spirit of the Middle Ages, with its old dark pictures, old tapestry, and antique *brazero*. A broad-plumed hat hung from a nail upon the wall above a matchlock used in guerilla warfare, and a heavy brigand's cloak. The kitchen lay immediately beyond this parlour, or living-room, where meals were served and cigars smoked; and Spaniards, talking round the smouldering brazier, would nurse hot wrath and hatred of the French in their hearts.

Silver jugs and valuable plate stood on the antique buffet, but the room was fitfully and scantily illuminated, so that the daylight scarcely did more than bring out faint sparkles from the brightest objects in the room; all the rest of it, and even the faces of its occupants, were as dark as a Dutch interior. Between the shop itself and this apartment, with its rich subdued tones and old-world aspect, a sufficiently ill-lit staircase led to a warehouse, where it was possible to examine the stuffs by the light from some ingeniously contrived windows. The merchant and his wife occupied the floor above this warehouse, and the apprentice and the maid-servant were lodged still higher in the attics immediately beneath the roof. This highest story overhung the street, and was supported by brackets, which gave a quaint look to the house front. On the coming of the officer, the merchant and his wife resigned their rooms to him and went up to these attics, doubtless to avoid friction.

Montefiore gave himself out to be a Spanish subject by birth, a victim to the tyranny of Napoleon, whom he was forced to serve against his will. These half-lies produced the intended effect. He was asked to join the family at meals, as befitted his birth and rank and the name he bore. He had his private reasons for wishing to conciliate the merchant's family. He felt the presence of his Madonna, much as the Ogre in the fairy tale smelt the tender flesh of little Thumbkin and his brothers; but though he succeeded in winning his host's confidence, the latter kept the secret of the Madonna so well that the captain not only saw no sign of the girl's existence during the first day spent beneath the honest Spaniard's roof, but heard no sound that could betray her presence in any part of the dwelling.   The old house was, however, almost entirely built of wood; every noise above or below could be heard through the walls and ceilings, and Montefiore hoped during the silence of the early hours of night to guess the young girl's whereabouts.   She was the only daughter of his host and hostess, he thought; probably they had shut her up in the attics, whither they themselves had retired during the military occupation of the town.   No indications, however, betrayed the hiding-place of the treasure.   The officer might stand with his face glued to the small leaded diamond-shaped panes of the window, looking out into the darkness of the yard below and the grim walls that rose up around it, but no light gleamed from any window save from those of the room overhead, where he could hear the old merchant and his wife talking, coughing, coming, and going.   There was not so much as a shadow of a girl to be seen.

Montefiore was too cunning to risk the future of his passion by prowling about the house of a night, by knocking softly at all the doors, or by other hazardous expedients.   His host was a hot patriot, a Spanish father, and an owner of bales of cloth; bound, therefore, in each character to be suspicious.   Discovery would be utter ruin, so Montefiore resolved to bide his time patiently, hoping everything from the carelessness of human nature; for if rogues, with the best of reasons for being cautious, will forget themselves in the long run, so still more will honest men.

Next day he discovered a kind of hammock slung in the

kitchen—evidently the servant slept there. The apprentice, it seemed, spent the night on the counter in the shop.

At supper-time, on the second day, Montefiore cursed Napoleon till he saw his host's sombre face relax somewhat. The man was a typical, swarthy Spaniard, with a head such as used to be carved on the head of a rebeck. A smile of gleeful hatred lurked among the wrinkles about his wife's mouth. The lamplight and fitful gleams from the brazier filled the stately room with capricious answering reflections. The hostess was just offering a cigarette to their semi-compatriot, when Montefiore heard the rustle of a dress, and a chair was overturned behind the tapestry hangings.

'There!' cried the merchant's wife, turning pale, 'may all the saints send that no misfortune has befallen us!'

'So you have some one in there, have you?' asked the Italian, who betrayed no sign of emotion.

The merchant let fall some injurious remarks as to girls. His wife, in alarm, opened a secret door, and brought in the Italian's Madonna, half dead with fear. The delighted lover scarcely seemed to notice the girl; but, lest he might overdo the affectation of indifference, he glanced at her, and turning to his host, asked in his mother tongue—

'Is she your daughter, señor?'

Perez de Lagounia (for that was the merchant's name) had had extensive business connections in Genoa, Florence, and Leghorn; he knew Italian, and replied in that language.

'No. If she had been my own daughter, I should have taken fewer precautions, but the child was put into our charge, and I would die sooner than allow the slightest harm to befall her. But what sense can you expect of a girl of eighteen?'

'She is very beautiful,' Montefiore said carelessly. He did not look at her again.

'The mother is sufficiently famous for her beauty,' answered the merchant. And they continued to smoke and to watch each other.

Montefiore had imposed upon himself the hard task of avoiding the least look that might compromise his attitude of indifference; but as Perez turned his head aside to spit, the Italian stole a glance at the girl, and again those sparkling eyes met his. In that one glance, with the experienced vision that gives to a voluptuary or a sculptor the power of discerning the outlines of the form beneath the draperies, he beheld a masterpiece created to know all the happiness of love. He saw a delicately fair face, which the sun of Spain had slightly tinged with a warm brown, that added to a seraphically calm expression a flush of pride, a suffused glow beneath the translucent fairness, due, perhaps, to the pure Moorish blood that brought animation and colour into it. Her hair, knotted on the crown of her head, fell in thick curls about transparent ears like a child's, surrounding them with dark shadows that made a framework for the white throat with its faint blue veins, in strong contrast with the fiery eyes and the red finely-curved mouth. The *basquina* of her country displayed the curving outlines of a figure as pliant as a branch of willow. This was no Madonna of Italian painters, but the Madonna of Spanish art, the Virgin of Murillo, the only artist daring enough to depict the rapture of the Conception, a delirious flight of the fervid imagination of the boldest and most sensuous of painters. Three qualities were blended in this young girl; any one of them would have sufficed to exalt a woman into a divinity—the purity of the pearl in the depths of the sea, the sublime exaltation of a Saint Theresa, and a voluptuous charm of which she was herself unconscious. Her presence had the power of a talisman. Everything in the ancient room seemed to have grown young to Montefiore's eyes since she entered it. But if the apparition was exquisite, the stay was brief; she was taken back to her mysterious abiding-place, and thither, shortly afterwards, the servant took a light and her supper, without any attempt at concealment.

'You do very wisely to keep her out of sight,' said Montefiore in Italian. 'I will keep your secret. The deuce! some of our generals would be quite capable of carrying her off by force.'

Montefiore, in his intoxication, went so far as to think of marrying the fair unknown. With this idea in his mind, he put some questions to his host. Perez willingly told him the strange chance that had given him his ward; indeed, the prudent Spaniard, knowing Montefiore's rank and name, of which he had heard in Italy, was anxious to confide the story to his guest, to show how strong were the barriers raised between the young girl and seduction. Although in the good man's talk there was a certain homely eloquence and force in keeping with his simple manner of life, and with that carbine shot at Montefiore from the window, his story will be better given in an abbreviated form.

When the French Republic revolutionised the manners of the inhabitants of the countries which served as the theatre of its wars, a *fille-de-joie*, driven from Venice after the fall of Venice, came to Taragona. Her life had been a tissue of romantic adventure and strange vicissitudes. On no woman belonging to her class had gold been showered so often; so often the caprice of some great lord, struck with her extraordinary beauty, had heaped jewels upon her, and all the luxuries of wealth, for a time. For her this meant flowers and carriages, pages and tire-women, palaces and pictures, insolent pride, journeys like a progress of Catherine ii., the life of an absolute queen, in fact, whose caprices were law, and whose whims were more than obeyed; and then— suddenly the gold would utterly vanish—how, neither she nor any one else, man of science, physicist, or chemist could tell, and she was returned again to the streets and to poverty, with nothing in the world save her all-powerful beauty. Yet through it all she lived without taking any thought for the past, the present, or the future. Thrown upon the world, and maintained in her extremity by some poor officer, a gambler, adored for his moustache, she would attach herself to him like a dog to his master, and console him for the hardships of a soldier's life, in all of which she shared, sleeping as lightly under the roof of a garret as beneath the richest of silk canopies. Whether she was in Spain or Italy, she punctually adhered to religious observances. More than once she had bidden love 'return to-morrow, to-day I am God's.'

But this clay in which gold and spices were mingled, this utter recklessness, these storms of passion, the religious faith lying in the heart like a diamond in the mud, the life begun and ended in the hospital, the continual game of hazard played with the soul and body as its stake; this Alchemy of Life, in short, with vice fanning the flame beneath the crucible in which great careers and fair inheritances and fortune and the honour of illustrious names were melted away; all these were the products of a peculiar genius, faithfully transmitted from mother to daughter from the times of the Middle Ages. The woman was called *La Marana*. In her family, whose descent since the thirteenth century was reckoned exclusively on the spindle side—the idea, person, authority, nay, the very name of a father, had been absolutely unknown. The name of *Marana* was for her what the dignity of *Stuart* was to the illustrious race of kings of Scotland, a title of honour substituted for the patronymic, when the office became hereditary in their family.

In former times, when France, Spain, and Italy possessed common interests, which at times bound them closely together, and at least as frequently embroiled all three in wars, the word Marana, in its widest acceptation, meant a courtesan. In those ages these women had a definite status of which no memory now exists. In France, Ninon de Lenclos and Marion Delorme alone played such a part as the Imperias, the Catalinas, and Maranas who in the preceding centuries exercised the powers of the cassock, the robe, and the sword. There is a church somewhere in Rome built by an Imperia in a fit of penitence, as Rhodope of old once built a pyramid in Egypt. The epithet by which this family of outcasts once was branded became at last their name in earnest, and even something like a patent of nobility for vice, by establishing its antiquity beyond cavil.

But for the La Marana of the nineteenth century there came a day, whether it was a day of splendour or of misery, no man knows, for the problem is a secret between her soul and God ; but it was surely in an hour of melancholy, when religion made its voice heard, that with her head in the skies she became conscious of the slough in which her feet were set. Then she cursed the blood in her veins ; she cursed herself ; she trembled to think that she should bear a daughter ; and vowed, as these women vow, with the honour and resolution of the convict, that is to say, with the strongest resolution, the most scrupulous honour to be found under the sun ; making her vow, therefore, before an altar, and consecrating it thereby, that her daughter should lead a virtuous and holy life, that of this long race of lost and sinful women there should come at last one angel who should appear for them in heaven. That vow made, the blood of the Marana regained its sway, and again the courtesan plunged into her life of adventure, with one more thought in her heart. At length she loved, with the violent love of the prostitute, as Henrietta Wilson loved Lord Ponsonby, as Mademoiselle Dupuis loved Bolingbroke, as the Marchesa di Pescara loved her husband ; nay, she did not love, she adored a fair-haired half-feminine creature, investing him with all the virtues that she had not, and taking all his vices upon herself. Of this mad union with a weakling, a union blessed neither of God nor man, only to be excused by the happiness it brings, but never absolved by happiness; a union for which the most brazen front must one day blush, a daughter was born, a daughter to be saved, a daughter for whom La Marana desired a stainless life, and, above all things, the instincts of womanliness which she herself had not. Thenceforward, in poverty or prosperity, La Marana bore within her heart a pure affection, the fairest of all human sentiments, because it is the least selfish. Love has its own tinge of egoism, but there is no trace of it in a mother's affection.

And La Marana's motherhood meant more to her than to other women. It was perhaps her hope of salvation, a plank to cling to in the shipwreck of her eternity. Was she not accomplishing part of her sacred task on earth by sending one more angel to heaven? Was not this a better thing than a tardy repentance? Was there any other way now left to her of sending up prayers from a pure heart to God?

When her daughter was given to her, her Maria-Juana-Pepita (the little one should have had the whole calendar for patron saints if the mother could have had her will), then La Marana set before herself so high an ideal of the dignity of motherhood that she sought a truce from her life of sin. She would live virtuously and alone. There should be no more midnight revels nor wanton days. All her fortunes, all her happiness lay in the child's fragile cradle. The sound of the little voice made an oasis for her amid the burning sands of her life. How should this love be compared with any other? Were not all human affections blended in it with every hope of heaven?

La Marana determined that no stain should rest upon her daughter's life, save that of the original sin of her birth, which she strove to cleanse by a baptism in all social virtues ; so she asked of the child's young father a sufficient fortune, and the name he bore. The child was no longer Juana Marana, but Juana dei Mancini.

At last, after seven years of joy and kisses, of rapture and bliss, the poor Marana must part with her darling, lest she also should be branded with her hereditary shame. The mother had force of soul sufficient to give up her child for her child's sake ; and sought out, not without dreadful pangs, another mother for her, a family whose manners she might learn, where good examples would be set before her. A mother's abdication is an act either atrocious or sublime ; in this case, was it not sublime ?

At Taragona, therefore, a lucky accident brought the Lagounias in her way, and in a manner that brought out all the honourable integrity of the Spaniard and the nobleness of his wife. For these two, La Marana appeared like an angel that unlocks the doors of a prison. The merchant's fortune and honour were in peril at the moment, and he needed prompt and secret help ; La Marana handed over to him the sum of money intended for Juana's dowry, asking neither for gratitude nor for interest. According to her peculiar notions of jurisprudence, a contract was a matter of the heart, a stiletto the remedy in the hands of the weak, and God the supreme Court of Appeal.

She told Doña Lagounia the story of her miserable situation, and confided her child and her child's fortune to the honour of old Spain, and the untarnished integrity that pervaded the old house. Doña Lagounia had no children of her own, and was delighted to have an adopted daughter to bring up. The courtesan took leave of her darling, feeling that the child's future was secure, and that she had found a mother for Juana, a mother who would train her up to be a Mancini, and not a Marana.

Poor Marana, poor bereaved mother, she went away

from the merchant's quiet and humble home, the abode of domestic and family virtue; and felt comforted in her grief as she pictured Juana growing up in that atmosphere of religion, piety, and honour, a maiden, a wife, and a mother, a happy mother, not for a few brief years, but all through a long lifetime. The tears that fell upon the threshold were tears that angels bear to heaven. Since that day of mourning and of hope La Marana had thrice returned to see her daughter, an irresistible presentiment each time bringing her back. The first time Juana had fallen dangerously ill.

'I knew it!' she said to Perez, as she entered his house.

Far away, and as she slept, she had dreamed that Juana was dying.

She watched over her daughter and tended her, and then one morning, when the danger was over, she kissed the sleeping girl's forehead, and went without revealing herself. The mother within her bade the courtesan depart.

A second time La Marana came,—this time to the church where Juana dei Mancini made her first Communion. The exiled mother, very plainly dressed, stood in the shadow behind a pillar, and saw her past self in her daughter, saw a divinely fair face like an angel's, pure as the newly fallen snow on the heights of the hills. Even in La Marana's love for her child there was a trace of the courtesan; a feeling of jealousy stronger than all love that she had known awoke in her heart, and she left the church; she could no longer control a wild desire to stab Doña Lagounia, who stood there with that look of happiness upon her face, too really a mother to her child.

The last meeting between the two had taken place at Milan, whither the merchant and his wife had gone. La Marana, sweeping along the Corso in almost queenly state, flashed like lightning upon her daughter's sight, and was not recognised. Her anguish was terrible. This Marana on whom kisses were showered must hunger for one kiss in vain, one for which she would have given all the others, the girlish glad caress a daughter gives her mother, her honoured mother, her mother in whom all womanly virtues shine. Juana as long as she lived was dead for her.

'What is it, love?' asked the Duc de Lina, and at the words a thought revived the courtesan's failing heart, a thought that gave her delicious happiness—Juana was safe henceforward! She might perhaps be one of the humblest of women, but not a shameless courtesan to whom any man might say, 'What is it, love?'

Indeed, the merchant and his wife had done their duty with scrupulous fidelity. Juana's fortune in their hands had been doubled. Perez de Lagounia had become the richest merchant in the province, and in his feeling towards the young girl there was a trace of superstition. Her coming had saved the old house from ruin and dishonour, and had not the presence of this angel brought unlooked-for prosperity? His wife, a soul of gold, a refined and gentle nature, had brought up her charge devoutly; the girl was as pure as she was beautiful. Juana was equally fitted to be the wife of a rich merchant or of a noble; she had every qualification for a brilliant destiny. But for the war that had broken out, Perez, who dreamed of living in Madrid, would ere now have given her in marriage to some Spanish grandee.

'I do not know where La Marana is at this moment,' he concluded; 'but wherever she may be, if she hears that our province is occupied by your armies, and that Taragona has been besieged, she is sure to be on her way hither to watch over her daughter.'

This story wrought a change in the captain's intentions; he no longer thought of making a Marchesa di Montefiore of Juana dei Mancini. He recognised the Marana blood in that swift glance the girl had exchanged with him from her shelter behind the blind, in the stratagem by which she had satisfied her curiosity, in that last look she had given him; and the libertine meant to marry a virtuous wife.

This would be a dangerous escapade, no doubt, but the perils were of the kind that never sinks the courage of the most pusillanimous, for love and its pleasures would reward them. There were obstacles everywhere: there was the apprentice who slept on the counter, and the servant-maid on the makeshift couch in the kitchen; Perez and his wife, who kept a dragon's watch by day, were old, and doubtless slept lightly; every sound echoed through the house, everything seemed to put the adventure beyond the range of possibilities. But as a set-off against these things, Montefiore had an ally—the blood of the Marana, which throbbed feverishly in the heart of the lovely Italian girl brought up as a Spaniard, the maiden athirst for love. Passion, the girl's nature, and Montefiore was a combination that might defy the whole world.

Prompted quite as strongly by the instincts of a chartered libertine as by the vague inexplicable hopes to which we give the name of presentiments, a word that describes them with such startling aptness—Montefiore took up his stand at his window, and spent the early hours of the night there, looking down in the presumed direction of the secret hiding-place, where the old couple had enshrined their darling, the joy of their old age.

The warehouse on the *entresol* (to make use of a French word that will perhaps make the disposition of the house clearer to the reader) separated the two young people, so it was idle for the captain to try to convey a message by means of tapping upon the floor, a shift for speech that all lovers can devise under such circumstances. Chance, however, came to his assistance, or was it the young girl herself? Just as he took his stand at the window he saw a circle of light that fell upon the grim opposite wall of the yard, and in the midst of it a dark silhouette, the form of Juana. Everything that she did was shadowed there ; from her attitude and the movement of her arms, she seemed to be arranging her hair for the night.

'Is she alone?' Montefiore asked himself. 'If I weight a letter with a few coins, will it be safe to dangle it by a thread against the round window that no doubt lights her cell?'

He wrote a note forthwith, a note characteristic of the officer, of the soldier sent for reasons of family expediency to the isle of Elba, of the former dilettante Marquis, fallen from his high estate, and become a captain on the clothing establishment. He wrapped some coins in the note, devised a string out of various odds and ends, tied up the packet and let it down, without a sound, into the very centre of that round brightness.

'If her mother or the servant is with her,' Montefiore thought, 'I shall see the shadows on the wall ; and if she is not alone, I will draw up the cord at once.'

But when, after pains innumerable, which can readily be imagined, the weighted packet tapped at the glass, only one shadow appeared, and it was the slender figure of Juana that flitted across the wall. Noiselessly the young girl opened the circular window, saw the packet, took it in, and stood for a while reading it.

Montefiore had written in his own name and entreated an interview. He offered, in the style of old romances, his heart and hand to Juana dei Mancini—a base and commonplace stratagem that nearly always succeeds ! At Juana's age, is not nobility of soul an added danger? A poet of our own days has gracefully said that 'only in her strength does woman yield.' Let a lover, when he is most beloved, feign doubts of the love that he inspires, and in her pride and her trust in him, a girl would invent sacrifices for his sake, knowing neither the world nor man's nature well enough to

I

retain her self-command when passion stirs within her, and to overwhelm with her scorn the lover who can accept a whole life offered to him to turn away a groundless reproach.

In our sublimely constituted society a young girl is placed in a painful dilemma between the forecasts of prudent virtue on the one hand, and the consequences of error upon the other. If she resists, it not seldom happens that she loses a lover and the first love, that is the most attractive of all; and if she is imprudent, she loses a marriage. Cast an eye over the vicissitudes of social life in Paris, and it is impossible to doubt the necessity of a religion that shall ensure that there are no more young girls seduced daily. And Paris is situated in the forty-eighth degree of latitude, while Taragona lies below the forty-first. The old question of climate is still useful to the novelist seeking an excuse for the suddenness of his catastrophe, and is made to explain the imprudence or the dilatoriness of a pair of lovers.

Montefiore's eyes were fixed meanwhile on the charming silhouette in the midst of the bright circle. Neither he nor Juana could see each other; an unlucky archway above her casement, with perverse malignity, cut off all chances of communication by signs, such as two lovers can contrive by leaning out of their windows. So the captain concentrated his whole mind and attention upon the round patch on the wall. Perhaps all unwittingly the girl's movements might betray her thoughts. Here again he was foiled. Juana's strange proceedings gave Montefiore no room for the faintest hope; she was amusing herself by cutting up the billet.

It often happens that virtue and discretion, in distrust, adopt shifts familiar to the jealous Bartholos of comedy. Juana, having neither paper, pen, nor ink, was scratching an answer with the point of a pair of scissors. In another moment she tied the scrap of paper to the string, the officer drew it in, opened it, held it up against the lamp, and read the perforated characters—'Come,' it said.

'"Come?"' said he to himself. 'Poison, and carbine, and Perez' dagger! And how about the apprentice hardly asleep on the counter by this time, and the servant in her hammock, and the house booming like a bass viol with every sound? why, I can hear old Perez snoring away upstairs! "Come!" . . . Then, has she nothing to lose?'

Acute reflection! Libertines alone can reason thus logically, and punish a woman for her devotion. The imagination of man has created Satan and Lovelace, but a maiden is an angelic being to whom he can lend nothing but his vices; so lofty, so fair is she, that he cannot set her higher nor add to her beauty; he has but the fatal power of blighting this creation by dragging it down to his miry level.

Montefiore waited till the drowsiest hour of the night, then in spite of his sober second thoughts, he crept down-stairs. He had taken off his shoes, and carried his pistols with him, and now he groped his way step by step, stopping to listen in the silence; trying each separate stair, straining his eyes till he almost saw in the darkness, and ready to turn back at any moment if the least thing befell him. He wore his handsomest uniform; he had perfumed his dark hair, and taken pains with the toilette that set off his natural good looks. On occasions like these, most men are as much a woman as any woman.

Montefiore managed to reach the door of the girl's secret hiding-place without difficulty. It was a little cabinet contrived in a corner which projected into another dwelling, a not unusual freak of the builder where ground-rents are high, and houses in conse-quence packed very tightly together. Here Juana lived alone, day and night, out of sight of all eyes. Hitherto she had slept near her adopted mother; but when Perez and his wife removed to the top of the house, the arrangements of the attics did not permit of their taking their ward thither also. So Doña Lagounia had left the girl to the guardianship of the lock of the secret door, to the protection of religious ideas, but so much the more powerful because they had become superstitions; and with the further safeguards of a natural pride, and the shrinking delicacy of the sensitive plant, which made Juana an exception among her sex, for to the most pathetic innocence Juana Mancini united no less the most passionate aspirations. It had needed a retired life and devout training to quiet and to cool the hot blood of the Maranas that glowed in her veins, the impulses that her adopted mother called temptations of the Evil One.

A faint gleam of light beneath the door in the panels discovered its whereabouts for Montefiore. He tapped softly with the tips of his finger-nails, and Juana let him in. Quivering from head to foot with excitement, he met the young girl's look of *naïve* curiosity, and read the most complete ignorance of her peril, and a sort of childlike admiration in her eyes. He stood, awed for a moment by the picture of the sanctuary before him.

The walls were hung with grey tapestry, covered with violet flowers. A small ebony chest, an antique mirror, a huge old-fashioned armchair, also made of ebony, and covered with tapestry; another chair beside the spindle-legged table, a pretty carpet on the floor—that was all. But there were flowers on the table, beside some embroidery work, and at the other end of the room stood the little narrow bed on which Juana dreamed; three pictures hung on the wall above it, and at the head stood a crucifix above a little holy water stoup, and a prayer framed and illuminated in gold. The room was full of the faint perfume of the flowers, of the soft light of the tapers; it all seemed so quiet, pure, and sacred. The subtle charm of Juana's dreamy fancies, nay, of Juana herself, seemed to pervade everything; her soul was revealed by her surroundings; the pearl lay there in its shell.

Juana, clad in white, with no ornament save her own loveliness, letting fall her rosary to call on the name of Love, would have inspired even Montefiore with reverence if it had not been for the night about them and the silence, if Juana had welcomed love less eagerly, if the little white bed had not displayed the turned-down coverlet—the pillow, confidante of innumerable vague longings. Montefiore stood there for long, intoxicated by joy hitherto unknown; such joy as Satan, it may be, would know at a glimpse of paradise if the cloud-veil that envelopes heaven was rent away for a moment.

'I loved you the first moment that I saw you,' he said, speaking pure Tuscan in the tones of his musical Italian voice. 'In you my soul and my life are set; if you so will it, they shall be yours for ever.'

To Juana listening, the air she breathed seemed to vibrate with the words grown magical upon her lover's tongue.

'Poor little girl! how have you breathed the atmosphere of this gloomy place so long, and lived? You, meant to reign like a queen in the world, to dwell in the palace of a prince, to pass from festival to festival, to feel in your own heart the joys that you create, to see the world at your feet, to make the fairest splendours pale before the glorious beauty that shall never be rivalled,—*you* have lived here in seclusion with this old tradesman and his wife!'

There was a purpose in his exclamation; he wanted to find out whether or no Juana had ever had a lover.

'Yes,' she answered. 'But who can have told you my inmost thoughts? For these twelve months past I have been weary to death of it. Yes, I would die rather than stay any longer in this house. Do you see this embroidery? I have set countless dreadful thoughts into every stitch of it. How often I have longed to run away and fling myself into the sea! Do you ask why? I have forgotten already. . . . Childish troubles, but very keenly felt in spite of their childishness. . . . Often at night when I kissed my mother, I have given her such a kiss as one gives for a last farewell, saying in my heart, "I will kill myself to-morrow." After all, I did not die. Suicides go to hell, and I was so much afraid of that, that I made up my mind to endure my life, to get up and go to bed, and do the same things hour after hour of every day. My life was not irksome, it was painful.—And yet, my father and mother worship me. Oh! I am wicked! indeed, I tell my confessor so.'

'Then have you always lived here without amuse-ments, without pleasures?'

'Oh! I have not always felt like this. Until I was fifteen years old, I enjoyed seeing the festivals of the Church; I loved the singing and the music. I was so happy, because I felt that, like the angels, I was sinless, so glad that I might take the sacrament every week, in short, I loved God then. But in these three years I have changed utterly, day by day. It began when I wanted flowers here in the house, and they gave me very beautiful ones; then I wanted. . . . But now I want nothing any longer,' she added, after a pause, and she smiled at Montefiore.

'Did you not tell me just now in your letter that you would love me for ever?'

'Yes, my Juana,' murmured Montefiore. He put his arm round the waist of this adorable girl, and pressed her closely to his heart. 'Yes. But let me speak to you as you pray to God. Are you not fairer than Our Lady in heaven? Hear me,' and he set a kiss in her hair, 'for me that forehead of yours is the fairest altar on earth; I swear to worship you, my idol, to pour out all the wealth of the world upon you. My carriages are yours, my palace in Milan is yours, yours all the jewels and the diamonds, the heirlooms of my ancient house; new ornaments and dresses every day, and all the countless pleasures and delights of the world.'

'Yes,' she said, 'I should like it all very much; but in my soul I feel that I should love my dear husband more than all things else in the world.'

Mio caro sposo! Italian was Juana's native speech, and it is impossible to put into two words of another language the wonderful tenderness, the winning grace with which that brief delicious phrase is invested by the accents of an Italian tongue. 'I shall find,' she said, and the purity of a seraph shone in her eyes, 'I shall find my beloved religion again in *him.* His and God's, God's and his! . . . But you are he, are you not?' she cried after a pause. 'Surely, surely you are he! Ah! come and see the picture that my father brought me from Italy.'

She took up a candle, beckoned to Montefiore, and showed him a picture that hung at the foot of the bed— Saint Michael trampling Satan underfoot.

'Look!' she cried, 'has he not your eyes? That made me think, as soon as I saw you in the street, that in the meeting I saw the finger of heaven. So often I have lain awake in the morning before my mother came to call me to prayer, thinking about that picture, looking at the angel, until at last I came to think that he was my husband. *Mon Dieu!* I am talking as I think to myself. What wild nonsense it must seem to you! but if you only knew how a poor recluse longs to pour out the thoughts that oppress her! I used to talk to these flowers and the woven garlands on the tapestry when I was alone; they understood me better, I think, than my father and mother—always so serious——'

'Juana,' said Montefiore, and as he took her hands and kissed them, passion shone in his eyes and overflowed in his gestures and in the sound of his voice, 'talk to me as if I were your husband, talk to me as you talk to yourself.

I have suffered all that you have suffered.   Few words
will be needed, when we talk together, to bring back the
whole past of either life before we met ; but there are
not words enough in language to tell of the bliss that
lies before us.   Lay your hand on my heart.   Do you
feel how it beats ?   Let us vow, before God, who sees
and hears us, to be faithful to each other all our lives.
Stay, take this ring.—Give me yours.'

'Give away my ring ?' she cried, startled.

'Why not ?' asked Montefiore, dismayed by so much
simplicity.

'Why, it came to me from our Holy Father the Pope.
When I was a little girl a beautiful lady set it on my
finger ; she took care of me, and brought me here, and
she told me to keep it always.'

'Then you do not love me, Juana ?'

'Ah! here it is,' she cried.   'Are you not more
myself than I ?'

She held out the ring, trembling as she did so, keeping
her fingers tightly clasped upon it as she looked at
Montefiore with clear, questioning eyes.   That ring
meant her whole self: she gave it to him.

'Oh! my Juana!' said Montefiore as he held her
closely in his arms, 'only a monster could be false to you.
. . . I will love you for ever . . .'

Juana grew dreamy.   Montefiore, thinking within
himself that, in his first interview, he must not run the
slightest risk of startling a girl so innocent, whose imprudence sprang rather from virtue than from desire, was
fain to content himself with thinking of the future, of
her beauty now that he had known its power, and of the
innocent marriage of the ring, that most sublime of
betrothals, the simplest and most binding of all ceremonies, the betrothal of the heart.

For the rest of the night, and all day long on the
morrow, Juana's imagination would surely become the
accomplice of his desires.   So he put constraint upon

himself, and tried to be as respectful as he was tender.
With these thoughts present in his mind, prompted by
his passion, and yet more by the desires that Juana inspired
in him, his words were insinuating and fervent. He
led the innocent child to plan out the new life before
them, painted the world for her in the most glowing colours, ·dwelt on the household details that
possess such a delightful interest for young girls, and
made with her the compacts over which lovers dispute,
the agreements that give rights and reality to love.
Then, when they had decided the hour for their nightly
tryst, he went, leaving a happy but a changed Juana.
The simple and innocent Juana no longer existed, already
there was more passion than a girl should reveal in the
last glance that she gave him, in the charming way that
she held up her forehead for the touch of her lover's lips.
It was all the result of solitude and irksome tasks upon
this nature ; if she was to be prudent and virtuous, the
knowledge of the world should either have come to her
gradually, or have been hidden from her for ever.

'How slowly the day will go to-morrow !' she said, as
another kiss, still respectfully given, was pressed upon her
forehead.

'But you will sit in the dining-room, will you not ?
and raise your voice a little when you talk, so that I may
hear you, and the sound may fill my heart.'

Montefiore, beginning to understand the life that
Juana led, was but the better pleased that he had managed
to restrain his desires that he might the better secure his
end. He returned to his room without mishap.

Ten days went by, and nothing occurred to disturb
the peace and quiet of the house. Montefiore, with the
persuasive manners of an Italian, had gained the good
graces of old Perez and Doña Lagounia ; indeed, he was
popular with the whole household—with the apprentice
and the maid-servant ; but in spite of the confidence that
he had succeeded in inspiring in them, he never attempted

to take advantage of it to ask to see Juana, or to open the door of that little sealed paradise. The Italian girl, in her longing to see her lover, had often besought him to do this, but from motives of prudence he had always refused. On the contrary, he had used the character he had gained and all his skill to lull the suspicions of the old couple; he had accustomed them to his habit of never rising till mid-day, soldier as he was. The captain gave out that his health was bad. So the two lovers only lived at night when all the household was asleep.

If Montefiore had not been a libertine to whom a long experience of pleasure had given presence of mind under all conditions, they would have been lost half a score of times in those ten days. A young lover, with the single-heartedness of first love, would have been tempted in his rapture into imprudences that were very hard to resist; but the Italian was proof even against Juana, against her pouting lips, her wild spirits, against a Juana who wound the long plaits of her hair about his throat to keep him by her side. The keenest observer would have been sorely puzzled to detect those midnight meetings. It may well be believed that the Italian, sure of his ultimate success, enjoyed prolonging the ineffable pleasure of this intrigue in which he made progress step by step, in fanning the flame that gradually waxed hotter, till everything must yield to it at last.

On the eleventh day, as they sat at dinner, he deemed it expedient to confide to Perez (under the seal of secrecy) the history of the disgrace into which he had fallen among his family. It was a mésalliance, he said.

There was something revolting in this lie, told as a confidence, while that midnight drama was in progress beneath the old man's roof. Montefiore, an experienced actor, was leading up to a catastrophe planned by himself; and, like an artist who loves his art, he enjoyed the thought of it. He meant very shortly to take leave of

the house and of his lady-love without regret. And
when Juana, risking her life it might be to ask the
question, should inquire of Perez what had become of
their guest, Perez would tell her, all unwittingly, that
'the Marchese di Montefiore has been reconciled with
his family; they have consented to receive his wife, and
he has taken her to them.'

And Juana? . . . The Italian never inquired of himself what would become of her; he had had ample
opportunity of knowing her nobleness, her innocence,
and her goodness, and felt sure that Juana would keep
silence.

He obtained a message to carry for some general or
other. Three days afterwards, on the night before he
must start, Montefiore went straight to Juana's room
instead of going first to his own. The same instinct
that bids the tiger leave no morsel of his prey, prompted
the Italian to lengthen the night of farewells. Juana,
the true daughter of two southern lands, with the passion
of Spain and of Italy in her heart, was enraptured by the
boldness that brought her lover to her and revealed the
ardour of his love. To know the delicious torment of an
illicit passion under the sanction of marriage, to conceal
her husband behind the bed-curtains, half deceiving the
adopted father and mother, to whom she could say in
case of discovery, 'I am the Marchesa di Montefiore,'
was not this a festival for the young and romantic girl
who, for three years past, had dreamed of love—love always
beset with perils? The curtains of the door fell, drawing
about their madness and their happiness a veil which it is
useless to raise.

It was nearly nine o'clock, the merchant and his wife
were reading the evening prayer, when suddenly the
sound of a carriage, drawn by several horses, came from
the narrow street without. Some one knocked hastily
and loudly at the door of the shop. The servant ran to
open it, and in a moment a woman sprang into the

quaint old room—a woman magnificently dressed, though her travelling carriage was besplashed by the mire of many roads, for she had crossed Italy and France and Spain. It was La Marana! La Marana, in spite of her thirty-six years and her riotous life, in the full pride of her *beltà folgorante*, to record the superb epithet invented for her in Milan by her enraptured adorers. La Marana, the openly avowed mistress of a King, had left Naples and its festivals and sunny skies, at the very height and summit of her strange career—had left gold and madrigals and silk and perfumes, and her royal lover, when she learned from him what was passing in Spain, and how that Taragona was besieged.

'Taragona!' she cried, 'and before the city is taken! I must be in Taragona in ten days!' And without another thought for courts or crowned heads, she had reached Taragona, provided with a passport that gave her something like the powers of an empress, and with gold that enabled her to cross the French empire with the speed and splendour of a rocket. There is no such thing as distance for a mother; she who is a mother, indeed, sees her child, and knows by instinct how he fares though they are as far as the poles apart.

'My daughter? my daughter?' cried La Marana.

At that cry, at this swift invasion of their house, and apparition of a queen travelling *incognito*, Perez and his wife let the prayer-book fall; that voice rang in their ears like a thunder-clap, and La Marana's eyes flashed lightnings.

'She is in there,' the merchant answered quietly, after a brief pause, during which they recovered from the shock of surprise caused by La Marana's sudden appearance, and by her look and tone. 'She is in there,' he said again, indicating the little hiding-place.

'Yes, but has she not been ill? Is she quite——'

'Perfectly well,' said Doña Lagounia.

'Oh, God!' cried La Marana, 'plunge me now in

hell for all eternity, if it be Thy pleasure,' and she sank down utterly exhausted into a chair.

The flush that anxiety had brought to her face faded suddenly; her cheeks grew white; she who had borne up bravely under the strain, had no strength left when it was over. The joy was too intolerable, a joy more intense than her previous distress, for she was still vibrating with dread, when bliss keen as anguish came upon her.

'But how have you done?' she asked. 'Taragona was taken by assault.'

'Yes,' answered Perez. 'But when you saw that I was alive, how could you ask such a question? How should any one reach Juana but over my dead body.'

The courtesan grasped Perez' horny hand on receiving this answer; tears gathered in her eyes and fell upon his fingers as she kissed them—the costliest of all things under the sun for her, who never wept.

'Brave Perez!' she said at last; 'but surely there are soldiers billeted upon you, are there not?'

'Only one,' answered the Spaniard. 'Luckily, we have one of the most honourable of men, an Italian by nationality, a Spaniard by birth, a hater of Bonaparte, a married man, a steady character. He rises late, and goes to bed early. He is in bad health, too, just now.'

'An Italian! What is his name?'

'Captain Montefiore, he——'

'Why, he is not the Marchese di Montefiore, is he?'

'Yes, señora, the very same.'

'Has he seen Juana?'

'No,' said Doña Lagounia.

'You are mistaken, wife,' said Perez. 'The Marquis must have seen Juana once, only for a moment, it is true, but I think he must have seen her that day when she came in at supper-time.'

'Ah!—I should like to see my daughter.'

'Nothing is easier,' said Perez. 'She is asleep. Though

if she has left the key in the lock, we shall have to wake her.

As the merchant rose to take down the duplicate key from its place, he happened to glance up through the tall window. The light from the large round pane-opening of Juana's cell fell upon the dark wall on the opposite side of the yard, tracing a gleaming circle there, and in the midst of the lighted space he saw two shadowy figures such as no sculptor till the time of the gifted Canova could have dreamed of. The Spaniard turned to the room again.

'I do not know,' he said to La Marana, 'where we have put the key——'

'You look very pale!' she exclaimed.

'I will soon tell you why,' he answered, as he sprang towards his dagger, caught it up, and beat violently on the door in the panelling. 'Open the door!' he shouted. 'Juana! open the door!'

There was an appalling despair in his tones that struck terror into the two women who heard him.

Juana did not open, because there was some delay in hiding Montefiore. She knew nothing of what had passed in the room without. The tapestry hangings on either side of the door deadened all sounds.

'Madame,' said Perez, turning to La Marana, 'I told you just now that I did not know where the key was. That was a lie. Here it is,' and he took it from the sideboard, 'but it is useless. 'Juana's key is in the lock, and her door is barricaded.—We are deceived, wife! There is a man in Juana's room.'

'By my hopes of salvation, the thing is impossible!' said Doña Lagounia.

'Do not perjure yourself, Doña Lagounia. Our honour is slain; and *she*' (he turned to La Marana, who had risen to her feet, and stood motionless as if thunder-struck by his words), 'she may well scorn us. She saved our lives, our fortune, and our honour, and we have barely guarded her money for her.—Juana, open the door!' he shouted, 'or I will break it down!'

The whole house rang with the cry; his voice grew louder and angrier; but he was cool and self-possessed. He held Montefiore's life in his hands, in another moment he would wash away his remorse in every drop of the Italian's blood.

'Go out! go out! go out! all of you!' cried La Marana, and springing upon the dagger like a tigress, she snatched it from the hands of the astonished Perez. 'Go out of this room, Perez,' she went on, speaking quite quietly now. 'Go out, you and your wife, and the maid and the apprentice. There will be a murder here directly, and you might all be shot down by the French for it. Do not you mix yourself up in it, it is my affair entirely. When my daughter and I meet, God alone should be present. As for the man, he is mine. The whole world should not snatch him out of my hands. There, there, go! I forgive you. I see it all. The girl is a Marana. My blood flows in her veins, and you, your religion, and your honour have been powerless against it.'

Her groan was dreadful to hear. She turned dry eyes upon them. She had lost everything, but she was accustomed to suffering; she was a courtesan. The door opened. La Marana henceforth heeded nothing else, and Perez, making a sign to his wife, could remain at his post. The old Spaniard, implacable where honour was concerned, determined to assist the wronged mother's vengeance. Juana, in her white draperies, stood quietly there in her room in the soft lamplight. 'What do you want with me?' she asked.

In spite of herself, a light shudder ran through La Marana.

'Perez,' she asked, 'is there any other way out of this closet?'

Perez shook his head; and on that the courtesan went into the room.

'Juana,' she said, 'I am your mother, your judge—you have put yourself in the one situation in which I can reveal myself to you. You have come to my level, you whom I had thought to raise to heaven. Oh! you have fallen very low! . . . You have a lover in your room.'

'Madame, no one but my husband should or could be there,' she answered. 'I am the Marchesa di Montefiore.'

'Then are there two of them?' asked old Perez sternly. 'He told me that he was married.'

'Montefiore! my love!' cried the girl, rending the curtains, and discovering the officer; 'come forward, these people are slandering you.'

The Italian's face was haggard and pale; he saw the dagger in La Marana's hand, and he knew La Marana. At one bound he sprang out of the chamber, and with a voice of thunder shouted, 'Help! help! murder! they are killing a Frenchman!—Soldiers of the Sixth of the line, run for Captain Diard! . . . Help!'

Perez had secured the Marquis, and was about to gag him by putting his large hand over the soldier's mouth, when the courtesan stopped him.

'Hold him fast,' she said, 'but let him call. Throw open the doors, and leave them open; and now go out, all of you, I tell you!—As for you,' she continued, addressing Montefiore, 'shout, and call for help. . . . As soon as there is a sound of your men's footsteps, this blade will be in your heart. . . . Are you married? Answer me.'

Montefiore, lying across the threshold of the door, two paces from Juana, heard nothing, and saw nothing, for the blinding gleam of the dagger blade.

'Then he meant to deceive me;' the words came slowly from Juana. 'He told me that he was free.'

'He told me that he was a married man,' said Perez, in the same stern tones as before.

'Holy Virgin!' exclaimed Doña Lagounia. La Marana stooped to mutter in the ear of the Marquis, 'Answer me, will you, soul of mud?'

'Your daughter . . .' Montefiore began.

'The daughter I once had is dead, or she soon will be,' said La Marana. 'I have no daughter now. Do not use that word again. Answer me, are you married?'

'No, Madame,' Montefiore said at last (he wished to gain time); 'I mean to marry your daughter.'

'My noble Montefiore!' cried Juana, with a deep breath.

'Then what made you fly and call for help?' demanded Perez.

Terrible perspicacity!

Juana said nothing, but she wrung her hands, went over to her armchair, and sat down. Even at that moment there was an uproar in the street, and in the deep silence that fell upon the parlour it was sufficiently easy to catch the sounds. A private soldier of the Sixth, who had chanced to pass along the street when Montefiore cried out for help, had gone to call up Diard. Luckily, the quartermaster was in his lodging, and came at once with several comrades.

'Why did I fly?' repeated Montefiore, who heard the sound of his friend's voice. 'Because I had told you the truth.—Diard! Diard!' he shrieked aloud.

But at a word from Perez, who meant that all in his house should share in the murder, the apprentice made the door fast, and the men were obliged to force it open. La Marana, therefore, could stab the guilty creature at her feet before they made an entrance; but her hand shook with pent-up wrath, and the blade slipped aside upon Montefiore's epaulette. Yet so heavy had been the blow, that the Italian rolled over almost at Juana's feet. The girl did not see him, but La Marana sprang upon her prey, and, lest she should fail this time, she held his throat in an iron grasp, and pointed the dagger at his heart.

'I am free!' he gasped. 'I will marry her! I swear it by God! by my mother! by all that is most sacred in

K

this world. . . . I am not married! I will marry her! Upon my word of honour, I will!' and he set his teeth in the courtesan's arm.

'That is enough, mother,' said Juana; 'kill him! I would not have such a coward for my husband if he were ten times more beautiful.'

'Ah! that is my daughter!' cried La Marana.

'What is going on here?' asked the quartermaster, looking about him.

'This,' shouted Montefiore; 'they are murdering me on that girl's account; she says that I am her lover; she trapped me, and now they want to force me to marry her against my will——'

'Against your will?' cried Diard, struck with the sublime beauty that indignation, scorn, and hate had lent to Juana's face, already so fair. 'You are very hard to please! If she must have a husband, here am I. Put up your dagger.'

La Marana grasped the Italian, pulled him to his feet, brought him to the bedside, and said in his ear—

'If I spare your life, you may thank that last speech of yours for it. But keep it in mind. If you say a word against my daughter, we shall see each other again. —What will her dowry amount to?' she asked of Perez.

'Two hundred thousand piastres down——'

'That will not be all, Monsieur,' said the courtesan, addressing Diard. 'Who are you?—You can go,' she added, turning to Montefiore.

But when the Marquis heard mention of two hundred thousand piastres down, he came forward, saying, 'I am really quite free——'

'You are really quite free to go,' said La Marana, and the Italian went.

'Alas! Monsieur,' the girl spoke, addressing Diard; 'I thank you, and I admire you. But my bridegroom is in heaven; I shall be the bride of Christ. To-morrow I shall enter the convent of——'

'Oh, hush! hush! Juana, my Juana!' cried her mother, holding the girl tightly in her arms. Then she whispered, 'You must take another bridegroom.'

Juana turned pale.

'Who are you, monsieur?' asked the mother of the Provençal.

'I am nothing as yet but a quartermaster in the Sixth Regiment of the line,' said he; 'but for such a wife, a man would feel that it lay in him to be a Marshal of France some day. My name is Pierre-François Diard. My father was a guild magistrate, so I am not a——'

'Eh! you are an honest man, are you not?' cried La Marana. 'If the Signorina Juana dei Mancini cares for you, you may both be happy.—Juana,' she went on gravely, 'when you are the wife of a good and worthy man, remember that you will be a mother. I have sworn that you shall set a kiss upon your child's forehead without a blush . . . (Here her tone changed somewhat.) I have sworn that you shall be a virtuous wife. So in this life, though many troubles await you, whatever happens to you, be a chaste and faithful wife to your husband; sacrifice everything to him; he will be the father of your children. . . . A father to your children! . . . Stay, between you and a lover your mother always will stand; I shall be your mother only when danger threatens. . . . Do you see Perez's dagger? *That* is part of your dower,' and she flung the weapon down on the bed. 'There I leave it as a guarantee of your honour, so long as I have eyes to see and hands that can strike a blow.—Farewell,' she said, keeping back the tears; 'heaven send that we never meet again,' and at that her tears flowed fast.

'Poor child! you have been very happy in this little cell, happier than you know.—Act in such a sort that she may never look back on it with regret,' she added, looking at her future son-in-law.

The story, which has been given simply by way of

introduction, is not by any means the subject of the following study; it has been told to explain, in the first place, how Montefiore and Diard became acquainted, how Captain Diard came to marry Juana dei Mancini, and to make known what passions filled Mme. Diard's heart, what blood flowed in her veins.

By the time that the quartermaster had been through the slow and tedious formalities indispensable for a French soldier who is obtaining leave to marry, he had fallen passionately in love with Juana dei Mancini, and Juana dei Mancini had had time to reflect on her fate. An appalling fate! Juana, who neither loved nor esteemed this Diard, was none the less bound to him by a promise, a rash promise no doubt, but there had been no help for it. The Provençal was neither handsome nor well made. His manners were totally lacking in distinction, and savoured of the camp, of his provincial bringing up and imperfect education. How should the young girl love Diard? With her perfect elegance and grace, her unconquerable instinct for luxury and refinement, her natural drawings were towards the higher spheres of society; and as for esteem, she could not bring herself to feel so much as esteem for this Diard who was to marry her, and precisely for that very reason.

The repugnance was very natural. Woman is a sacred and gracious being, almost always misunderstood; the judgments passed upon her are almost always unjust, because she is not understood. If Juana had loved Diard, she would have esteemed him. Love creates a new self within a woman; the old self passes away with the dawn of love, and in the wedding-robe of a passion that shall last as long as life itself, her life is invested with whiteness and purity. After this new birth, this revival of modesty and virtue, she has no longer a past; it is utterly forgotten; she turns wholly to the future that she may learn all things afresh. In this sense, the words of the famous line that a modern poet has put into the mouth of Marion Delorme, a line moreover that Corneille might well have written, are steeped in truth—

' *And Love gives back my maidenhood to me.*'

Does it not read like a reminiscence of some tragedy of Corneille's? The style of the father of French drama, so forceful, owing so little to epithet, seems to be revived again in the words. And yet the writer, the poet of our own day, has been compelled to sacrifice it to the taste of a public only capable of appreciating vaudevilles.

So Juana, loveless, was still the same Juana, betrayed, humiliated, brought very low. How should this Juana respect a man who could take her thus? With the high-minded purity of youth, she felt the force of a distinction, subtle in appearance, but real and immutable, a binding law upon the heart, which even the least thoughtful women instinctively apply to all their sentiments. Life had opened out before Juana, and the prospect saddened her inmost soul.

Often she looked at Perez and Doña Lagounia, her eyes full of the tears she was too proud to let fall; they understood the bitter thoughts contained in those tears, but they said no word. Were not reproaches useless? And why should they seek to comfort her? The keener the sympathy, the wider the pent-up sorrow would spread.

One evening, as Juana sat in her little cell in a dull stupor of wretchedness, she heard the husband and wife talking together. They thought that the door was shut, and a wail broke from her adopted mother.

'The poor child will die of grief!'

'Yes,' answered Perez in a faltering voice; 'but what can we do? Can I go now to boast of my ward's chaste beauty to the Comte d'Arcos, to whom I hoped to marry her?'

'There is a difference between one slip and vice,' said

the old woman, indulgent as an angel could have been.

'Her mother gave her to him,' objected Perez.

'All in a minute, and without consulting her!' cried Doña Lagounia.

'She knew quite well what she was doing——'

'Into what hands our pearl will pass!'

'Not a word more, or I will go and pick a quarrel with that —— Diard!'

'And then there would be one more misfortune.'

Juana, listening to these terrible words, knew at last the value of the happy life that had flowed on untroubled until her error ended it. So the innocent hours in her peaceful retreat were to have been crowned by a brilliant and splendid existence; the delights so often dreamed of would have been hers. Those dreams had caused her ruin. She had fallen from the heights of social greatness to the feet of *Monsieur* Diard! Juana wept; her thoughts almost drove her mad. For several seconds she hesitated between a life of vice and religion. Vice offered a prompt solution; religion, a life made up of suffering. The inward debate was stormy and solemn. To-morrow was the fatal day, the day fixed for this marriage. It was not too late; Juana might be Juana still. If she remained free, she knew the utmost extent of her calamities; but when married, she could not tell what might lie in store for her. Religion gained the day. Doña Lagounia came to watch and pray by her daughter's side, as she might have done by a dying woman's bed.

'It is the will of God,' she said to Juana. Nature gives to a woman a power peculiarly her own, that enables her to endure suffering, a power succeeded in turn by weakness that counsels resignation. Juana submitted without an after-thought. She determined to fulfil her mother's vow, to cross the desert of life, and so reach heaven, knowing that no flowers could spring in the

thorny paths that lay before her. She married
Diard.

As for the quartermaster, though Juana judged him
pitilessly, who else would not have forgiven him? He
was intoxicated with love. La Marana, with the quick
instinct natural to her, had felt passion in the tones of
his voice, and seen in him the abrupt temper, the impulsive generosity of the South. In the paroxysm of her
great anger, she had seen Diard's good qualities, and these
only, and thought that these were sufficient guarantees
for her daughter's happiness.

And to all appearance the early days of this marriage
were happy. But to lay bare the underlying facts of the
case, the miserable secrets that women bury in the depths
of their souls, Juana had determined that she would not
overcloud her husband's joy. All women who are victims
of an ill-assorted marriage, come sooner or later to play
a double part—a part terrible to play, and Juana had
already taken up her rôle. Of such a life, a man can
only record the facts; and women's hearts alone can divine
the inner life of sentiments. Is it not a story impossible
to relate in all its truth? Juana, struggling every hour
against her own nature, half Spanish, half Italian; Juana,
shedding tears in secret till she had no tears left to shed,
was a typical creation, a living symbol, destined to represent the uttermost extent of woman's misfortunes. The
minute detail required to depict that life of restless pain
would be without interest for those who crave melo-
dramatic sensation. And would not an analysis, in which
every wife would discover some of her own experience,
require an entire volume if it were to be given in full?
Such a book, by its very nature, would be impossible to
write, for its merits must consist in half-tones and in
subtle shades of colour that critics would consider vague
and indistinct. And besides, who that does not bear
another heart within his heart can touch on the pathetic,
deeply-hidden tragedies that some women take with them

to their graves; the heartache, understood of none—not even of those who cause it; the sighs in vain; the devotion that, here on earth at least, meets with no return; unappreciated magnanimities of silence and scorn of vengeance; unfailing generosity, lavished in vain; longings for happiness destined to be unfulfilled; angelic charity that blesses in secret; all the beliefs held sacred, all the inextinguishable love? This life Juana knew; fate spared her in nothing. Hers was to be in all things the lot of a wronged and unhappy wife, always forgiving her wrongs; a woman pure as a flawless diamond, though through her beauty, as flawless and as dazzling as the diamond, a way of revenge lay open to her. Of a truth, she need not dread the dagger in her dower.

But at first, under the influence of love, of a passion that for a while at least can work a change in the most depraved nature, and bring to light all that is noblest in a human soul, Diard behaved like a man of honour. He compelled Montefiore to go out of the regiment, and even out of that division of the army, that his wife might not be compelled to meet the Marquis during the short time that she was to remain in Spain. Then the quarter-master asked to change his regiment, and managed to exchange into the Imperial Guard. He meant at all costs to gain a title; he would have honours and a great position to match his great fortune. With this thought in his mind, he displayed great courage in one of our bloodiest battles in Germany, and was so badly wounded that he could no longer stay in the service. For a time it was feared that he might have to lose his leg, and he was forced to retire, with his pension indeed, but without the title of baron or any of the rewards which he had hoped for, and very likely would have won, if his name had not been Diard.

These events, together with his wound and his dis-appointed hopes, made a changed man of the late quarter-

master.   The Provençal's energy, wrought for a time to
a fever pitch, suddenly deserted him.   At first, however,
his wife sustained his courage; his efforts, his bravery,
and his ambition had given her some belief in her husband; and surely it behoved her, of all women, to play a
woman's part, to be a tender consoler for the troubles
of life.

Juana's words put fresh heart into the Major.   He
went to live in Paris, determined to make a high
position for himself in the Administration; the quartermaster of the Sixth Line Regiment should be forgotten, and some day Madame Diard should wear a
splendid title.   His passion for his charming wife had
made him quick to guess her inmost wishes.   Juana did
not speak of them, but he understood her; he was not
loved as a man dreams of being loved—he knew it, and
longed to be looked up to and loved and caressed.   The
luckless man anticipated happiness with a wife who was
at all times so submissive and so gentle; but her gentleness and her submission meant nothing but that resignation to her fate which had given Juana to him.
Resignation and religion, were these love?   Diard could
often have wished for a refusal instead of that wifely
obedience; often he would have given his soul if Juana
would but have deigned to weep upon his breast, and
ceased to conceal her feelings with the smile that she
wore proudly as a mask upon her face.

Many a man in his youth (for after a certain time we
give up struggling) strives to triumph over an evil destiny
that brings the thunder-clouds from time to time above
the horizon of his life; and when he falls into the depths
of misfortune, those unrequited struggles should be taken
into account.   Like many another, Diard tried all ways,
and found all ways barred against him.   His wealth
enabled him to surround his wife with all the luxuries
that can be enjoyed in Paris.   She had a great mansion
and vast drawing-rooms, and presided over one of those

houses frequented by some few artists who are uncritical
by nature, by a great many schemers, by the frivolous
folk who are ready to go anywhere to be amused, and by
certain men of fashion, attracted by Juana's beauty.
Those who make themselves conspicuous in Paris must
either conquer Paris or fall victims. Diard's character
was not strong enough, nor compact enough, nor persistent enough, to impress itself upon the society of a
time when every one else was likewise bent upon
reaching a high position. Ready-made social classifica-
tions are not improbably a great blessing, even for the
people. Napoleon's *Memoirs* have informed us of the
pains he was at to impose social conventions upon a
Court composed for the most part of subjects who had
once been his equals. But Napoleon was a Corsican,
Diard was a Provençal.

If the two men had been mentally equal—an islander
is always a more complete human being than a man born
and bred on the mainland; and though Provence and
Corsica lie between the same degrees of latitude, the
narrow stretch of sea that keeps them apart is, in spite of
man's inventions, a whole ocean that makes two different
countries of them both.

From this false position, which Diard falsified yet
further, grave misfortunes arose. Perhaps there is a
useful lesson to be learned by tracing the chain of inter-
dependent facts that imperceptibly brought about the
catastrophe of the story.

In the first place, Parisian scoffers could not see the
pictures that adorned the late quartermaster's mansion
without a significant smile. The recently purchased
masterpieces were all condemned by the unspoken slur
cast upon the pictures that had been the spoils of war
in Spain; by this slur, self-love avenged itself for the
involuntary offence of Diard's wealth. Juana understood
the meaning of some of the ambiguous compliments in
which the French excel. Acting upon her advice, there-

fore, her husband sent the Spanish pictures back to
Taragona. But the world of Paris, determined to put
the worst construction on the matter, said, 'That fellow
Diard is shrewd; he has sold his pictures,' and the good
folk continued to believe that the paintings which still
hung on the walls had not been honestly come by.
Then some ill-natured women inquired how a *Diard*
had come to marry a young wife so rich and so beautiful.
Comments followed, endless absurdities were retailed,
after the manner of Paris. If Juana rose above it all,
even above the scandal, and met with nothing but the
respect due to her pure and devout life, that respect
ended with her, and was not accorded to her husband.
Her shining eyes glanced over her rooms, and her
woman's clear-sightedness brought her nothing but
pain. And yet—the disparagement was quite explic-
able. Military men, for all the virtues with which
romance endows them, could not forgive the quondam
quartermaster for his wealth and his determination to
cut a figure in Paris, and for that very reason.

There is a world in Paris that lies between the furthest
house in the Faubourg Saint-Germain on the one hand,
and the last mansion in the Rue Saint-Lazare on the
other; between the rising ground of the Luxembourg
and the heights of Montmartre; a world that dresses
and gossips, dresses to go out, and goes out to gossip; a
world of petty and great airs; a world of mean and poor
ambitions, masquerading in insolence; a world of envy
and of fawning arts. It is made up of gilded rank, and
rank that has lost its gilding, of young and old, of
nobility of the fourth century and titles of yesterday, of
those who laugh at the expense of a *parvenu*, and others
who fear to be contaminated by him, of men eager for
the downfall of a power, though none the less they will
bow the knee to it if it holds its own; and all these ears
hear, and all these tongues repeat, and all these minds
are informed in the course of an evening of the birth-

place, education, and previous history of each new aspirant for its high places. If there is no High Court of Justice in this exalted sphere, it boasts the most ruthless of *procureurs-généraux*, an intangible public opinion that dooms the victim and carries out the sentence, that accuses and brands the delinquent. Do not hope to hide anything from this tribunal, tell everything at once yourself, for it is determined to go to the bottom of everything, and knows everything. Do not seek to understand the mysterious operation by which intelligence is flashed from place to place, so that a story, a scandal, or a piece of news is known everywhere simultaneously in the twinkling of an eye. Do not ask who set the machinery in motion; it is a social mystery, no observer can do more than watch its phenomena, and its working is rapid beyond belief. A single example shall suffice. The murder of the Duc de Berri, at the Opéra, was known in the furthest part of the Ile Saint-Louis ten minutes after the crime was committed. The opinion of the Sixth Regiment of the Line concerning Diard permeated this world of Paris on the very evening of his first ball.

So Diard himself could accomplish nothing. Henceforward his wife, and his wife alone, might make a way for him. Strange portent of a strange civilisation! If a man can do nothing by himself in Paris, he has still some chance of rising in the world if his wife is young and clever. There are women, weak to all appearance, invalids who, without rising from their sofas or leaving their rooms, make their influence felt in society; and by bringing countless secret springs into play, gain for their husbands the position which their own vanity desires. But Juana, whose girlhood had been spent in the quaint simplicity of the narrow house in Taragona, knew nothing of the corruption, the baseness, or the opportunities afforded by life in Paris; she looked out upon it with girlish curiosity, and learned from it no

worldly wisdom save the lessons taught her by her
wounded pride and susceptibilities. Juana, moreover,
possessed the quick instinct of a maiden heart, and was
as swift to anticipate an impression as a sensitive plant.
The lonely girl had become a woman all at once. She
saw that if she endeavoured to compel society to honour
her husband, it must be after the Spanish fashion, of
telling a lie, carbine in hand. Did not her own constant
watchfulness tell her how necessary her manifold precautions were? A gulf yawned for Diard between the
failure to make himself respected and the opposite
danger of being respected but too much. Then as
suddenly as before, when she had foreseen her life, there
came a revelation of the world to her; she beheld on all
sides the vast extent of an irreparable misfortune. Then
came the tardy recognition of her husband's peculiar
weaknesses, his total unfitness to play the parts he had
assigned to himself, the incoherency of his ideas, the
mental incapacity to grasp this society as a whole, or to
comprehend the subtleties that are all-important there.
Would not tact effect more for a man in his position
than force of character? But the tact that never fails
is perhaps the greatest of all forces.

So far from effacing the blot upon the Diard scutcheon,
the Major was at no little pains to make matters worse.
For instance, as it had not occurred to him that the
Empire was passing through a phase that required careful study, he tried, though he was only a major, to
obtain an appointment as prefect. At that time almost
every one believed in Napoleon; his favour had increased
the importance of every post. The prefectures, those
empires on a small scale, could only be filled by men
with great names, by the gentlemen of the household of
his Majesty the Emperor and King. The prefects by
this time were Grand Viziers. These minions of the
great man laughed at Major Diard's artless ambitions,
and he was fain to solicit a sub-prefecture. His modest

pretensions were ludicrously disproportioned to his vast
wealth.   After this ostentatious display of luxury, how
could the millionaire leave the royal splendours of his
house in Paris for Issoudun or Savenay?   Would it not
be a descent unworthy of his fortunes?   Juana, who all
too late had come to understand our laws, and the
manners and customs of our administration, too late
enlightened her husband.   Diard, in his desperation,
went begging to all the powers that be; but Diard met
with nothing but rebuffs, no way was open to him.
Then people judged him as the Government had judged
him, and passed his own verdict upon himself.   Diard
had been badly wounded on the field of battle, and Diard
had not been decorated.   The quartermaster, who had
gained wealth, but no esteem, found no place under the
government, and society quite logically refused him the
social position to which he had aspired.   In short, in his
own house the unfortunate man continually felt that his
wife was his superior.   He had come to feel it in spite
of the 'velvet glove' (if the metaphor is not too bold)
that disguised from her husband the supremacy that
astonished her herself, while she felt humiliated by it.   It
produced its effect upon Diard at last.

A man who plays a losing game like this is bound to
lose heart, and to grow either a greater or a worse man
for it; Diard's courage, or his passion, was sure to
diminish, after repeated blows dealt to his self-love, and he
made mistake upon mistake.   From the first everything
had been against him, even his own habits and his own
character.   The vices and virtues of the impulsive Provençal were equally patent.   The fibres of his nature
were like harp strings, and every old friend had a place
in his heart.   He was as prompt to relieve a comrade in
abject poverty as the distress of another of high rank;
in short, he never forgot a friend, and filled his gilded
rooms with poor wretches down on their luck.   Beholding which things, the general of the old stamp (a species

that will soon be extinct) was apt to greet Diard in an offhand fashion, and address him with a patronising, 'Well, my dear fellow!' when they met.   If the generals of the Empire concealed their insolence beneath an assumption of a soldier's bluff familiarity, the few people of fashion whom Diard met showed him the polite and well-bred contempt against which a self-made man is nearly always powerless.   Diard's behaviour and speech, like his half-Italian accent, his dress, and everything about him, combined to lower him in the eyes of ordinary minds; for the unwritten code of good manners and good taste is a binding tradition that only the greatest power can shake off.   Such is the way of the world.

These details give a very imperfect idea of Juana's martyrdom.   The pangs were endured one by one.   Every social species contributed its pin-prick, and hers was a soul that would have welcomed dagger-thrusts in preference.   It was intolerably painful to watch Diard receiving insults that he did not feel, insults that Juana must feel though they were not meant for her.   A final and dreadful illumination came at last for her; it cast a light upon the future, and she knew all the sorrows that it held in store.   She had seen already that her husband was quite incapable of mounting to the highest rungs of the social ladder, but now she saw the inevitable depths to which he must fall when he should lose heart; and then a feeling of pity for Diard came over her.

The future that lay before her was very dark.   Juana had never ceased to feel an overhanging dread of some evil, though whence it should come she knew not. This presentiment haunted her inmost soul, as contagion hovers in the air; but she was able to hide her anguish with smiles.   She had reached the point when she no longer thought of herself.

Juana used her influence to persuade Diard to renounce his social ambitions, pointing out to him as a refuge the

peaceful and gracious life of the domestic hearth. All
their troubles came from without; why should they not
shut out the world? In his own home Diard would
find peace and respect; he should reign there. She felt
that she had courage enough to undertake the trying
task of making him happy, this man dissatisfied with
himself. Her energy had increased with the difficulties of her life; she had within her the heroic spirit
needed by a woman in her position, and felt the stirrings
of those religious aspirations which are cherished by the
guardian angel appointed to watch over a Christian soul,
for this poetic superstitious fancy is an allegory that
expresses the idea of the two natures within us.

Diard renounced his ambitions, closed his house, and
literally shut himself up in it, if it is allowable to make
use of so familiar a phrase. But therein lay the danger.
Diard was one of those centrifugal souls who must
always be moving about. The luckless soldier's turn of
mind was such that no sooner had he arrived in a place
than this restless instinct forthwith drove him to depart.
Natures of this kind have but one end in life; they must
come and go unceasingly like the wheels spoken of in
the Scriptures. It may have been that Diard would fain
have escaped from himself. He was not weary of Juana;
she had given him no cause to blame her, but with
possession his passion for her had grown less absorbing,
and his character asserted itself again.

Thenceforward his moments of despondency came
more frequently; he gave way more often to his quick
southern temper. The more virtuous and irreproachable
a woman is, the more a man delights to find her in
fault, if only to demonstrate his titular superiority; but
if by chance she compels his respect, he must needs
fabricate faults, and so between the husband and wife
nothings are exaggerated, and trifles become mountains.
But Juana's meek patience and gentleness, untinged with
the bitterness that women can infuse into their sub-

mission, gave no handle to this fault-finding of set purpose, the most unkind of all. Hers was, moreover, one of those noble natures for whom it is impossible to fail in duty; her pure and holy life shone in those eyes with the martyr's expression in them that haunted the imagination. Diard first grew weary, then he chafed, and ended by finding this lofty virtue an intolerable yoke. His wife's discretion left him no room for violent sensations, and he craved excitement. Thousands of such dramas lie hidden away in the souls of men and women, beneath the uninteresting surface of apparently simple and commonplace lives. It is difficult to choose an example from among the many scenes that last for so short a time, and leave such ineffaceable traces in a life; scenes that are almost always precursors of the calamity that is written in the destiny of most marriages. Still one scene may be described, because it sharply marks the first beginnings of a misunderstanding between these two, and may in some degree explain the catastrophe of the story.

Juana had two children; luckily for her, they were both boys. The oldest was born seven months after her marriage; he was named Juan, and was like his mother. Two years after they came to Paris her second son was born; he resembled Diard and Juana, but he was more like Diard, whose names he bore. Juana had given the most tender care to little Francisco. For the five years of his life, his mother was absorbed in this child; he had more than his share of kisses and caresses and playthings; and besides and beyond all this, his mother's penetrating eyes watched him continually. Juana studied his character even in the cradle, noticing heedfully his cries and movements, that she might direct his education. Juana seemed to have but that one child. The Provençal, seeing that Juan was almost neglected, began to take notice of the older boy. He would not ask himself whether the little one was the

L

offspring of the short-lived love affair to which he owed Juana, and by a piece of rare flattery made of Juan his Benjamin.   Of all the race inheritance of passions which preyed upon her, Mme. Diard gave way but to one—a mother's love; she loved her children with the same vehemence and intensity that La Marana had shown for her child in the first part of this story; but to this love she added a gracious delicacy of feeling, a quick and keen comprehension of the social virtues that it had been her pride to practise, in which she had found her recompense.   The secret thought of the conscientious fulfilment of the duties of motherhood had been a crude element of poetry that left its impress on La Marana's life; but Juana could be a mother openly, it was her hourly consolation.   Her own mother had been virtuous as other women are criminal, by stealth; she had stolen her illicit happiness, she had not known all the sweetness of secure possession.   But Juana, whose life of virtue was as dreary as her mother's life of sin, knew every hour the ineffable joys for which that mother had longed in vain.   For her, as for La Marana, motherhood summed up all earthly affection, and both the Maranas from opposite causes had but this one comfort in their desolation.   Perhaps Juana's love was the stronger, because, shut out from all other love, her children became all in all to her, and because a noble passion has this in common with vice : it grows by what it feeds upon.   The mother and the gambler are alike insatiable.

Juana was touched by the generous pardon extended over Juan's head by Diard's fatherly affection, and thenceforward the relations between husband and wife were changed; the interest which Diard's Spanish wife had taken in him from a sense of duty only, became a deep and sincere feeling.   Had he been less inconsequent in his life, if fickleness and spasmodic changes of feeling on his part had not quenched that flicker of timid but real sympathy, Juana must surely have loved him; but, unluckily, Diard's character belonged to the quick-witted southern type, that has no continuity in its ideas; such men will be capable of heroic actions over night, and sink into nonentities on the morrow; often they are made to suffer for their virtues, often their worst defects contribute to their success; and for the rest, they are great when their good qualities are pressed into the service of an unflagging will. For two years Diard had been a prisoner in his home, a prisoner bound by the sweetest of all chains. He lived, almost against his will, beneath the influence of a wife who kept him amused, and was always bright and cheerful for him, a wife who devoted all her powers of coquetry to beguiling him into the ways of virtue; and yet all her ingenuity could not deceive him, and he knew this was not love.

Just about that time a murder caused a great sensation in Paris. A captain of the armies of the Republic had killed a woman in a paroxysm of debauchery. Diard told the story to Juana when he came home to dine. The officer, he said, had taken his own life to avoid the ignominy of a trial and the infamous death of a criminal. At first Juana could not understand the reason for his conduct, and her husband was obliged to explain to her the admirable provision of the French law, which takes no proceedings against the dead.

'But, papa, didn't you tell us the other day that the King can pardon anybody?' asked Francisco.

'The King can only grant *life*,' said Juan, nettled.

Diard and Juana watched this little scene with very different feelings. The tears of happiness in Juana's eyes as she glanced at her oldest boy let her husband see with fatal clearness into the real secrets of that hitherto inscrutable heart. Her older boy was Juana's own child; Juana knew his nature; she was sure of him and of his future; she worshipped him, and her great love was a secret known only to her child and to God. Juan, in his secret heart, gladly endured his mother's sharp speeches.

What if she seemed to frown upon him in the presence of his father and brother, when she showered passionate kisses upon him when they were alone? Francisco was Diard's child, and Juana's care meant that she wished to check the growth of his father's faults in him, and to develop his good qualities.

Juana, unconscious that she had spoken too plainly in that glance, took little Francisco on her knee; and, her sweet voice faltering somewhat with the gladness that Juan's answer had caused her, gave the younger boy the teaching suited to his childish mind.

'His training requires great care,' the father said, speaking to Juana.

'Yes,' she answered simply.

'But *Juan!*'

The tone in which the two words were uttered startled Mme. Diard. She looked up at her husband.

'Juan was born perfection,' he added, and having thus delivered himself, he sat down, and looked gloomily at his wife. She was silent, so he went on, 'You love one of *your* children more than the other.'

'You know it quite well,' she said.

'No!' returned Diard. 'Until this moment I did not know which of them you loved the most.'

'But neither of them has as yet caused me any sorrow,' she answered quickly.

'No, but which of them has given you more joys?' he asked still more quickly.

'I have not kept any reckoning of them.'

'Women are very deceitful!' cried Diard. 'Do you dare to tell me that Juan is not the darling of your heart?'

'And if he were,' she said, with gentle dignity, 'do you mean that it would be a misfortune?'

'You have never loved me! If you had chosen, I might have won kingdoms for you with my sword. You know all that I have tried to do, sustained by one

thought—a longing that you might care for me.   Ah!
if you had but loved me——'

'A woman who loves,' said Juana, 'lives in solitude far
from the world.   Is not that what we are doing?'

'Oh! I know, Juana, that you are never in the
wrong.'

The words, spoken with such intense bitterness,
brought about a coolness between them that lasted the
rest of their lives.

On the morrow of that fatal day, Diard sought out
one of his old cronies, and with him sought distraction at
the gaming-table.   Unluckily, he won a great deal of
money, and he began to play regularly.   Little by little
he slipped back into his old dissipated life.   After a short
time he no longer dined at home.   A few months were
spent in the enjoyment of the first pleasures of freedom;
he made up his mind that he would not part with it, left
the large apartments of the house to his wife, and took
up his abode separately on the *entresol*.   By the end of
the year Diard and Juana only met once a day—at
breakfast time.

In a few words, like all gamblers, he had runs of good
and bad luck; but as he was reluctant to touch his
capital, he wished to have entire control of their income,
and his wife accordingly ceased to take any part in the
management of the household economy.   Mistrust had
succeeded to the boundless confidence that he had once
placed in her.   As to money matters, which had formerly
been arranged by both husband and wife, he adopted the
plan of a monthly allowance for her own expenses; they
settled the amount of it together in the last of the con-
fidential talks that form one of the most attractive charms
of marriage.

The barrier of silence between two hearts is a real
divorce, accomplished on the day when husband and wife
say *we* no longer.   When that day came, Juana knew
that she was no longer a wife, but a mother; she was

not unhappy, and did not seek to guess the reason of the misfortune. It was a great pity. Children consolidate, as it were, the lives of their parents, and the life that her husband led apart was to weave sadness and anguish for others as well as for Juana. Diard lost no time in making use of his newly regained liberty; he played high, and lost and won enormous sums. He was a good and bold player, and gained a great reputation. The respect which he had failed to win in society in the days of the Empire was accorded now to the wealth that was risked upon a green table, to a talent for all and any of the games of chance of that period. Ambassadors, financiers, men with large fortunes, jaded pleasure-seekers in quest of excitement and extreme sensations, admired Diard's play at their clubs; they rarely asked him to their houses, but they all played with him. Diard became the fashion. Once or twice during the winter his independent spirit led him to give a fête to return the courtesies that he had received, and by glimpses Juana saw something of society again; there was a brief return of balls and banquets, of luxury and brilliantly-lighted rooms; but all these things she regarded as a sort of duty levied upon her happiness and solitude.

The queen of these high festivals appeared in them like some creature fallen from an unknown world. Her simplicity that nothing had spoiled, a certain maidenliness of soul with which the changed conditions of her life had invested her, her beauty, her unaffected modesty, won sincere admiration. But Juana saw few women among her guests; and it was plain to her mind that if her husband had ordered his life differently without taking her into his confidence, he had not risen in the esteem of the world.

Diard was not always lucky. In three years he had squandered three-fourths of his fortune; but he drew from his passion for gambling sufficient energy to satisfy it. He had a large circle of acquaintance, and was hand

and glove with certain swindlers on the Stock Exchange —gentry who, since the Revolution, have established the principle that robbery on a large scale is a mere *peccadillo*, transferring to the language of the counting-house the brazen epithets of the license of the eighteenth century.

Diard became a speculator, engaged in the peculiar kinds of business described as 'shady' in the slang of the Palais. He managed to get hold of poor wretches ignorant of commercial red-tape, and weary of everlasting proceedings in liquidation ; he would buy up their claims on the debtor's estate for a small sum, arrange the matter with the assignees in the course of an evening, and divide the spoil with the latter. When liquefiable debts were not to be found, he looked out for floating debts ; he unearthed and revived claims in abeyance in Europe and America and uncivilised countries. When at the Restoration the debts incurred by the princes, the Republic, and the Empire were all paid, he took commissions on loans, on contracts for public works and enterprises of all kinds. In short, he committed legal robbery, like many another carefully masked delinquent behind the scenes in the theatre of politics. Such thefts, if perpetrated by the light of a street lamp, would send the luckless offender to the hulks ; but there is a virtue in the glitter of chandeliers and gilded ceilings that absolves the crimes committed beneath them.

Diard forestalled and regrated sugars ; he sold places ; to him belongs the credit of the invention of the *warming-pan* ; he installed lay-figures in lucrative posts that must be held for a time to secure still better positions. Then he fell to meditating on bounties ; he studied the loop-holes of the law, and carried on contraband trades against which no provision had been made. This traffic in high places may be briefly described as a sort of commission agency ; he received 'so much per cent.' on the purchase of fifteen votes which passed in a single night from the benches on the left to the benches on the right of the legislative chamber.　In these days such things are neither misdemeanours nor felony; exploiting industry, the art of government, financial genius—these are the names by which they are called.

Public opinion put Diard in the pillory, where more than one clever man stood already to keep him company; there, indeed, you will find the aristocracy of this kind of talent—the Upper Chamber of civilised rascality.

Diard, therefore, was no commonplace gambler, no vulgar spendthrift who ends his career, in melodramas, as a beggar.　Above a certain social altitude that kind of gambler is not to be found.　In these days a bold scoundrel of this kind will die gloriously in the harness of vice in all the trappings of success: he will blow out his brains in a coach and six, and all that has been intrusted to him vanishes with him.　Diard's talent determined him not to buy remorse too cheaply, and he joined this privileged class.　He learned all the springs of government, made himself acquainted with all the secrets and the weaknesses of men in office, and held his own in the fiery furnace into which he had cast himself.

Mme. Diard knew nothing of the infernal life that her husband led.　She was well content to be neglected, and did not ponder overmuch the reasons for his neglect. Her time was too well filled.　She devoted all the money that she had to the education of her children; a very clever tutor was engaged for them, besides various masters.　She meant to make men of her boys, to develop in them the faculty of reasoning clearly, but not at the expense of their imaginative powers.　Nothing affected her now save through her children, and her own colourless life depressed her no longer.　Juan and Francisco were for her what children are for a time for many mothers—a sort of expansion of her own existence.　Diard had come to be a mere accident in her life.　Since Diard had ceased to be a father and the head of the family, nothing bound Juana to her husband any longer, save a regard for appearances demanded by social conventions ; yet she brought up her children to respect their father, shadowy and unreal as that fatherhood had become ; indeed, her husband's continual absence from home helped her to maintain the fiction of his high character. If Diard had lived in the house, all Juana's efforts must have been in vain. Her children were too quick and bright not to judge their father, and this process is a moral parricide.

At length, however, Juana's indifference changed to a feeling of dread. She felt that sooner or later her husband's manner of life must affect the children's future. Day by day that old presentiment of coming evil gathered definiteness and strength. On the rare occasions when Juana saw her husband, she would glance at his hollow cheeks, at his face grown haggard with the vigils he kept, and wrinkled with violent emotions ; and Diard almost trembled before the clear, penetrating eyes. At such times her husband's assumed gaiety alarmed her even more than the dark look that his face wore in repose, when for a moment he happened to forget the part that he was playing. He feared his wife as the criminal fears the headsman. Juana saw in him a disgrace on her children's name ; and Diard dreaded her, she was like some passionless Vengeance, a Justice with unchanging brows, with the arm that should one day strike always suspended above him.

One day, about fifteen years after his marriage, Diard found himself without resources. He owed a hundred thousand crowns, and was possessed of a bare hundred thousand francs. His mansion (all that he possessed beside ready money) was mortgaged beyond its value. A few more days, and the prestige of enormous wealth must fade ; and when those days of grace had expired, no helping hand would be stretched out, no purse would be open for him. Nothing but unlooked-for luck could save him now from the slough into which he must fall ;

and he would but sink the deeper in it, men would scorn him the more because for a while they had estimated him at more than his just value.

Very opportunely, therefore, he learned that with the beginning of the season diplomatists and foreigners of distinction flocked to watering-places in the Pyrenees, that play ran high at these resorts, and that the visitors were doubtless well able to pay their losings. So he determined to set out at once for the Pyrenees. He had no mind to leave his wife in Paris; some of his creditors might enlighten her as to his awkward position, and he wished to keep it secret, so he took Juana and the two children. He would not allow the tutor to go with them, and made some difficulties about Juana's maid, who, with a single man-servant, composed their travelling suite. His tone was curt and peremptory; his energy seemed to have returned to him. This hasty journey sent a shiver of dread to Juana's soul; her penetration was at fault, she could not imagine the why and wherefore of their leaving Paris. Her husband seemed to be in high spirits on the way; and during the time spent together perforce in the travelling carriage, he took more and more notice of the children, and was more kindly to the children's mother. And yet—every day brought new and dark forebodings for Juana, the forebodings of a mother's heart. These inward warnings, even when there is no apparent reason for them, are seldom vain, and the veil that hides the future grows thin for a mother's eyes.

Diard took a house, not large, but very nicely furnished, situated in one of the quietest parts of Bordeaux. It happened to be a corner house with a large garden, surrounded on three sides by streets, and on the fourth by the wall of a neighbouring dwelling. Diard paid the rent in advance, and installed his wife and family, leaving Juana fifty louis, a sum barely sufficient to meet the housekeeping expenses for three months. Mme. Diard made no comment on this unwonted niggardliness. When her husband told her that he was about to go to the Baths, and that she was to remain in Bordeaux, she made up her mind that the children should learn the Spanish and Italian languages thoroughly, and that they should read with her the great masterpieces of either tongue.

With this object in view, Juana's life should be retired and simple, and in consequence her expenses would be few. Her own woman waited upon them; and, to simplify the housekeeping, she arranged on the morrow of Diard's departure to have their meals sent in from a restaurant. Everything was provided for until her husband's return, and she had no money left. Her amusements must consist in occasional walks with the children. She was now a woman of thirty-three; her beauty had developed to its fullest extent, she was in the full splendour of her maturity. Scarcely had she appeared in Bordeaux before people talked of nothing but the lovely Spanish lady. She received a first love-letter, and thenceforth confined her walks to her own garden.

At first Diard had a run of luck at the Baths. He won three hundred thousand francs in two months; but it never occurred to him to send any money to his wife, he meant to keep as large a sum as possible by him, and to play for yet higher stakes. Towards the end of the last month a Marchese di Montefiore came to the Baths, preceded by a reputation for a fine figure, and great wealth, for the match that he had made with an English lady of family, and most of all for a passion for gaming. Diard waited for his old comrade in arms, to add the spoils to his winnings. A gambler with something like four hundred thousand francs at his back can command most things; Diard felt confident in his luck, and renewed his acquaintance with Montefiore. That gentleman received him coldly, but they played together, and Diard lost everything.

'Montefiore, my dear fellow,' said the sometime quartermaster, after a turn round the room in which he had ruined himself, 'I owe you a hundred thousand francs; but I have left my money at Bordeaux, where my wife is staying.'

As a matter of fact, Diard had notes for the amount in his pockets at that moment, but, with the self-possession of a man accustomed to take in all the possibilities of a situation at a glance, he still hoped something from the incalculable chances of the gaming-table. Montefiore had expressed a desire to see something of Bordeaux; and if Diard were to settle at once with him, he would have nothing left, and could not have his 'revenge.' A 'revenge' will sometimes more than make good all previous losses. All these burning hopes depended on the answer that the Marquis might give.

'Let it stand, my dear fellow,' said Montefiore; 'we will go to Bordeaux together. I am rich enough now in all conscience; why should I take an old comrade's money?'

Three days later, Diard and the Italian were at Bordeaux. Montefiore offered the Provençal his revenge. In the course of an evening, which Diard began by paying down the hundred thousand francs, he lost two hundred thousand more upon parole. He was as light-hearted over his losses as if he could swim in gold. It was eleven o'clock, and a glorious night, surely Montefiore must wish to breathe the fresh air under the open sky, and to take a walk to cool down a little after the excitement of play; Diard suggested that the Italian should accompany him to his house and take a cup of tea there when the money was paid over.

'But Mme. Diard!' queried Montefiore.

'Pshaw!' answered the Provençal.

They went downstairs together; but before leaving the house, Diard went into the dining-room, asked for a glass of water, and walked about the room as he waited for it. In this way he managed to secrete a tiny steel knife with a handle of mother-of-pearl, such as is used at dessert for fruit; the thing had not yet been put away in its place.

'Where do you live?' asked Montefiore, as they crossed the court; 'I must leave word, so as to have the carriage sent round for me.'

Diard gave minute directions.

'Of course, I am perfectly safe as long as I am with you, you see,' said Montefiore in a low voice, as he took Diard's arm; 'but if I came back by myself, and some scamp were to follow me, I should be worth killing.'

'Then have you money about you?'

'Oh! next to nothing,' said the cautious Italian, 'only my winnings. But they would make a pretty fortune for a penniless rascal; he might take brevet rank as an honest man afterwards for the rest of his life, that I know.'

Diard took the Italian into a deserted street. He had noticed the gateway of a single house in it at the end of a sort of avenue of trees, and that there were high dark walls on either side. Just as they reached the end of this road he had the audacity to ask his friend, in soldierly fashion, to walk on. Montefiore understood Diard's meaning, and turned to go with him. Scarcely had they set foot in the shadow, when Diard sprang like a tiger upon the Marquis, tripped him up, boldly set his foot on his victim's throat, and plunged the knife again and again into his heart, till the blade snapped off short in his body. Then he searched Montefiore, took his money, his pocket-book, and everything that the Marquis had.

But though Diard had set about his work in a frenzy that left him perfectly clear-headed, and completed it with the deftness of a pickpocket; though he had taken his victim adroitly by surprise, Montefiore had had time to shriek 'Murder!' once or twice, a shrill, far-reaching cry that must have sent a thrill of horror through many sleepers, and his dying groans were fearful to hear.

Diard did not know that even as they turned into the avenue a crowd of people returning home from the theatre had reached the upper end of the street. They had heard Montefiore's dying cries, though the Provençal had tried to stifle the sounds, never relaxing the pressure of his foot upon the murdered man's throat, until at last they ceased.

The high walls still echoed with dying groans which guided the crowd to the spot whence they came. The sound of many feet filled the avenue and rang through Diard's brain. The murderer did not lose his head; he came out from under the trees, and walked very quietly along the street, as if he had been drawn thither by curiosity, and saw that he had come too late to be of any use. He even turned to make sure of the distance that separated him from the new-comers, and saw them all rush into the avenue, save one man, who not unnaturally stood still to watch Diard's movements.

'There he lies! There he lies!' shouted voices from the avenue. They had caught sight of Montefiore's dead body in front of the great house. The gateway was shut fast, and after diligent search they could not find the murderer in the alley.

As soon as he heard the shout, Diard knew that he had got the start; he seemed to have the strength of a lion in him and the fleetness of a stag; he began to run, nay, he flew. He saw, or fancied that he saw, a second crowd at the other end of the road, and darted down a side street. But even as he fled, windows were opened, and rows of heads were thrust out, lights and shouting issued from every door; to Diard, running for dear life, it seemed as if he were rushing through a tumult of cries and swaying lights. As he fled straight along the road before him, his legs stood him in such good stead that he left the crowd behind; but he could not keep out of sight of the windows, nor avoid the watchful eyes that traversed the length and breadth of a street faster than he could fly.

In the twinkling of an eye, soldiers, gendarmes, and householders were all astir. Some in their zeal had gone to wake up Commissaries of Police, others stood by the dead body. The alarm spread out into the suburbs in the direction of the fugitive (whom it followed like a conflagration from street to street) and into the heart of the town, where it reached the authorities. Diard heard as in a dream the hurrying feet, the yells of a whole horror-stricken city. But his ideas were still clear; he still preserved his presence of mind, and he rubbed his hands against the walls as he ran.

At last he reached the garden wall of his own house. He thought that he had thrown his pursuers off the scent. The place was perfectly silent save for the far-off murmur of the city, scarcely louder there than the sound of the sea. He dipped his hands into a runnel of clear water and drank. Then, looking about him, he saw a heap of loose stones by the roadside, and hastened to bury his spoils beneath it, acting on some dim notion such as crosses a criminal's mind when he has not yet found a consistent tale to account for his actions, and hopes to establish his innocence by lack of proofs against him. When this was accomplished, he tried to look serene and calm, forced a smile, and knocked gently at his own door, hoping that no one had seen him. He looked up at the house front and saw a light in his wife's windows. And then in his agitation of spirit visions of Juana's peaceful life rose before him; he saw her sitting there in the candlelight with her children on either side of her, and the vision smote his brain like a blow from a hammer. The waiting-woman opened the door, Diard entered, and hastily shut it to again. He dared to breathe more freely, but he remembered that he was covered with perspiration, and sent the maid up to Juana, while he stayed below in the darkness.   He wiped his face with a handkerchief and set his clothes in order, as a coxcomb smooths his coat before calling upon a pretty woman ; then for a moment he stood in the moonlight examining his hands; he passed them over his face, and with unspeakable joy found that there was no trace of blood upon him, doubtless his victim's wounds had bled internally.

He went up to Juana's room, and his manner was as quiet and composed as if he had come home after the theatre, to sleep.   As he climbed the stairs, he could think over his position, and summed it up in a phrase— he must leave the house and reach the harbour.   These ideas did not cross his brain in words; he saw them written in letters of fire upon the darkness.   Once down at the harbour, he could lie in hiding during the day, and return at night for his treasure ; then he would creep with it like a rat into the hold of some vessel, and leave the port, no one suspecting that he was on board. For all these things money was wanted in the first place.   And he had nothing.   The waiting-woman came with a light.

' Félicie,' he said, ' do you not hear that noise ? people are shouting in the street.   Go and find out what it is and let me know———'

His wife in her white dressing-gown was sitting at a table, reading Cervantes in Spanish with Francisco and Juan ; the two children's eyes followed the text while their mother read aloud.   All three of them stopped and looked up at Diard, who stood with his hands in his pockets, surprised perhaps by the surroundings, the peaceful scene, the fair faces of the woman and the children in the softly lit room.   It was like a living picture of a Madonna with her son and the little Saint John on either side.

' Juana, I have something to say to you.'

'What is it?' she asked. In her husband's wan and sallow face she read the news of this calamity that she had expected daily; it had come at last.

'Nothing, but I should like to speak to you—to you, quite alone,' and he fixed his eyes on the two little boys.

'Go to your room, my darlings, and go to bed,' said Juana. 'Say your prayers without me.'

The two boys went away in silence, with the uninquisitive obedience of children who have been well brought up.

'Dear Juana,' Diard began in coaxing tones, 'I left you very little money, and I am very sorry for it now. Listen, since I relieved you of the cares of your household by giving you an allowance, perhaps you may have saved a little money, as all women do?'

'No,' answered Juana, 'I have nothing. You did not allow anything for the expenses of the children's education. I am not reproaching you at all, dear; I only remind you that you forgot about it, to explain how it is that I have no money. All that you gave me I spent on lessons and masters——'

'That will do!' Diard broke in. '*Sacré tonnerre!* time is precious. Have you no jewels?'

'You know quite well that I never wear them.'

'Then there is not a *sou* in the house!' cried Diard, like a man bereft of his senses.

'Why do you cry out?' she asked.

'Juana,' he began, 'I have just killed a man!'

Juana rushed to the children's room, and returned, shutting all the doors after her.

'Your sons must not hear a word of this,' she said; 'but whom can you have fought with?'

'Montefiore,' he answered.

'Ah!' she said, and a sigh broke from her; 'he is the one man whom you had a right to kill——'

'There were plenty of reasons why he should die by my hand. But let us lose no time. Money, I want

M

money, in God's name ! They may be on my track. We did not fight, Juana, I—I killed him.'

'Killed him !' she cried. 'But how——? '

'Why, how does one kill a man ? He had robbed me of all I had at play; and I have taken it back again. Juana, since we have no money, you might go now, while everything is quiet, and look for my money under the heap of stones at the end of the road ; you know the place.'

'Then,' said Juana, 'you have robbed him.'

'What business is it of yours ? Fly I must, mustn't I ? Have you any money ? . . . They are after me !'

'Who ? '

'The authorities.'

Juana left the room, and came back suddenly.

'Here,' she cried, holding out a trinket, but standing at a distance from him; 'this is Doña Lagounia's cross. There are four rubies in it, and the stones are very valuable; so I have been told. Be quick, fly, fly—— why don't you go ? '

'Félicie has not come back,' he said, in dull amazement. 'Can they have arrested her ? '

Juana dropped the cross on the edge of the table, and sprang towards the windows that looked out upon the street. Outside in the moonlight she saw a row of soldiers taking their places in absolute silence along the walls. She came back again ; to all appearance she was perfectly calm.

'You have not a minute to lose,' she said to her husband ; 'you must escape through the garden. Here is the key of the little door.'

A last counsel of prudence led her, however, to give a glance over the garden. In the shadows under the trees she saw the silvery gleam of the metal rims of the gendarmes' caps. She even heard a vague murmur of a not far-distant crowd ; sentinels were keeping back the people gathered together by curiosity at the further ends of the streets by which the house was approached.

As a matter of fact, Diard had been seen from the windows of the houses; the maid-servant had been frightened, and afterwards arrested; and, acting on this information, the military and the crowd had soon blocked the ends of the streets that lay on two sides of the house. A dozen gendarmes, coming off duty at the theatres, were posted outside; others had climbed the wall, and were searching the garden, a proceeding authorised by the serious nature of the crime.

'Monsieur,' said Juana, 'it is too late. The whole town is aroused.'

Diard rushed from window to window with the wild recklessness of a bird that dashes frantically against every pane. Juana stood absorbed in her thoughts.

'Where can I hide?' he asked.

He looked at the chimney, and Juana stared at the two empty chairs. To her it seemed only a moment since her children were sitting there. Just at that moment the gate opened, and the courtyard echoed with the sound of many footsteps.

'Juana, dear Juana, for pity's sake, tell me what to do.'

'I will tell you,' she said; 'I will save you.'

'Ah! you will be my good angel!'

Again Juana returned with one of Diard's pistols; she held it out to him, and turned her head away. Diard did not take it. Juana heard sounds from the courtyard; they had brought in the dead body of the Marquis to confront the murderer. She came away from the window and looked at Diard; he was white and haggard; his strength failed him; he made as if he would sink into a chair.

'For your children's sake,' she said, thrusting the weapon into his hands.

'But, my dear Juana, my little Juana, do you really

believe that . . . ?   Juana, is there such need of haste ? . . .
I would like to kiss you before . . .'

The gendarmes were on the stairs.   Then Juana took
up the pistol, held it at Diard's head ; with a firm grasp
on his throat she held him tightly in spite of his cries,
fired, and let the weapon fall to the ground.

The door was suddenly flung open at that moment.
The public prosecutor, followed by a magistrate and his
clerk, a doctor, and the gendarmes, all the instruments of
man's justice, appeared upon the scene.

'What do you want ?' she asked.

'Is that M. Diard ?' answered the public prosecutor,
pointing to the body lying bent double upon the floor.

'Yes, monsieur.'

'Your dress is covered with blood, madame——'

'Do you not understand how it is ?' asked Juana.

She went over to the little table and sat down there,
and took up the volume of Cervantes ; her face was
colourless ; she strove to control her inward nervous
agitation.

'Leave the room,' said the public prosecutor to the
gendarmes.   He made a sign to the magistrate and the
doctor, and they remained.

'Madame, under the circumstances, we can only con-
gratulate you on your husband's death.   If he was
carried away by passion, at any rate he has died like
a soldier, and it is vain for justice to pursue him now.
Yet little as we may desire to intrude upon you at such
a time, the law obliges us to inquire into a death by
violence.   Permit us to do our duty.'

'May I change my dress ?' she asked, laying down
the volume.

'Yes, madame, but you must bring it here.   The
doctor will doubtless require it——'

'It would be too painful to Mme. Diard to be present
while I go through my task,' said the doctor, understanding the public prosecutor's suspicions.   'Will you

permit her, gentlemen, to remain in the adjoining room ? '

The two functionaries approved the kindly doctor's suggestion, and Félicie went to her mistress. Then the magistrate and the public prosecutor spoke together for a while in a low voice. It is the unhappy lot of administrators of justice to be in duty bound to suspect everybody and everything. By dint of imagining evil motives, and every possible combination that they may bring about, so as to discover the truth that lurks beneath the most inconsistent actions, it is impossible but that their dreadful office should in course of time dry up the source of the generous impulses to which they may never yield. If the sensibilities of the surgeon who explores the mysteries of the body are blunted by degrees, what becomes of the inner sensibility of the judge who is compelled to probe the intricate recesses of the human conscience ? Magistrates are the first victims of their profession ; their progress is one perpetual mourning for their lost illusions, and the crimes that hang so heavily about the necks of criminals weigh no less upon their judges. An old man seated in the tribunal of justice is sublime ; but do we not shudder to see a young face there ? In this case the magistrate was a young man, and it was his duty to say to the public prosecutor, ' Was the woman her husband's accomplice, do you think ? Must we take proceedings ? Ought she, in your opinion, to be examined ? '

By way of reply, the public prosecutor shrugged his shoulders ; apparently it was a matter of indifference.

'Montefiore and Diard,' he remarked, ' were a pair of notorious scamps. The servant-girl knew nothing about the crime. We need not go any further.'

The doctor was making his examination of Diard's body, and dictating his report to the clerk. Suddenly he rushed into Juana's room.

' Madame——'

Juana, who had changed her blood-stained dress, confronted the doctor.

'You shot your husband, did you not?' he asked, bending to say the words in her ear.

'Yes, monsieur,' the Spaniard answered.

'*And from circumstantial evidence*' (the doctor went on dictating) '*we conclude that the said Diard has taken his life by his own act.*—Have you finished?' he asked the clerk after a pause.

'Yes,' answered the scribe.

The doctor put his signature to the document. Juana glanced at him, and could scarcely keep back the tears that, for a moment, filled her eyes.

'Gentlemen,' she said, and she turned to the public prosecutor, 'I am a stranger, a Spaniard. I do not know the law. I know no one in Bordeaux. I entreat you to do me this kindness, will you procure me a passport for Spain?'

'One moment!' exclaimed the magistrate. 'Madame, what has become of the sum of money that was stolen from the Marquis di Montefiore?'

'M. Diard said something about a heap of stones beneath which he had hidden it,' she answered.

'Where?'

'In the street.'

The two functionaries exchanged glances. Juana's involuntary start was sublime. She appealed to the doctor.

'Can they suspect me?' she said in his ear; 'suspect *me* of some villainy? The heap of stones is sure to be somewhere at the end of the garden. Go yourself, I beg of you, and look for it and find the money.

The doctor went, accompanied by the magistrate, and found Montefiore's pocket-book.

Two days later Juana sold her golden cross to meet the expenses of the journey. As she went with her two children to the diligence in which they were about to travel to the Spanish frontier, some one called her name in the street. It was her dying mother, who was being taken to the hospital ; she had caught a glimpse of her daughter through a slit in the curtains of the stretcher on which she lay. Juana bade them carry the stretcher into a gateway, and there for the last time the mother and daughter met. Low as their voices were while they spoke together, Juan overheard these words of farewell—

'Mother, die in peace ; I have suffered for you all.'

PARIS, *November* 1832.

EL VERDUGO

To Martinez de la Rosa

MIDNIGHT had just sounded from the belfry tower of the little town of Menda. A young French officer, leaning over the parapet of the long terrace at the further end of the castle gardens, seemed to be unusually absorbed in deep thought for one who led the reckless life of a soldier; but it must be admitted that never was the hour, the scene, and the night more favourable to meditation.

The blue dome of the cloudless sky of Spain was overhead; he was looking out over the coy windings of a lovely valley lit by the uncertain starlight and the soft radiance of the moon. The officer, leaning against an orange tree in blossom, could also see, a hundred feet below him, the town of Menda, which seemed to nestle for shelter from the north wind at the foot of the crags on which the castle itself was built. He turned his head and caught sight of the sea; the moonlit waves made a broad frame of silver for the landscape.

There were lights in the castle windows. The mirth and movement of a ball, the sounds of the violins, the laughter of the officers and their partners in the dance was borne towards him, and blended with the far-off murmur of the waves. The cool night had a certain bracing effect upon his frame, wearied as he had been by the heat of the day. He seemed to bathe in the air, made fragrant by the strong, sweet scent of flowers and of aromatic trees in the gardens.

184

The castle of Menda belonged to a Spanish grandee, who was living in it at that time with his family. All through the evening the oldest daughter of the house had watched the officer with such a wistful interest that the Spanish lady's compassionate eyes might well have set the young Frenchman dreaming. Clara was beautiful; and although she had three brothers and a sister, the broad lands of the Marqués de Légañès appeared to be sufficient warrant for Victor Marchand's belief that the young lady would have a splendid dowry. But how could he dare to imagine that the most fanatical believer in blue blood in all Spain would give his daughter to the son of a grocer in Paris? Moreover, the French were hated. It was because the Marquis had been suspected of an attempt to raise the country in favour of Ferdinand VII. that General G——, who governed the province, had stationed Victor Marchand's battalion in the little town of Menda to overawe the neighbouring districts which received the Marqués de Légañès' word as law. A recent despatch from Marshal Ney had given ground for fear that the English might ere long effect a landing on the coast, and had indicated the Marquis as being in correspondence with the Cabinet in London.

In spite, therefore, of the welcome with which the Spaniards had received Victor Marchand and his soldiers, that officer was always on his guard. As he went towards the terrace, where he had just surveyed the town and the districts confided to his charge, he had been asking himself what construction he ought to put upon the friendliness which the Marquis had invariably shown him, and how to reconcile the apparent tranquillity of the country with his General's uneasiness. But a moment later these thoughts were driven from his mind by the instinct of caution and very legitimate curiosity. It had just struck him that there was a very fair number of lights in the town below. Although it was the Feast of Saint James, he himself had issued orders that very morning that all lights must be put out in the town at the hour prescribed by military regulations. The castle alone had been excepted in this order. Plainly here and there he saw the gleam of bayonets, where his own men were at their accustomed posts; but in the town there was a solemn silence, and not a sign that the Spaniards had given themselves up to the intoxication of a festival. He tried vainly for a while to explain this breach of the regulations on the part of the inhabitants; the mystery seemed but so much the more obscure because he had left instructions with some of his officers to do police duty that night, and make the rounds of the town.

With the impetuosity of youth, he was about to spring through a gap in the wall preparatory to a rapid scramble down the rocks, thinking to reach a small guard-house at the nearest entrance into the town more quickly than by the beaten track, when a faint sound stopped him. He fancied that he could hear the light footstep of a woman along the gravelled garden walk. He turned his head and saw no one; for one moment his eyes were dazzled by the wonderful brightness of the sea, the next he saw a sight so ominous that he stood stock-still with amazement, thinking that his senses must be deceiving him. The white moonbeams lighted the horizon, so that he could distinguish the sails of ships still a considerable distance out at sea. A shudder ran through him; he tried to persuade himself that this was some optical delusion brought about by chance effects of moonlight on the waves; and even as he made the attempt, a hoarse voice called to him by name. The officer glanced at the gap in the wall; saw a soldier's head slowly emerge from it, and knew the grenadier whom he had ordered to accompany him to the castle.

'Is that you, Commandant?'

'Yes. What is it?' returned the young officer in a low voice. A kind of presentiment warned him to act cautiously.

'Those beggars down there are creeping about like worms; and, by your leave, I came as quickly as I could to report my little reconnoitring expedition.'

'Go on,' answered Victor Marchand.

'I have just been following a man from the castle who came round this way with a lantern in his hand. A lantern is a suspicious matter with a vengeance! I don't imagine that there was any need for that good Christian to be lighting tapers at this time of night. Says I to myself, "They mean to gobble us up!" and I set myself to dogging his heels; and that is how I found out that there is a pile of faggots, sir, two or three steps away from here.'

Suddenly a dreadful shriek rang through the town below, and cut the man short. A light flashed in the Commandant's face, and the poor grenadier dropped down with a bullet through his head. Ten paces away a bonfire flared up like a conflagration. The sounds of music and laughter ceased all at once in the ballroom; the silence of death, broken only by groans, succeeded to the rhythmical murmur of the festival. Then the roar of cannon sounded from across the white plain of the sea.

A cold sweat broke out on the young officer's forehead. He had left his sword behind. He knew that his men had been murdered, and that the English were about to land. He knew that if he lived he would be dishonoured; he saw himself summoned before a court-martial. For a moment his eyes measured the depth of the valley; the next, just as he was about to spring down, Clara's hand caught his.

'Fly!' she cried. 'My brothers are coming after me to kill you. Down yonder at the foot of the cliff you will find Juanito's Andalusian. Go!'

She thrust him away. The young man gazed at her in dull bewilderment; but obeying the instinct of self-preservation, which never deserts even the bravest, he rushed across the park in the direction pointed out to him, springing from rock to rock in places unknown to any save the goats. He heard Clara calling to her brothers to pursue him; he heard the footsteps of the murderers; again and again he heard their balls whistling about his ears; but he reached the foot of the cliff, found the horse, mounted, and fled with lightning speed.

A few hours later the young officer reached General G——'s quarters, and found him at dinner with the staff.

'I put my life in your hands!' cried the haggard and exhausted Commandant of Menda.

He sank into a seat, and told his horrible story. It was received with an appalling silence.

'It seems to me that you are more to be pitied than to blame,' the terrible General said at last. 'You are not answerable for the Spaniard's crimes, and unless the Marshal decides otherwise, I acquit you.'

These words brought but cold comfort to the unfortunate officer.

'When the Emperor comes to hear about it!' he cried.

'Oh, he will be for having you shot,' said the General, 'but we shall see. Now we will say no more about this,' he added severely, 'except to plan a revenge that shall strike a salutary terror into this country, where they carry on war like savages.'

An hour later a whole regiment, a detachment of cavalry, and a convoy of artillery were upon the road. The General and Victor marched at the head of the column. The soldiers had been told of the fate of their comrades, and their rage knew no bounds. The distance between headquarters and the town of Menda was crossed at a well-nigh miraculous speed. Whole villages by the way were found to be under arms; every one of the wretched hamlets was surrounded, and their inhabitants decimated.

It so chanced that the English vessels still lay out at sea, and were no nearer the shore, a fact inexplicable until it was known afterwards that they were artillery transports which had outsailed the rest of the fleet. So the townsmen of Menda, left without the assistance on which they had reckoned when the sails of the English appeared, were surrounded by French troops almost before they had had time to strike a blow. This struck such terror into them that they offered to surrender at discretion. An impulse of devotion, no isolated instance in the history of the Peninsula, led the actual slayers of the French to offer to give themselves up; seeking in this way to save the town, for from the General's reputation for cruelty it was feared that he would give Menda over to the flames, and put the whole population to the sword. General G—— took their offer, stipulating that every soul in the castle from the lowest servant to the Marquis should likewise be given up to him. These terms being accepted, the General promised to spare the lives of the rest of the townsmen, and to prohibit his soldiers from pillaging or setting fire to the town. A heavy contribution was levied, and the wealthiest inhabitants were taken as hostages to guarantee payment within twenty-four hours.

The General took every necessary precaution for the safety of his troops, provided for the defence of the place, and refused to billet his men in the houses of the town. After they had bivouacked, he went up to the castle and entered it as a conqueror. The whole family of Léganès and their household were gagged, shut up in the great ballroom, and closely watched. From the windows it was easy to see the whole length of the terrace above the town.

The staff was established in an adjoining gallery, where the General forthwith held a council as to the best means of preventing the landing of the English. An aide-de-camp was despatched to Marshal Ney, orders were issued to plant batteries along the coast, and then the General and his staff turned their attention to their prisoners. The two hundred Spaniards given up by the townsfolk were shot down then and there upon the terrace. And after this military execution, the General gave orders to erect gibbets to the number of the prisoners in the ball-room in the same place, and to send for the hangman out of the town. Victor took advantage of the interval before dinner to pay a visit to the prisoners. He soon came back to the General.

'I am come in haste,' he faltered out, 'to ask a favour.'

'*You!*' exclaimed the General, with bitter irony in his tones.

'Alas!' answered Victor, 'it is a sorry favour. The Marquis has seen them erecting the gallows, and hopes that you will commute the punishment for his family; he entreats you to have the nobles beheaded.'

'Granted,' said the General.

'He further asks that they may be allowed the consolations of religion, and that they may be unbound; they give you their word that they will not attempt to escape.'

'That I permit,' said the General, 'but you are answerable for them.'

'The old noble offers you all that he has if you will pardon his youngest son.'

'Really!' cried the Commander. 'His property is forfeit already to King Joseph.' He paused; a contemptuous thought set wrinkles in his forehead, as he added, 'I will do better than they ask. I understand what he means by that last request of his. Very good. Let him hand down his name to posterity; but whenever it is mentioned, all Spain shall remember his treason and its punishment! I will give the fortune and his life to any one of the sons who will do the executioner's office. . . . There, don't talk any more about them to me.'

Dinner was ready. The officers sat down to satisfy an appetite whetted by hunger. Only one among them was absent from the table — that one was Victor Marchand. After long hesitation, he went to the ball-room, and heard the last sighs of the proud house of Léganès. He looked sadly at the scene before him. Only last night, in this very room, he had seen their faces whirled past him in the waltz, and he shuddered to think that those girlish heads with those of the three young brothers must fall in a brief space by the executioner's sword. There sat the father and mother, their three sons and two daughters, perfectly motionless, bound to their gilded chairs. Eight serving men stood with their hands tied behind them. These fifteen prisoners, under sentence of death, exchanged grave glances; it was difficult to read the thoughts that filled them from their eyes, but profound resignation and regret that their enterprise should have failed so completely was written on more than one brow.

The impassive soldiers who guarded them respected the grief of their bitter enemies. A gleam of curiosity lighted up all faces when Victor came in. He gave orders that the condemned prisoners should be unbound, and himself unfastened the cords that held Clara a prisoner. She smiled mournfully at him. The officer could not refrain from lightly touching the young girl's arm; he could not help admiring her dark hair, her slender waist. She was a true daughter of Spain, with a Spanish complexion, a Spaniard's eyes, blacker than the raven's wing beneath their long curving lashes.

'Did you succeed?' she asked, with a mournful smile, in which a certain girlish charm still lingered.

Victor could not repress a groan. He looked from the faces of the three brothers to Clara, and again at the three young Spaniards. The first, the oldest of the family, was a man of thirty. He was short, and some-what ill made; he looked haughty and proud, but a certain distinction was not lacking in his bearing, and he was apparently no stranger to the delicacy of feeling for which in olden times the chivalry of Spain was famous. His name was Juanito. The second son, Felipe, was about twenty years of age ; he was like his sister Clara ; and the youngest was a child of eight. In the features of the little Manuel a painter would have discerned something of that Roman steadfastness which David has given to the children's faces in his Republican *genre* pictures. The old Marquis, with his white hair, might have come down from some canvas of Murillo's. Victor threw back his head in despair after this survey ; how should one of these accept the General's offer ! nevertheless he ventured to intrust it to Clara. A shudder ran through the Spanish girl, but she recovered herself almost instantly, and knelt before her father.

'Father,' she said, 'bid Juanito swear to obey the commands that you shall give him, and we shall be content.'

The Marquesa trembled with hope, but as she leant towards her husband and learned Clara's hideous secret, the mother fainted away. Juanito understood it all, and leapt up like a caged lion. Victor took it upon himself to dismiss the soldiers, after receiving an assurance of entire submission from the Marquis. The servants were led away and given over to the hangman and their fate. When only Victor remained on guard in the room, the old Marqués de Légañès rose to his feet.

'Juanito,' he said. For all answer Juanito bowed his head in a way that meant refusal ; he sank down into his chair, and fixed tearless eyes upon his father and mother in an intolerable gaze. Clara went over to him and sat on his knee ; she put her arms about him, and pressed kisses on his eyelids, saying gaily—

'Dear Juanito, if you but knew how sweet death at your hands will be to me ! I shall not be compelled to submit to the hateful touch of the hangman's fingers. You will snatch me away from the evils to come and . . .

Dear, kind Juanito, you could not bear the thought of my belonging to any one—well, then?'

The velvet eyes gave Victor a burning glance; she seemed to try to awaken in Juanito's heart his hatred for the French.

'Take courage,' said his brother Felipe, 'or our well-nigh royal line will be extinct.'

Suddenly Clara sprang to her feet. The group round Juanito fell back, and the son who had rebelled with such good reason was confronted with his aged father.

'Juanito, I command you!' said the Marquis solemnly.

The young Count gave no sign, and his father fell on his knees; Clara, Manuel, and Felipe unconsciously followed his example, stretching out suppliant hands to him who must save their family from oblivion, and seeming to echo their father's words.

'Can it be that you lack the fortitude of a Spaniard and true sensibility, my son? Do you mean to keep me on my knees? What right have you to think of your own life and of your own sufferings?—Is this my son, madam?' the old Marquis added, turning to his wife.

'He will consent to it,' cried the mother in agony of soul. She had seen a slight contraction of Juanito's brows which she, his mother, alone understood.

Mariquita, the second daughter, knelt, with her slender clinging arms about her mother; the hot tears fell from her eyes, and her little brother Manuel upbraided her for weeping. Just at that moment the castle chaplain came in; the whole family surrounded him and led him up to Juanito. Victor felt that he could endure the sight no longer, and with a sign to Clara he hurried from the room to make one last effort for them. He found the General in boisterous spirits; the officers were still sitting over their dinner and drinking together; the wine had loosened their tongues.

N

An hour later, a hundred of the principal citizens of Menda were summoned to the terrace by the General's orders to witness the execution of the family of Légañès. A detachment had been told off to keep order among the Spanish townsfolk, who were marshalled beneath the gallows whereon the Marquis's servants hung ; the feet of those martyrs of their cause all but touched the citizens' heads. Thirty paces away stood the block ; the blade of a scimitar glittered upon it, and the executioner stood by in case Juanito should refuse at the last.

The deepest silence prevailed, but before long it was broken by the sound of many footsteps, the measured tramp of a picket of soldiers, and the jingling of their weapons. Mingled with these came other noises—loud talk and laughter from the dinner-table where the officers were sitting ; just as the music and the sound of the dancers' feet had drowned the preparations for last night's treacherous butchery.

All eyes turned to the castle, and beheld the family of nobles coming forth with incredible composure to their death. Every brow was serene and calm. One alone among them, haggard and overcome, leant on the arm of the priest, who poured forth all the consolations of religion for the one man who was condemned to live. Then the executioner, like the spectators, knew that Juanito had consented to perform his office for a day. The old Marquis and his wife, Clara and Mariquita, and their two brothers knelt a few paces from the fatal spot. Juanito reached it, guided by the priest. As he stood at the block the executioner plucked him by the sleeve, and took him aside, probably to give him certain instructions. The confessor so placed the victims that they could not witness the executions, but one and all stood upright and fearless, like Spaniards, as they were.

Clara sprang to her brother's side before the others.

'Juanito,' she said to him, 'be merciful to my lack of courage. Take me first !'

As she spoke, the footsteps of a man running at full speed echoed from the walls, and Victor appeared upon the scene. Clara was kneeling before the block; her white neck seemed to appeal to the blade to fall. The officer turned faint, but he found strength to rush to her side.

'The General grants you your life if you will consent to marry me,' he murmured.

The Spanish girl gave the officer a glance full of proud disdain.

'Now, Juanito!' she said in her deep-toned voice.

Her head fell at Victor's feet. A shudder ran through the Marquesa de Légañès, a convulsive tremor that she could not control, but she gave no other sign of her anguish.

'Is this where I ought to be, dear Juanito? Is it all right?' little Manuel asked his brother.

'Oh, Mariquita, you are weeping!' Juanito said when his sister came.

'Yes,' said the girl; 'I am thinking of you, poor Juanito; how unhappy you will be when we are gone.'

Then the Marquis's tall figure approached. He looked at the block where his children's blood had been shed, turned to the mute and motionless crowd, and said in a loud voice as he stretched out his hands to Juanito—

'Spaniards! I give my son a father's blessing.— Now, *Marquis*, strike "without fear"; thou art "without reproach."'

But when his mother came near, leaning on the confessor's arm—'She fed me from her breast!' Juanito cried, in tones that drew a cry of horror from the crowd. The uproarious mirth of the officers over their wine died away before that terrible cry. The Marquesa knew that Juanito's courage was exhausted; at one bound she sprang to the balustrade, leapt forth, and was dashed to pieces on the rocks below.   A cry of admiration broke from the spectators.   Juanito swooned.

'General,' said an officer, half drunk by this time, 'Marchand has just been telling me something about this execution ; I will wager that it was not by your orders——'

'Are you forgetting, gentlemen, that in a month's time five hundred families in France will be in mourning, and that we are still in Spain ? ' cried General G——. ' Do you want us to leave our bones here ? '

But not a man at the table, not even a subaltern, dared to empty his glass after that speech.

In spite of the respect in which all men hold the Marqués de Légañès, in spite of the title of *El Verdugo* (the executioner) conferred upon him as a patent of nobility by the King of Spain, the great noble is consumed by a gnawing grief. He lives a retired life, and seldom appears in public. The burden of his heroic crime weighs heavily upon him, and he seems to wait impatiently till the birth of a second son shall release him, and he may go to join the Shades that never cease to haunt him.

PARIS, *October* 1820.

FAREWELL

To Prince Friedrich von Schwarzenberg

'COME, Deputy of the Centre, come along ! We shall have to mend our pace if we mean to sit down to dinner when every one else does, and that's a fact ! Hurry up ! Jump, Marquis ! That's it ! Well done ! You are bounding over the furrows just like a stag ! '

These words were uttered by a sportsman seated much at his ease on the outskirts of the Forêt de l'Isle-Adam ; he had just finished a Havannah cigar, which he had smoked while he waited for his companion, who had evidently been straying about for some time among the forest undergrowth. Four panting dogs by the speaker's side likewise watched the progress of the personage for whose benefit the remarks were made. To make their sarcastic import fully clear, it should be added that the second sportsman was both short and stout ; his ample girth indicated a truly magisterial corpulence, and in consequence his progress across the furrows was by no means easy. He was striding over a vast field of stubble ; the dried corn-stalks underfoot added not a little to the difficulties of his passage, and to add to his discomforts, the genial influence of the sun that slanted into his eyes brought great drops of perspiration into his face. The uppermost thought in his mind being a strong desire to keep his balance, he lurched to and fro much like a coach jolted over an atrocious road.

It was one of those September days of almost tropical heat that finishes the work of summer and ripens the grapes. Such heat forebodes a coming storm; and though as yet there were wide patches of blue between the dark rain-clouds low down on the horizon, pale golden masses were rising and scattering with ominous swiftness from west to east, and drawing a shadowy veil across the sky. The wind was still, save in the upper regions of the air, so that the weight of the atmosphere seemed to compress the steamy heat of the earth into the forest glades. The tall forest trees shut out every breath of air so completely that the little valley across which the sportsman was making his way was as hot as a furnace; the silent forest seemed parched with the fiery heat. Birds and insects were mute; the topmost twigs of the trees swayed with scarcely perceptible motion. Any one who retains some recollection of the summer of 1819 must surely compassionate the plight of the hapless supporter of the ministry who toiled and sweated over the stubble to rejoin his satirical comrade. That gentleman, as he smoked his cigar, had arrived, by a process of calculation based on the altitude of the sun, to the conclusion that it must be about five o'clock.

'Where the devil are we?' asked the stout sportsman. He wiped his brow as he spoke, and propped himself against a tree in the field opposite his companion, feeling quite unequal to clearing the broad ditch that lay between them.

'And you ask that question of *me*!' retorted the other, laughing from his bed of tall brown grasses on the top of the bank. He flung the end of his cigar into the ditch, exclaiming, 'I swear by Saint Hubert that no one shall catch *me* risking myself again in a country that I don't know with a magistrate, even if, like you, my dear d'Albon, he happens to be an old schoolfellow.'

'Why, Philip, have you really forgotten your own language? You surely must have left your wits behind you in Siberia,' said the stouter of the two, with a glance half-comic, half-pathetic at a guide-post distant about a hundred paces from them.

'I understand,' replied the one addressed as Philip. He snatched up his rifle, suddenly sprang to his feet, made but one jump of it into the field, and rushed off to the guide-post. 'This way, d'Albon, here you are! left about!' he shouted, gesticulating in the direction of the high-road. '*To Baillet and l'Isle-Adam!*' he went on; 'so if we go along here, we shall be sure to come upon the cross-road to Cassan.'

'Quite right, Colonel,' said M. d'Albon, putting the cap with which he had been fanning himself back on his head.

'Then *forward*! highly respected Councillor,' returned Colonel Philip, whistling to the dogs, that seemed already to obey him rather than the magistrate their master.

'Are you aware, my lord Marquis, that two leagues yet remain before us?' inquired the malicious soldier. 'That village down yonder must be Baillet.'

'Great heavens!' cried the Marquis d'Albon. 'Go on to Cassan by all means, if you like; but if you do, you will go alone. I prefer to wait here, storm or no storm; you can send a horse for me from the château. You have been making game of me, Sucy. We were to have a nice day's sport by ourselves; we were not to go very far from Cassan, and go over ground that I knew. Pooh! Instead of a day's fun, you have kept me running like a greyhound since four o'clock this morning, and nothing but a cup or two of milk by way of breakfast. Oh! if ever you find yourself in a court of law, I will take care that the day goes against you if you were in the right a hundred times over.'

The dejected sportsman sat himself down on one of the stumps at the foot of the guide-post, disencumbered himself of his rifle and empty game-bag, and heaved a prolonged sigh.

'Oh, France, behold thy Deputies!' laughed Colonel de Sucy. 'Poor old d'Albon; if you had spent six months at the other end of Siberia as I did . . .'

He broke off, and his eyes sought the sky, as if the story of his troubles was a secret between himself and God.

'Come, march!' he added. 'If you once sit down, it is all over with you.'

'I can't help it, Philip! It is such an old habit in a magistrate! I am dead beat, upon my honour. If I had only bagged one hare though!'

Two men more different are seldom seen together. The civilian, a man of forty-two, seemed scarcely more than thirty; while the soldier, at thirty years of age, looked to be forty at the least. Both wore the red rosette that proclaimed them to be officers of the Legion of Honour. A few locks of hair, mingled white and black, like a magpie's wing, had strayed from beneath the Colonel's cap; while thick, fair curls clustered about the magistrate's temples. The Colonel was tall, spare, dried up, but muscular; the lines in his pale face told a tale of vehement passions or of terrible sorrows; but his comrade's jolly countenance beamed with health, and would have done credit to an Epicurean. Both men were deeply sunburnt. Their high gaiters of brown leather carried souvenirs of every ditch and swamp that they crossed that day.

'Come, come,' cried M. de Sucy, 'forward! One short hour's march, and we shall be at Cassan with a good dinner before us.'

'You never were in love, that is positive,' returned the Councillor, with a comically piteous expression. 'You are as inexorable as Article 304 of the Penal Code!'

Philip de Sucy shuddered violently. Deep lines appeared in his broad forehead, his face was overcast like the sky above them; but though his features seemed to contract with the pain of an intolerably bitter memory,

no tears came to his eyes. Like all men of strong
character, he possessed the power of forcing his emotions
down into some inner depth, and, perhaps, like many
reserved natures, he shrank from laying bare a wound
too deep for any words of human speech, and winced at
the thought of ridicule from those who do not care to
understand. M. d'Albon was one of those who are
keenly sensitive by nature to the distress of others, who
feel at once the pain they have unwittingly given by
some blunder. He respected his friend's mood, rose to
his feet, forgot his weariness, and followed in silence,
thoroughly annoyed with himself for having touched on
a wound that seemed not yet healed.

'Some day I will tell you my story,' Philip said at
last, wringing his friend's hand, while he acknowledged
his dumb repentance with a heartrending glance. 'To-
day, I cannot.'

They walked on in silence. As the Colonel's distress
passed off the Councillor's fatigue returned. Instinctively,
or rather urged by weariness, his eyes explored the depths
of the forest around them; he looked high and low
among the trees, and gazed along the avenues, hoping to
discover some dwelling where he might ask for hospitality. They reached a place where several roads met;
and the Councillor, fancying that he saw a thin film of
smoke rising through the trees, made a stand and looked
sharply about him. He caught a glimpse of the dark
green branches of some firs among the other forest trees,
and finally, 'A house! a house!' he shouted. No
sailor could have raised the cry of 'Land a-head!' more
joyfully than he.

He plunged at once into undergrowth, somewhat of
the thickest; and the Colonel, who had fallen into deep
musings, followed him unheedingly.

'I would rather have an omelette here and home-made
bread, and a chair to sit down in, than go further for a
sofa, truffles, and Bordeaux wine at Cassan.'

This outburst of enthusiasm on the Councillor's part was caused by the sight of the whitened wall of a house in the distance, standing out in strong contrast against the brown masses of knotted tree-trunks in the forest.

'Aha! This used to be a priory, I should say,' the Marquis d'Albon cried once more, as they stood before a grim old gateway. Through the grating they could see the house itself standing in the midst of some considerable extent of park land; from the style of the architecture it appeared to have been a monastery once upon a time.

'Those knowing rascals of monks knew how to choose a site!'

This last exclamation was caused by the magistrate's amazement at the romantic hermitage before his eyes. The house had been built on a spot half-way up the hillside on the slope below the village of Nerville, which crowned the summit. A huge circle of great oak-trees, hundreds of years old, guarded the solitary place from intrusion. There appeared to be about forty acres of the park. The main building of the monastery faced the south, and stood in a space of green meadow, picturesquely intersected by several tiny clear streams, and by larger sheets of water so disposed as to have a natural effect. Shapely trees with contrasting foliage grew here and there. Grottos had been ingeniously contrived; and broad terraced walks, now in ruin, though the steps were broken and the balustrades eaten through with rust, gave to this sylvan Thebaïd a certain character of its own. The art of man and the picturesqueness of nature had wrought together to produce a charming effect. Human passions surely could not cross that boundary of tall oak-trees which shut out the sounds of the outer world, and screened the fierce heat of the sun from this forest sanctuary.

'What neglect!' said M. d'Albon to himself, after the first sense of delight in the melancholy aspect of the ruins in the landscape, which seemed blighted by a curse.

It was like some haunted spot, shunned of men. The twisted ivy stems clambered everywhere, hiding everything away beneath a luxuriant green mantle. Moss and lichens, brown and grey, yellow and red, covered the trees with fantastic patches of colour, grew upon the benches in the garden, overran the roof and the walls of the house. The window-sashes were weather-worn and warped with age, the balconies were dropping to pieces, the terraces in ruins. Here and there the folding shutters hung by a single hinge. The crazy doors would have given way at the first attempt to force an entrance.

Out in the orchard the neglected fruit-trees were running to wood, the rambling branches bore no fruit save the glistening mistletoe berries, and tall plants were growing in the garden walks. All this forlornness shed a charm across the picture that wrought on the spectator's mind with an influence like that of some enchanting poem, filling his soul with dreamy fancies A poet must have lingered there in deep and melancholy musings, marvelling at the harmony of this wilderness, where decay had a certain grace of its own.

In a moment a few gleams of sunlight struggled through a rift in the clouds, and a shower of coloured light fell over the wild garden. The brown tiles of the roof glowed in the light, the mosses took bright hues, strange shadows played over the grass beneath the trees ; the dead autumn tints grew vivid, bright unexpected contrasts were evoked by the light, every leaf stood out sharply in the clear, thin air. Then all at once the sunlight died away, and the landscape that seemed to have spoken grew silent and gloomy again, or rather, it took grey soft tones like the tenderest hues of autumn dusk.

'It is the palace of the Sleeping Beauty,' the Councillor said to himself (he had already begun to look at the place from the point of view of an owner of property). 'Whom can the place belong to, I wonder. He must be a great fool not to live on such a charming little estate ! '

Just at that moment, a woman sprang out from under a walnut tree on the right-hand side of the gateway, and passed before the Councillor as noiselessly and swiftly as the shadow of a cloud. This apparition struck him dumb with amazement.

' Hallo, d'Albon, what is the matter ? ' asked the Colonel.

' I am rubbing my eyes to find out whether I am awake or asleep,' answered the magistrate, whose countenance was pressed against the grating in the hope of catching a second glimpse of the ghost.

' In all probability she is under that fig-tree,' he went on, indicating, for Philip's benefit, some branches that over-topped the wall on the left-hand side of the gateway.

' She ?   Who ? '

' Eh ! how should I know ? ' answered M. d'Albon. ' A strange-looking woman sprang up there under my very eyes just now,' he added, in a low voice ; ' she looked to me more like a ghost than a living being. She was so slender, light, and shadowy that she might be transparent. Her face was as white as milk, her hair, her eyes, and her dress were black. She gave me a glance as she flitted by. I am not easily frightened, but that cold stony stare of hers froze the blood in my veins.'

' Was she pretty ? ' inquired Philip.

' I don't know. I saw nothing but those eyes in her head.'

' The devil take dinner at Cassan ! ' exclaimed the Colonel ; ' let us stay here. I am as eager as a boy to see the inside of this queer place. The window-sashes are painted red, do you see ? There is a red line round the panels of the doors and the edges of the shutters. It might be the devil's own dwelling ; perhaps he took it over when the monks went out. Now, then, let us

give chase to the black and white lady ; come along !'
cried Philip, with forced gaiety.

He had scarcely finished speaking when the two
sportsmen heard a cry as if some bird had been taken
in a snare. They listened. There was a sound like
the murmur of rippling water, as something forced its
way through the bushes ; but diligently as they lent
their ears, there was no footfall on the path, the earth
kept the secret of the mysterious woman's passage, if
indeed she had moved from her hiding-place.

' This is very strange !' cried Philip.

Following the wall of the park, the two friends reached
before long a forest road leading to the village of Chauvry ;
they went along this track in the direction of the high-
way to Paris, and reached another large gateway.
Through the railings they had a complete view of the
façade of the mysterious house. From this point of
view, the dilapidation was still more apparent. Huge
cracks had riven the walls of the main body of the
house built round three sides of a square. Evidently
the place was allowed to fall to ruin ; there were holes
in the roof, broken slates and tiles lay about below.
Fallen fruit from the orchard trees was left to rot on
the ground ; a cow was grazing over the bowling-green
and trampling the flowers in the garden beds ; a goat
browsed on the green grapes and young vine-shoots on
the trellis.

' It is all of a piece,' remarked the Colonel. ' The
neglect is in a fashion systematic.' He laid his hand
on the chain of the bell-pull, but the bell had lost its
clapper. The two friends heard no sound save the
peculiar grating creak of the rusty spring. A little
door in the wall beside the gateway, though ruinous, held good against all their efforts to force it
open.

' Oho ! all this is growing very interesting,' Philip said
to his companion.

'If I were not a magistrate,' returned M. d'Albon, 'I should think that the woman in black is a witch.'

The words were scarcely out of his mouth when the cow came up to the railings and held out her warm damp nose, as if she were glad of human society. Then a woman, if so indescribable a being could be called a woman, sprang up from the bushes, and pulled at the cord about the cow's neck. From beneath the crimson handkerchief about the woman's head, fair matted hair escaped, something as tow hangs about a spindle. She wore no kerchief at the throat. A coarse black-and-grey striped woollen petticoat, too short by several inches, left her legs bare. She might have belonged to some tribe of Redskins in Fenimore Cooper's novels; for her neck, arms, and ankles looked as if they had been painted brick-red. There was no spark of intelligence in her featureless face; her pale, bluish eyes looked out dull and expression-less from beneath the eyebrows with one or two straggling white hairs on them. Her teeth were prominent and uneven, but white as a dog's.

'Hallo, good woman,' called M. de Sucy.

She came slowly up to the railing, and stared at the two sportsmen with a contorted smile painful to see.

'Where are we? What is the name of the house yonder? Whom does it belong to? Who are you? Do you come from hereabouts?'

To these questions, and to a host of others poured out in succession upon her by the two friends, she made no answer save gurgling noises in the throat, more like animal sounds than anything uttered by a human voice.

'Don't you see that she is deaf and dumb?' said M. d'Albon.

'*Minorites!*' the peasant woman said at last.

'Ah! she is right. The house looks as though it might once have been a Minorite convent,' he went on.

Again they plied the peasant woman with questions, but, like a wayward child, she coloured up, fidgeted with

her sabot, twisted the rope by which she held the cow
that had fallen to grazing again, stared at the sportsmen,
and scrutinised every article of clothing upon them ; she
gibbered, grunted, and clucked, but no articulate word
did she utter.

'Your name ?' asked Philip, fixing her with his eyes
as if he were trying to bewitch the woman.

'Geneviève,' she answered, with an empty laugh.

'The cow is the most intelligent creature we have
seen so far,' exclaimed the magistrate. 'I shall fire a
shot, that ought to bring somebody out.'

D'Albon had just taken up his rifle when the Colonel
put out a hand to stop him, and pointed out the
mysterious woman who had aroused such lively curiosity
in them. She seemed to be absorbed in deep thought,
as she went along a green alley some little distance
away, so slowly that the friends had time to take a good
look at her. She wore a threadbare black satin gown,
her long hair curled thickly over her forehead, and fell
like a shawl about her shoulders below her waist.
Doubtless she was accustomed to the dishevelment of her
locks, for she seldom put back the hair on either side of
her brows ; but when she did so, she shook her head with
a sudden jerk that had not to be repeated to shake away
the thick veil from her eyes or forehead. In everything that she did, moreover, there was a wonderful
certainty in the working of the mechanism, an unerring
swiftness and precision, like that of an animal, well nigh
marvellous in a woman.

The two sportsmen were amazed to see her spring up
into an apple-tree and cling to a bough lightly as a bird.
She snatched at the fruit, ate it, and dropped to the
ground with the same supple grace that charms us in a
squirrel. The elasticity of her limbs took all appearance of awkwardness or effort from her movements.
She played about upon the grass, rolling in it as a young
child might have done ; then, on a sudden, she lay still

and stretched out her feet and hands, with the languid natural grace of a kitten dozing in the sun.

There was a threatening growl of thunder far away, and at this she started up on all fours and listened, like a dog who hears a strange footstep. One result of this strange attitude was to separate her thick black hair into two masses, that fell away on either side of her face and left her shoulders bare; the two witnesses of this singular scene wondered at the whiteness of the skin that shone like a meadow daisy, and at the neck that indicated the perfection of the rest of her form.

A wailing cry broke from her; she rose to her feet, and stood upright. Every successive movement was made so lightly, so gracefully, so easily, that she seemed to be no human being, but one of Ossian's maids of the mist. She went across the grass to one of the pools of water, deftly shook off her shoe, and seemed to enjoy dipping her foot, white as marble, in the spring; doubtless it pleased her to make the circling ripples, and watch them glitter like gems. She knelt down by the brink, and played there like a child, dabbling her long tresses in the water, and flinging them loose again to see the water drip from the ends, like a string of pearls in the sunless light.

'She is mad!' cried the Councillor.

A hoarse cry rang through the air; it came from Geneviève, and seemed to be meant for the mysterious woman. She rose to her feet in a moment, flinging back the hair from her face, and then the Colonel and d'Albon could see her features distinctly. As soon as she saw the two friends she bounded to the railings with the swiftness of a fawn.

'*Farewell!*' she said in low, musical tones, but they could not discover the least trace of feeling, the least idea in the sweet sounds that they had awaited impatiently.

M. d'Albon admired the long lashes, the thick, dark eyebrows, the dazzling fairness of a skin untinged by any trace of red. Only the delicate blue veins contrasted with that uniform whiteness.

But when the Marquis turned to communicate his surprise at the sight of so strange an apparition, he saw the Colonel stretched on the grass like one dead. M. d'Albon fired his gun into the air, shouted for help, and tried to raise his friend. At the sound of the shot, the strange lady, who had stood motionless by the gate, fled away, crying out like a wounded wild creature, circling round and round in the meadow, with every sign of unspeakable terror.

M. d'Albon heard a carriage rolling along the road to l'Isle Adam, and waved his handkerchief to implore help. The carriage immediately came towards the Minorite convent, and M. d'Albon recognised neighbours, M. de and Mme. de Grandville, who hastened to alight and put their carriage at his disposal. Colonel de Sucy inhaled the salts which Mme. de Grandville happened to have with her; he opened his eyes, looked towards the mysterious figure that still fled wailing through the meadow, and a faint cry of horror broke from him; he closed his eyes again, with a dumb gesture of entreaty to his friends to take him away from this scene. M. and Mme. de Grandville begged the Councillor to make use of their carriage, adding very obligingly that they themselves would walk.

'Who can the lady be?' inquired the magistrate, looking towards the strange figure.

'People think that she comes from Moulins,' answered M. de Grandville. 'She is a Comtesse de Vandières; she is said to be mad; but as she has only been here for two months, I cannot vouch for the truth of all this hearsay talk.'

M. d'Albon thanked M. and Mme. de Grandville, and they set out for Cassan.

'It is she!' cried Philip, coming to himself.

'She? who?' asked d'Albon.

'Stéphanie. . . . Ah! dead and yet living still; still alive, but her mind is gone!   I thought the sight would kill me.'

The prudent magistrate, recognising the gravity of the crisis through which his friend was passing, refrained from asking questions or exciting him further, and grew impatient of the length of the way to the château, for the change wrought in the Colonel's face alarmed him. He feared lest the Countess's terrible disease had communicated itself to Philip's brain.   When they reached the avenue at l'Isle-Adam, d'Albon sent the servant for the local doctor, so that the Colonel had scarcely been laid in bed before the surgeon was beside him.

'If Monsieur le Colonel had not been fasting, the shock must have killed him,' pronounced the leech.   'He was overtired, and that saved him,' and with a few directions as to the patient's treatment, he went to prepare a composing draught himself.   M. de Sucy was better the next morning, but the doctor had insisted on sitting up all night with him.

'I confess, Monsieur le Marquis,' the surgeon said, 'that I feared for the brain.   M. de Sucy has had some very violent shock; he is a man of strong passions, but, with his temperament, the first shock decides everything. He will very likely be out of danger to-morrow.'

The doctor was perfectly right.   The next day the patient was allowed to see his friend.

'I want you to do something for me, dear d'Albon,' Philip said, grasping his friend's hand.   'Hasten at once to the Minorite convent, find out everything about the lady whom we saw there, and come back as soon as you can; I shall count the minutes till I see you again.'

M. d'Albon called for his horse, and galloped over to the old monastery.   When he reached the gateway he found some one standing there, a tall, spare man with a kindly face, who answered in the affirmative when he was asked if he lived in the ruined house. M. d'Albon explained his errand.

'Why, then, it must have been you, sir, who fired that unlucky shot! You all but killed my poor invalid.'

'Eh! I fired into the air!'

'If you had actually hit Madame la Comtesse, you would have done less harm to her.'

'Well, well, then, we can neither of us complain, for the sight of the Countess all but killed my friend, M. de Sucy.'

'The Baron de Sucy, is it possible?' cried the doctor, clasping his hands. 'Has he been in Russia? was he in the Beresina?'

'Yes,' answered d'Albon. 'He was taken prisoner by the Cossacks and sent to Siberia. He has not been back in this country a twelvemonth.'

'Come in, Monsieur,' said the other, and he led the way to a drawing-room on the ground-floor. Everything in the room showed signs of capricious destruction.

Valuable china jars lay in fragments on either side of a clock beneath a glass shade, which had escaped. The silk hangings about the windows were torn to rags, while the muslin curtains were untouched.

'You see about you the havoc wrought by a charming being to whom I have dedicated my life. She is my niece; and though medical science is powerless in her case, I hope to restore her to reason, though the method which I am trying is, unluckily, only possible to the wealthy.'

Then, like all who live much alone and daily bear the burden of a heavy trouble, he fell to talk with the magistrater. This is the story that he told, set in order, and with the many digressions made by both teller and hearer omitted.

When, at nine o'clock at night, on the 28th of November 1812, Marshal Victor abandoned the heights

of Studzianka, which he had held through the day, he left
a thousand men behind with instructions to protect, till
the last possible moment, the two pontoon bridges over
the Beresina that still held good. This rearguard was
to save if possible an appalling number of stragglers, so
numbed with the cold, that they obstinately refused
to leave the baggage-waggons. The heroism of the
generous band was doomed to fail; for, unluckily, the
men who poured down to the eastern bank of the
Beresina found carriages, caissons, and all kinds of property which the Army had been forced to abandon during
its passage on the 27th and 28th days of November.
The poor, half-frozen wretches, sunk almost to the level
of brutes, finding such unhoped-for riches, bivouacked in
the deserted space, laid hands on the military stores,
improvised huts out of the material, lighted fires with
anything that would burn, cut up the carcases of the
horses for food, tore out the linings of the carriages,
wrapped themselves in them, and lay down to sleep,
instead of crossing the Beresina in peace under cover of
night—the Beresina that even then had proved, by an
incredible fatality, so disastrous to the Army. Such
apathy on the part of the poor fellows can only be understood by those who remember tramping across those
vast deserts of snow, with nothing to quench their thirst
but snow, snow for their bed, snow as far as the horizon
on every side, and no food but snow, a little frozen
beetroot, horseflesh, or a handful of meal.

The miserable creatures were dropping down, overcome by hunger, thirst, weariness, and sleep, when they
reached the shores of the Beresina and found fuel and fire
and victuals, countless waggons and tents, a whole improvised town, in short. The whole village of Studzianka had been removed piecemeal from the heights to
the plain, and the very perils and miseries of this
dangerous and doleful habitation smiled invitingly to the
wayfarers, who beheld no prospect beyond it but the

awful Russian deserts. A huge hospice, in short, was erected for twenty hours of existence. Only one thought —the thought of rest—appealed to men weary of life or rejoicing in unlooked-for comfort.

They lay right in the line of fire from the cannon of the Russian left; but to that vast mass of human creatures, a patch upon the snow, sometimes dark, sometimes breaking into flame, the indefatigable grape-shot was but one discomfort the more. For them it was only a storm, and they paid the less attention to the bolts that fell among them because there were none to strike down there save dying men, the wounded, or perhaps the dead. Stragglers came up in little bands at every moment. These walking corpses instantly separated, and wandered begging from fire to fire; and meeting, for the most part, with refusals, banded themselves together again, and took by force what they could not otherwise obtain. They were deaf to the voices of their officers prophesying death on the morrow, and spent the energy required to cross the swamp in building shelters for the night and preparing a meal that often proved fatal. The coming death no longer seemed an evil, for it gave them an hour of slumber before it came. Hunger and thirst and cold —these were evils, but not death.

At last wood and fuel and canvas and shelters failed, and hideous brawls began between destitute late comers and the rich already in possession of a lodging. The weaker were driven away, until a few last fugitives before the Russian advance were obliged to make their bed in the snow, and lay down to rise no more.

Little by little the mass of half-dead humanity became so dense, so deaf, so torpid,—or perhaps it should be said so happy—that Marshal Victor, their heroic defender against twenty thousand Russians under Wittgenstein, was actually compelled to cut his way by force through this forest of men, so as to cross the Beresina with the five thousand heroes whom he was leading to the Emperor.

The miserable creatures preferred to be trampled and crushed to death rather than stir from their places, and died without a sound, smiling at the dead ashes of their fires, forgetful of France.

Not before ten o'clock that night did the Duc de Belluno reach the other side of the river. Before committing his men to the pontoon bridges that led to Zembin, he left the fate of the rearguard at Studzianka in Eblé's hands, and to Eblé the survivors of the calamities of the Beresina owed their lives.

About midnight, the great General, followed by a courageous officer, came out of his little hut by the bridge, and gazed at the spectacle of this camp between the bank of the Beresina and the Borizof road to Studzianka. The thunder of the Russian cannonade had ceased. Here and there faces that had nothing human about them were lighted up by countless fires that seemed to grow pale in the glare of the snowfields, and to give no light. Nearly thirty thousand wretches, belonging to every nation that Napoleon had hurled upon Russia, lay there hazarding their lives with the indifference of brute beasts.

'We have all these to save,' the General said to his subordinate. 'To-morrow morning the Russians will be in Studzianka. The moment they come up we shall have to set fire to the bridge; so pluck up heart, my boy! Make your way out and up yonder through them, and tell General Fournier that he has barely time to evacuate his post and cut his way through to the bridge. As soon as you have seen him set out, follow him down, take some able-bodied men, and set fire to the tents, waggons, caissons, carriages, anything and everything, without pity, and drive these fellows on to the bridge. Compel everything that walks on two legs to take refuge on the other bank. We must set fire to the camp; it is our last resource. If Berthier had let me burn those d——d waggons sooner, no lives need have been lost in the river except my poor pontooners, my fifty heroes, who saved the Army, and will be forgotten.'

The General passed his hand over his forehead and said no more. He felt that Poland would be his tomb, and foresaw that afterwards no voice would be raised to speak for the noble fellows who had plunged into the stream—into the waters of the Beresina!—to drive in the piles for the bridges. And, indeed, only one of them is living now, or, to be more accurate, starving, utterly forgotten in a country village! The brave officer had scarcely gone a hundred paces towards Studzianka, when General Eblé roused some of his patient pontooners, and began his work of mercy by setting fire to the camp on the side nearest the bridge, so compelling the sleepers to rise and cross the Beresina. Meanwhile the young aide-de-camp, not without difficulty, reached the one wooden house yet left standing in Studzianka.

'So the box is pretty full, is it, messmate?' he said to a man whom he found outside.

'You will be a knowing fellow if you manage to get inside,' the officer returned, without turning round or stopping his occupation of hacking at the woodwork of the house with his sabre.

'Philip, is that you?' cried the aide-de-camp, recognising the voice of one of his friends.

'Yes. Aha! is it you, old fellow?' returned M. de Sucy, looking round at the aide-de-camp, who like himself was not more than twenty-three years old. 'I fancied you were on the other side of this confounded river. Do you come to bring us sweetmeats for dessert? You will get a warm welcome,' he added, as he tore away a strip of bark from the wood and gave it to his horse by way of fodder.

'I am looking for your Commandant. General Eblé has sent me to tell him to file off to Zembin. You have only just time to cut your way through that mass

of dead men ; as soon as you get through, I am going to
set fire to the place to make them move——'

'You almost make me feel warm ! Your news has
put me in a fever ; I have two friends to bring through.
Ah ! but for those marmots, I should have been dead
before now, old fellow. On their account I am taking
care of my horse instead of eating him. But have you
a crust about you, for pity's sake ? It is thirty hours
since I have stowed any victuals. I have been fighting
like a madman to keep up a little warmth in my body
and what courage I have left.'

'Poor Philip ! I have nothing—not a scrap !—But is
your General in there ?'

'Don't attempt to go in. The barn is full of our
wounded. Go up a bit higher, and you will see a sort
of pigsty to the right—that is where the General is.
Good-bye, my dear fellow. If ever we meet again in a
quadrille in a ballroom in Paris——'

He did not finish the sentence, for the treachery of
the north-east wind that whistled about them froze
Major Philip's lips, and the aide-de-camp kept moving
for fear of being frost-bitten. Silence soon prevailed,
scarcely broken by the groans of the wounded in the
barn, or the stifled sounds made by M. de Sucy's horse
crunching the frozen bark with famished eagerness.
Philip thrust his sabre into the sheath, caught at the
bridle of the precious animal that he had managed to
keep for so long, and drew her away from the miserable
fodder that she was bolting with apparent relish.

'Come along, Bichette ! come along ! It lies with
you now, my beauty, to save Stéphanie's life. There,
wait a little longer, and they will let us lie down and die,
no doubt ;' and Philip, wrapped in a pelisse, to which
doubtless he owed his life and energies, began to run,
stamping his feet on the frozen snow to keep them
warm. He was scarce five hundred paces away before
he saw a great fire blazing on the spot where he had left

his carriage that morning with an old soldier to guard it. A dreadful misgiving seized upon him. Many a man under the influence of a powerful feeling during the Retreat summoned up energy for his friend's sake when he would not have exerted himself to save his own life; so it was with Philip. He soon neared a hollow, where he had left a carriage sheltered from the cannonade, a carriage that held a young woman, his playmate in childhood, dearer to him than any one else on earth.

Some thirty stragglers were sitting round a tremendous blaze, which they kept up with logs of wood, planks wrenched from the floors of the caissons, and wheels, and panels from carriage bodies. These had been, doubtless, among the last to join the sea of fires, huts, and human faces that filled the great furrow in the land between Studzianka and the fatal river, a restless living sea of almost imperceptibly moving figures, that sent up a smothered hum of sound blended with frightful shrieks. It seemed that hunger and despair had driven these forlorn creatures to take forcible possession of the carriage, for the old General and his young wife, whom they had found warmly wrapped in pelisses and travelling cloaks, were now crouching on the earth beside the fire, and one of the carriage doors was broken.

As soon as the group of stragglers round the fire heard the footfall of the Major's horse, a frenzied yell of hunger went up from them. 'A horse!' they cried. 'A horse!'

All the voices went up as one voice.

'Back! back! Look out!' shouted two or three of them, levelling their muskets at the animal.

'I will pitch you neck and crop into your fire, you blackguards!' cried Philip, springing in front of the mare. 'There are dead horses lying up yonder; go and look for them!'

'What a rum customer the officer is!—Once, twice, will you get out of the way?' returned a giant grenadier. 'You won't? All right then, just as you please.'

A woman's shriek rang out above the report. Luckily, none of the bullets hit Philip; but poor Bichette lay in the agony of death. Three of the men came up and put an end to her with thrusts of the bayonet.

'Cannibals! leave me the rug and my pistols,' cried Philip in desperation.

'Oh! the pistols if you like; but as for the rug, there is a fellow yonder who has had nothing to wet his whistle these two days, and is shivering in his coat of cobwebs, and that's our General.'

Philip looked up and saw a man with worn-out shoes and a dozen rents in his trousers; the only covering for his head was a ragged foraging cap, white with rime. He said no more after that, but snatched up his pistols.

Five of the men dragged the mare to the fire, and began to cut up the carcase as dexterously as any journeymen butchers in Paris. The scraps of meat were distributed and flung upon the coals, and the whole process was magically swift. Philip went over to the woman who had given the cry of terror when she recognised his danger, and sat down by her side. She sat motionless upon a cushion taken from the carriage, warming herself at the blaze; she said no word, and gazed at him without a smile. He saw beside her the soldier whom he had left mounting guard over the carriage; the poor fellow had been wounded; he had been overpowered by numbers, and forced to surrender to the stragglers who had set upon him, and, like a dog who defends his master's dinner till the last moment, he had taken his share of the spoil, and had made a sort of cloak for himself out of a sheet. At that particular moment he was busy toasting a piece of horseflesh, and in his face the major saw a gleeful anticipation of the coming feast.

The Comte de Vandières, who seemed to have grown

quite childish in the last few days, sat on a cushion close
to his wife, and stared into the fire. He was only just
beginning to shake off his torpor under the influence of
the warmth. He had been no more affected by Philip's
arrival and danger than by the fight and subsequent
pillage of his travelling carriage.

At first Sucy caught the young Countess's hand in his,
trying to express his affection for her, and the pain that
it gave him to see her reduced like this to the last
extremity of misery ; but he said nothing as he sat by
her side on the thawing heap of snow, he gave himself
up to the pleasure of the sensation of warmth, forgetful
of danger, forgetful of all things else in the world. In
spite of himself his face expanded with an almost fatuous
expression of satisfaction, and he waited impatiently till
the scrap of horseflesh that had fallen to his soldier's
share should be cooked. The smell of the charred
flesh stimulated his hunger. Hunger clamoured within
him and silenced his heart, his courage, and his love.
He coolly looked round on the results of the spolia-
tion of his carriage. Not a man seated round the fire
but had shared the booty, the rugs, cushions, pelisses,
dresses,—articles of clothing that belonged to the Count
and Countess or to himself. Philip turned to see
if anything worth taking was left in the berline. He
saw by the light of the flames, gold, and diamonds, and
silver lying scattered about ; no one had cared to
appropriate the least particle. There was something
hideous in the silence among those human creatures
round the fire ; none of them spoke, none of them
stirred, save to do such things as each considered
necessary for his own comfort.

It was a grotesque misery. The men's faces were
warped and disfigured with the cold, and plastered over
with a layer of mud ; you could see the thickness of the
mask by the channel traced down their cheeks by the
tears that ran from their eyes, and their long slovenly

kept beards added to the hideousness of their appearance. Some were wrapped round in women's shawls, others in horse-cloths, dirty blankets, rags stiffened with melting hoar-frost; here and there a man wore a boot on one foot and a shoe on the other, in fact, there was not one of them but wore some ludicrously odd costume. But the men themselves with such matter for jest about them were gloomy and taciturn.

The silence was unbroken save by the crackling of the wood, the roaring of the flames, the far-off hum of the camp, and the sound of sabres hacking at the carcase of the mare. Some of the hungriest of the men were still cutting tit-bits for themselves. A few miserable creatures, more weary than the others, slept outright; and if they happened to roll into the fire, no one pulled them back. With cut-and-dried logic their fellows argued that if they were not dead, a scorching ought to be sufficient warning to quit and seek out more comfortable quarters. If the poor wretch woke to find himself on fire, he was burned to death, and nobody pitied him. Here and there the men exchanged glances, as if to excuse their indifference by the carelessness of the rest; the thing happened twice under the young Countess's eyes, and she uttered no sound. When all the scraps of horse-flesh had been broiled upon the coals, they were devoured with a ravenous greediness that would have been disgusting in wild beasts.

'And now we have seen thirty infantry-men on one horse for the first time in our lives!' cried the grenadier who had shot the mare, the one solitary joke that sustained the Frenchmen's reputation for wit.

Before long the poor fellows huddled themselves up in their clothes, and lay down on planks of timber, on anything but the bare snow, and slept—heedless of the morrow. Major de Sucy having warmed himself and satisfied his hunger, fought in vain against the drowsiness that weighed upon his eyes. During this brief struggle he gazed at the sleeping girl who had turned her face to the fire, so that he could see her closed eyelids and part of her forehead. She was wrapped round in a furred pelisse and a coarse horseman's cloak, her head lay on a blood-stained cushion; a tall astrakhan cap tied over her head by a handkerchief knotted under the chin protected her face as much as possible from the cold, and she had tucked up her feet in the cloak. As she lay curled up in this fashion, she bore no likeness to any creature.

Was this the lowest of camp-followers? Was this the charming woman, the pride of her lover's heart, the queen of many a Parisian ballroom? Alas! even for the eyes of this most devoted friend, there was no discernible trace of womanhood in that bundle of rags and linen, and the cold was mightier than the love in a woman's heart.

Then for the major the husband and wife came to be like two distant dots seen through the thick veil that the most irresistible kind of slumber spread over his eyes. It all seemed to be part of a dream—the leaping flames, the recumbent figures, the awful cold that lay in wait for them three paces away from the warmth of the fire that glowed for a little while. One thought that could not be stifled haunted Philip—'If I go to sleep, we shall all die; I will not sleep,' he said to himself.

He slept. After an hour's slumber M. de Sucy was awakened by a hideous uproar and the sound of an explosion. The remembrance of his duty, of the danger of his beloved, rushed upon his mind with a sudden shock. He uttered a cry like the growl of a wild beast. He and his servant stood upright above the rest. They saw a sea of fire in the darkness, and against it moving masses of human figures. Flames were devouring the huts and tents. Despairing shrieks and yelling cries reached their ears; they saw thousands upon thousands of wild and desperate faces; and through this inferno a column of soldiers was cutting its way to the bridge, between two hedges of dead bodies.

'Our rearguard is in full retreat,' cried the major. 'There is no hope left!'

'I have spared your travelling carriage, Philip,' said a friendly voice.

Sucy turned and saw the young aide-de-camp by the light of the flames.

'Oh, it is all over with us,' he answered. 'They have eaten my horse. And how am I to make this sleepy general and his wife stir a step?'

'Take a brand, Philip, and threaten them.'

'Threaten the Countess? . . .'

'Good-bye,' cried the aide-de-camp; 'I have only just time to get across that unlucky river, and go I must, there is my mother in France! . . . What a night! This herd of wretches would rather lie here in the snow, and most of them would sooner be burned alive than get up. . . . It is four o'clock, Philip! In two hours the Russians will begin to move, and you will see the Beresina covered with corpses a second time, I can tell you. You haven't a horse, and you cannot carry the Countess, so come along with me,' he went on, taking his friend by the arm.

'My dear fellow, how am I to leave Stéphanie!'

Major de Sucy grasped the Countess, set her on her feet, and shook her roughly; he was in despair. He compelled her to wake, and she stared at him with dull fixed eyes.

'Stéphanie, we must go, or we shall die here!'

For all answer the Countess tried to sink down again and sleep on the earth. The aide-de-camp snatched a brand from the fire and shook it in her face.

'We must save her in spite of herself,' cried Philip, and he carried her in his arms to the carriage. He came back to entreat his friend to help him, and the two young men took the old general and put him beside his

wife, without knowing whether he were alive or dead.
The major rolled the men over as they crouched on the
earth, took away the plundered clothing, and heaped it
upon the husband and wife, then he flung some of the
broiled fragments of horse-flesh into a corner of the
carriage.

'Now, what do you mean to do?' asked the aide-de-
camp.

'Drag them along!' answered Sucy.

'You are mad!'

'You are right!' exclaimed Philip, folding his arms
on his breast.

Suddenly a desperate plan occurred to him.

'Look you here!' he said, grasping his sentinel by the
unwounded arm, 'I leave her in your care for one hour.
Bear in mind that you must die sooner than let any one,
no matter whom, come near the carriage!'

The major seized a handful of the lady's diamonds,
drew his sabre, and violently battered those who seemed
to him to be the bravest among the sleepers. By this
means he succeeded in rousing the gigantic grenadier
and a couple of men whose rank and regiment were
undiscoverable.

'It is all up with us!' he cried.

'Of course it is,' returned the grenadier; 'but that is
all one to me.'

'Very well then, if die you must, isn't it better
to sell your life for a pretty woman, and stand a chance
of going back to France again?'

'I would rather go to sleep,' said one of the men,
dropping down into the snow; 'and if you worry me
again, major, I shall stick my toasting-iron into your
belly!'

'What is it all about, sir?' asked the grenadier.
'The man's drunk. He is a Parisian, and likes to lie in
the lap of luxury.'

'You shall have these, good fellow,' said the major,

holding out a *rivière* of diamonds, 'if you will follow me and fight like a madman. The Russians are not ten minutes away; they have horses; we will march up to the nearest battery and carry off two stout ones.'

'How about the sentinels, major?'

'One of us three——' he began; then he turned from the soldier and looked at the aide-de-camp.—'You are coming, aren't you, Hippolyte?'

Hippolyte nodded assent.

'One of us,' the major went on, 'will look after the sentry. Besides, perhaps those blessed Russians are also fast asleep.'

'All right, major; you are a good sort! But will you take me in your carriage?' asked the grenadier.

'Yes, if you don't leave your bones up yonder.—If I come to grief, promise me, you two, that you will do everything in your power to save the Countess.'

'All right,' said the grenadier.

They set out for the Russian lines, taking the direction of the batteries that had so cruelly raked the mass of miserable creatures huddled together by the river bank. A few minutes later the hoofs of two galloping horses rang on the frozen snow, and the awakened battery fired a volley that passed over the heads of the sleepers; the hoof-beats rattled so fast on the iron ground that they sounded like the hammering in a smithy. The generous aide-de-camp had fallen; the stalwart grenadier had come off safe and sound; and Philip himself had received a bayonet thrust in the shoulder while defending his friend. Notwithstanding his wound, he clung to his horse's mane, and gripped him with his knees so tightly that the animal was held as in a vice.

'God be praised!' cried the major, when he saw his soldier still on the spot, and the carriage standing where he had left it.

'If you do the right thing by me, sir, you will get me

the cross for this. We have treated them to a sword dance to a pretty tune from the rifle, eh ? '

'We have done nothing yet ! Let us put the horses in. Take hold of these cords.'

'They are not long enough.'

'All right, grenadier, just go and overhaul those fellows sleeping there; take their shawls, sheets, any-thing——'

'I say ! the rascal is dead,' cried the grenadier, as he plundered the first man who came to hand. 'Why, they are all dead ! how queer !'

'All of them ?'

'Yes, every one. It looks as though horseflesh *à la neige* was indigestible.'

Philip shuddered at the words. The night had grown twice as cold as before.

'Great heaven ! to lose her when I have saved her life a score of times already.'

He shook the countess, 'Stéphanie ! Stéphanie !' he cried.

She opened her eyes.

'We are saved, madame !'

'Saved !' she echoed, and fell back again.

The horses were harnessed after a fashion at last. The major held his sabre in his unwounded hand, took the reins in the other, saw to his pistols, and sprang on one of the horses, while the grenadier mounted the other. The old sentinel had been pushed into the carriage, and lay across the knees of the general and the Countess ; his feet were frozen. Urged on by blows from the flat of the sabre, the horses dragged the carriage at a mad gallop down to the plain, where endless difficulties awaited them. Before long it became almost impossible to advance without crushing sleeping men, women, and even children at every step, all of whom declined to stir when the grenadier awakened them. In vain M. de Sucy looked for the track that the rearguard had cut

P

through this dense crowd of human beings; there was no more sign of their passage than of the wake of a ship in the sea. The horses could only move at a foot pace, and were stopped most frequently by soldiers, who threatened to kill them.

'Do you mean to get there?' asked the grenadier.

'Yes, if it costs every drop of blood in my body! if it costs the whole world!' the major answered.

'Forward, then! . . . You can't have the omelette without breaking eggs.' And the grenadier of the Garde urged on the horses over the prostrate bodies, and upset the bivouacs; the blood-stained wheels ploughing that field of faces left a double furrow of dead. But in justice it should be said that he never ceased to thunder out his warning cry, 'Carrion! look out!'

'Poor wretches!' exclaimed the major.

'Bah! That way, or the cold, or the cannon!' said the grenadier, goading on the horses with the point of his sword.

Then came the catastrophe, which must have happened sooner but for miraculous good fortune; the carriage was overturned, and all further progress was stopped at once.

'I expected as much!' exclaimed the imperturbable grenadier. 'Oho! he is dead!' he added, looking at his comrade.

'Poor Laurent!' said the major.

'Laurent! Wasn't he in the Fifth Chasseurs?'

'Yes.'

'My own cousin.—Pshaw! this beastly life is not so pleasant that one need be sorry for him as things go.'

But all this time the carriage lay overturned, and the horses were only released after great and irreparable loss of time. The shock had been so violent that the Countess had been awakened by it, and the subsequent commotion aroused her from her stupor. She shook off the rugs and rose.

'Where are we, Philip?' she asked in musical tones, as she looked about her.

'About five hundred paces from the bridge. We are just about to cross the Beresina. When we are on the other side, Stéphanie, I will not tease you any more; I will let you go to sleep; we shall be in safety, we can go on to Wilna in peace. God grant that you may never know what your life has cost!'

'You are wounded!'

'A mere trifle.'

The hour of doom had come. The Russian cannon announced the day. The Russians were in possession of Studzianka, and thence were raking the plain with grape-shot; and by the first dim light of the dawn the major saw two columns moving and forming above on the heights. Then a cry of horror went up from the crowd, and in a moment every one sprang to his feet. Each instinctively felt his danger, and all made a rush for the bridge, surging towards it like a wave.

Then the Russians came down upon them, swift as a conflagration. Men, women, children, and horses all crowded towards the river. Luckily for the major and the Countess, they were still at some distance from the bank. General Éblé had just set fire to the bridge on the other side; but in spite of all the warnings given to those who rushed towards the chance of salvation, not one among them could or would draw back. The overladen bridge gave way, and not only so, the impetus of the frantic living wave towards that fatal bank was such that a dense crowd of human beings was thrust into the water as if by an avalanche. The sound of a single human cry could not be distinguished; there was a dull crash as if an enormous stone had fallen into the water—and the Beresina was covered with corpses.

The violent recoil of those in front, striving to escape this death, brought them into hideous collision with those behind them, who were pressing towards the bank, and many were suffocated and crushed. The Comte and Comtesse de Vandières owed their lives to the carriage. The horses that had trampled and crushed so many dying men were crushed and trampled to death in their turn by the human maelstrom which eddied from the bank. Sheer physical strength saved the major and the grenadier. They killed others in self-defence. That wild sea of human faces and living bodies, surging to and fro as by one impulse, left the bank of the Beresina clear for a few moments. The multitude had hurled themselves back on the plain. Some few men sprang down from the banks toward the river, not so much with any hope of reaching the opposite shore, which for them meant France, as from dread of the wastes of Siberia. For some bold spirits despair became a panoply. An officer leapt from hummock to hummock of ice, and reached the other shore; one of the soldiers scrambled over miraculously on the piles of dead bodies and drift ice. But the immense multitude left behind saw at last that the Russians would not slaughter twenty thousand unarmed men, too numb with the cold to attempt to resist them, and each awaited his fate with dreadful apathy. By this time the major and his grenadier, the old general and his wife, were left to themselves not very far from the place where the bridge had been. All four stood dry-eyed and silent among the heaps of dead. A few able-bodied men and one or two officers, who had recovered all their energy at this crisis, gathered about them. The group was sufficiently large; there were about fifty men all told. A couple of hundred paces from them stood the wreck of the artillery bridge, which had broken down the day before; the major saw this, and 'Let us make a raft!' he cried.

The words were scarcely out of his mouth before the whole group hurried to the ruins of the bridge. A crowd of men began to pick up iron clamps and to hunt for planks and ropes—for all the materials for a raft, in short.

A score of armed men and officers, under command of the major, stood on guard to protect the workers from any desperate attempt on the part of the multitude if they should guess their design. The longing for freedom, which inspires prisoners to accomplish impossibilities, cannot be compared with the hope which lent energy at that moment to these forlorn Frenchmen.

'The Russians are upon us! Here are the Russians!' the guard shouted to the workers.

The timbers creaked, the raft grew larger, stronger, and more substantial. Generals, colonels, and common soldiers all alike bent beneath the weight of waggon-wheels, chains, coils of rope, and planks of timber; it was a modern realisation of the building of Noah's ark. The young Countess, sitting by her husband's side, looked on, regretful that she could do nothing to aid the workers, though she helped to knot the lengths of rope together.

At last the raft was finished. Forty men launched it out into the river, while ten of the soldiers held the ropes that must keep it moored to the shore. The moment that they saw their handiwork floating on the Beresina, they sprang down on to it from the bank with callous selfishness. The major, dreading the frenzy of the first rush, held back Stéphanie and the general; but a shudder ran through him when he saw the landing place black with people, and men crowding down like play-goers into the pit of a theatre.

'It was I who thought of the raft, you savages!' he cried. 'I have saved your lives, and you will not make room for me!'

A confused murmur was the only answer. The men at the edge took up stout poles, thrust them against the bank with all their might, so as to shove the raft out and gain an impetus at its starting upon a journey across a sea of floating ice and dead bodies towards the other shore.

'*Tonnerre de Dieu!* I will knock some of you off into the water if you don't make room for the major and his two companions,' shouted the grenadier. He raised his sabre threateningly, delayed the departure, and made the men stand closer together, in spite of threatening yells.

'I shall fall in! . . . I shall go overboard! . . .' his fellows shouted.

'Let us start! Put off!'

The major gazed with tearless eyes at the woman he loved; an impulse of sublime resignation raised her eyes to heaven.

'To die with you!' she said.

In the situation of the folk upon the raft there was a certain comic element. They might utter hideous yells, but not one of them dared to oppose the grenadier, for they were packed together so tightly that if one man were knocked down, the whole raft might capsize. At this delicate crisis, a captain tried to rid himself of one of his neighbours; the man saw the hostile intention of his officer, collared him, and pitched him overboard. 'Aha! The duck has a mind to drink. . . . Over with you! — There is room for two now!' he shouted. 'Quick, major! throw your little woman over, and come! Never mind that old dotard; he will drop off to-morrow!'

'Be quick!' cried a voice, made up of a hundred voices.

'Come, major! Those fellows are making a fuss, and well they may!'

The Comte de Vandières flung off his ragged blankets, and stood before them in his general's uniform.

'Let us save the Count,' said Philip.

Stéphanie grasped his hand tightly in hers, flung her arms about, and clasped him close in an agonised embrace.

'Farewell,' she said.

Then each knew the other's thoughts. The Comte

de Vandières recovered his energies and presence of mind sufficiently to jump on to the raft, whither Stéphanie followed him after one last look at Philip.

'Major, won't you take my place? I do not care a straw for life; I have neither wife, nor child, nor mother belonging to me——'

'I give them into your charge,' cried the major, indicating the Count and his wife.

'Be easy; I will take as much care of them as of the apple of my eye.'

Philip stood stock-still on the bank. The raft sped so violently towards the opposite shore that it ran aground with a violent shock to all on board. The count, standing on the very edge, was shaken into the stream; and as he fell, a mass of ice swept by and struck off his head, and sent it flying like a ball.

'Hey! major!' shouted the grenadier.

'Farewell!' a woman's voice called aloud.

An icy shiver of dread ran through Philip de Sucy, and he dropped down where he stood, overcome with cold and sorrow and weariness.

'My poor niece went out of her mind,' the doctor added after a brief pause. 'Ah! monsieur,' he went on, grasping M. d'Albon's hand, 'what a fearful life for the poor little thing, so young, so delicate! An unheard-of misfortune separated her from that grenadier of the Garde (Fleuriot by name), and for two years she was dragged on after the army, the laughing-stock of a rabble of outcasts. She went barefoot, I heard, ill-clad, neglected, and starved for months at a time; sometimes confined in a hospital, sometimes living like a hunted animal. God alone knows all the misery which she endured, and yet she lives. She was shut up in a mad-house in a little German town, while her relations, believing her to be dead, were dividing her property here in France.

'In 1816 the grenadier Fleuriot recognised her in an inn in Strasbourg. She had just managed to escape from captivity. Some peasants told him that the Countess had lived for a whole month in a forest, and how that they had tracked her and tried to catch her without success.

'I was at that time not many leagues from Strasbourg; and hearing the talk about this girl in the wood, I wished to verify the strange facts that had given rise to absurd stories. What was my feeling when I beheld the Countess? Fleuriot told me all that he knew of the piteous story. I took the poor fellow with my niece into Auvergne, and there I had the misfortune to lose him. He had some ascendency over Mme. de Vandières. He alone succeeded in persuading her to wear clothes; and in those days her one word of human speech—*Farewell*—she seldom uttered. Fleuriot set himself to the task of awakening certain associations; but there he failed completely; he drew that one sorrowful word from her a little more frequently, that was all. But the old grenadier could amuse her, and devoted himself to playing with her, and through him I hoped; but——' here Stéphanie's uncle broke off. After a moment he went on again.

'Here she has found another creature with whom she seems to have an understanding—an idiot peasant girl, who once, in spite of her plainness and imbecility, fell in love with a mason. The mason thought of marrying her because she had a little bit of land, and for a whole year poor Geneviève was the happiest of living creatures. She dressed in her best, and danced on Sundays with Dallot; she understood love; there was room for love in her heart and brain. But Dallot thought better of it. He found another girl who had all her senses and rather more land than Geneviève, and he forsook Geneviève for her. Then the poor thing lost the little intelligence that love had developed in her; she can do nothing now but cut grass and look after the cattle. My niece and the poor girl are in some sort bound to each other by the invisible chain of their common destiny, and by their madness due to the same cause. Just come here a moment; look!' and Stéphanie's uncle led the Marquis d'Albon to the window.

There, in fact, the magistrate beheld the pretty Countess sitting on the ground at Geneviève's knee, while the peasant girl was wholly absorbed in combing out Stéphanie's long, black hair with a huge comb. The Countess submitted herself to this, uttering low smothered cries that expressed her enjoyment of the sensation of physical comfort. A shudder ran through M. d'Albon as he saw her attitude of languid abandonment, the animal supineness that revealed an utter lack of intelligence.

'Oh! Philip, Philip!' he cried, 'past troubles are as nothing. Is it quite hopeless?' he asked.

The doctor raised his eyes to heaven.

'Good-bye, monsieur,' said M. d'Albon, pressing the old man's hand. 'My friend is expecting me; you will see him here before very long.'

'Then it is Stéphanie herself?' cried Sucy when the Marquis had spoken the first few words. 'Ah! until now I did not feel sure!' he added. Tears filled the dark eyes that were wont to wear a stern expression.

'Yes; she is the Comtesse de Vandières,' his friend replied.

The colonel started up, and hurriedly began to dress.

'Why, Philip!' cried the horrified magistrate. 'Are you going mad?'

'I am quite well now,' said the colonel simply. 'This news has soothed all my bitterest grief; what pain could hurt me while I think of Stéphanie? I am going over to the Minorite convent, to see her and speak to her, to restore her to health again. She is free; ah, surely, surely, happiness will smile on us, or there is no Providence above.   How can you think that she could hear my voice, poor Stéphanie, and not recover her reason ? '

'She has seen you once already, and she did not recognise you,' the magistrate answered gently, trying to suggest some wholesome fears to this friend, whose hopes were visibly too high.

The colonel shuddered, but he began to smile again, with a slight involuntary gesture of incredulity.   Nobody ventured to oppose his plans, and a few hours later he had taken up his abode in the old priory, to be near the doctor and the Comtesse de Vandières.

' Where is she ? ' he cried at once.

' Hush ! ' answered M. Fanjat, Stéphanie's uncle.   ' She is sleeping.   Stay ; here she is.'

Philip saw the poor distraught sleeper crouching on a stone bench in the sun.   Her thick hair, straggling over her face, screened it from the glare and heat ; her arms dropped languidly to the earth ; she lay at ease as gracefully as a fawn, her feet tucked up beneath her ; her bosom rose and fell with her even breathing ; there was the same transparent whiteness as of porcelain in her skin and complexion that we so often admire in children's faces.   Geneviève sat there motionless, holding a spray that Stéphanie doubtless had brought down from the top of one of the tallest poplars ; the idiot girl was waving the green branch above her, driving away the flies from her sleeping companion, and gently fanning her.

She stared at M. Fanjat and the colonel as they came up ; then, like a dumb animal that recognises its master, she slowly turned her face towards the countess, and watched over her as before, showing not the slightest sign of intelligence or of astonishment.   The air was scorching.   The glittering particles of the stone bench shone like sparks of fire ; the meadow sent up the quivering vapours that hover above the grass and gleam like golden dust when they catch the light, but Geneviève did not seem to feel the raging heat.

The colonel wrung M. Fanjat's hands; the tears that gathered in the soldier's eyes stole down his cheeks, and fell on the grass at Stéphanie's feet.

'Sir,' said her uncle, 'for these two years my heart has been broken daily. Before very long you will be as I am; if you do not weep, you will not feel your anguish the less.'

'You have taken care of her!' said the colonel, and jealousy no less than gratitude could be read in his eyes.

The two men understood one other. They grasped each other by the hand again, and stood motionless, gazing in admiration at the serenity that slumber had brought into the lovely face before them. Stéphanie heaved a sigh from time to time, and this sigh, that had all the appearance of sensibility, made the unhappy colonel tremble with gladness.

'Alas!' M. Fanjat said gently, 'do not deceive yourself, monsieur; as you see her now, she is in full possession of such reason as she has.'

Those who have sat for whole hours absorbed in the delight of watching over the slumber of some tenderly-beloved one, whose waking eyes will smile for them, will doubtless understand the bliss and anguish that shook the colonel. For him this slumber was an illusion, the waking must be a kind of death, the most dreadful of all deaths.

Suddenly a kid frisked in two or three bounds towards the bench, and snuffed at Stéphanie. The sound awakened her; she sprang lightly to her feet without scaring away the capricious creature; but as soon as she saw Philip she fled, followed by her four-footed playmate, to a thicket of elder-trees; then she uttered a little cry like the note of a startled wild-bird, the same sound that the colonel had heard once before near the grating, when the Countess appeared to M. d'Albon for the first time. At length she climbed into a laburnum-tree, ensconced herself in the feathery greenery, and peered out at the *strange man* with as much interest as the most inquisitive nightingale in the forest.

'Farewell, farewell, farewell,' she said, but the soul sent no trace of expression of feeling through the words, spoken with the careless intonation of a bird's notes.

'She does not know me!' the colonel exclaimed in despair. 'Stéphanie! Here is Philip, your Philip! . . . Philip!' and the poor soldier went towards the laburnum-tree; but when he stood three paces away, the Countess eyed him almost defiantly, though there was timidity in her eyes; then at a bound she sprang from the laburnum to an acacia, and thence to a spruce-fir, swinging from bough to bough with marvellous dexterity.

'Do not follow her,' said M. Fanjat, addressing the colonel. 'You would arouse a feeling of aversion in her which might become insurmountable; I will help you to make her acquaintance and to tame her. Sit down on the bench. If you pay no heed whatever to her, poor child, it will not be long before you will see her come nearer by degrees to look at you.'

'That *she* should not know me! that *she* should fly from me!' the colonel repeated, sitting down on a rustic bench and leaning his back against a tree that overshadowed it.

He bowed his head. The doctor remained silent. Before very long the Countess stole softly down from her high refuge in the spruce fir, flitting like a will-of-the-wisp; for as the wind stirred the boughs, she lent herself at times to the swaying movements of the trees. At each branch she stopped and peered at the stranger; but as she saw him sitting motionless, she at length jumped down to the grass, stood a while, and came slowly across the meadow. When she took up her position by a tree about ten paces from the bench, M. Fanjat spoke to the colonel in a low voice.

'Feel in my pocket for some lumps of sugar,' he said, 'and let her see them, she will come; I willingly give up to you the pleasure of giving her sweetmeats. She is passionately fond of sugar, and by that means you will accustom her to come to you and to know you.'

'She never cared for sweet things when she was a woman,' Philip answered sadly.

When he held out the lump of sugar between his thumb and finger, and shook it, Stéphanie uttered the wild note again, and sprang quickly towards him; then she stopped short, there was a conflict between longing for the sweet morsel and instinctive fear of him; she looked at the sugar, turned her head away, and looked again like an unfortunate dog forbidden to touch some scrap of food, while his master slowly recites the greater part of the alphabet until he reaches the letter that gives permission. At length animal appetite conquered fear; Stéphanie rushed to Philip, held out a dainty brown hand to pounce upon the coveted morsel, touched her lover's fingers, snatched the piece of sugar, and vanished with it into a thicket. This painful scene was too much for the colonel; he burst into tears, and took refuge in the drawing-room.

'Then has love less courage than affection?' M. Fanjat asked him. 'I have hope, Monsieur le Baron. My poor niece was once in a far more pitiable state than at present.'

'Is it possible?' cried Philip.

'She would not wear clothes,' answered the doctor.

The colonel shuddered, and his face grew pale. To the doctor's mind this pallor was an unhealthy symptom; he went over to him and felt his pulse, M. de Sucy was in a high fever; by dint of persuasion, he succeeded in putting the patient in bed, and gave him a few drops of laudanum to gain repose and sleep.

The Baron de Sucy spent nearly a week, in a constant struggle with a deadly anguish, and before long he had

no tears left to shed.   He was often well nigh heart-
broken; he could not grow accustomed to the sight of
the Countess's madness; but he made terms for himself,
as it were, in this cruel position, and sought alleviations
in his pain.   His heroism was boundless.   He found
courage to overcome Stéphanie's wild shyness by choosing
sweetmeats for her, and devoted all his thoughts to this,
bringing these dainties, and following up the little
victories that he set himself to gain over Stéphanie's
instincts (the last gleam of intelligence in her), until he
succeeded to some extent—she grew *tamer* than ever
before.   Every morning the colonel went into the park;
and if, after a long search for the Countess, he could not
discover the tree in which she was rocking herself
gently, nor the nook where she lay crouching at play
with some bird, nor the roof where she had perched herself, he would whistle the well-known air *Partant pour la
Syrie*, which recalled old memories of their love, and
Stéphanie would run towards him lightly as a fawn.
She saw the colonel so often that she was no longer
afraid of him; before very long she would sit on his
knee with her thin, lithe arms about him.   And while
thus they sat as lovers love to do, Philip doled out
sweetmeats one by one to the eager Countess.   When
they were all finished, the fancy often took Stéphanie to
search through her lover's pockets with a monkey's quick
instinctive dexterity, till she had assured herself that there
was nothing left, and then she gazed at Philip with vacant
eyes; there was no thought, no gratitude in their clear
depths.   Then she would play with him.   She tried to
take off his boots to see his foot; she tore his gloves to
shreds, and put on his hat; and she would let him pass
his hands through her hair, and take her in his arms,
and submit passively to his passionate kisses, and at last,
if he shed tears, she would gaze silently at him.
    She quite understood the signal when he whistled
Partant pour la Syrie, but he could never succeed in

inducing her to pronounce her own name—*Stéphanie*.
Philip persevered in his heartrending task, sustained by
a hope that never left him. If on some bright autumn
morning he saw her sitting quietly on a bench under a
poplar tree, grown brown now as the season wore, the
unhappy lover would lie at her feet and gaze into her
eyes as long as she would let him gaze, hoping that some
spark of intelligence might gleam from them. At times
he lent himself to an illusion; he would imagine that he
saw the hard, changeless light in them falter, that there
was a new life and softness in them, and he would cry,
'Stéphanie! oh, Stéphanie! you hear me, you see me,
do you not?'

But for her the sound of his voice was like any other
sound, the stirring of the wind in the trees, or the lowing
of the cow on which she scrambled; and the colonel wrung
his hands in a despair that lost none of its bitterness; nay,
time and these vain efforts only added to his anguish.

One evening, under the quiet sky, in the midst of the
silence and peace of the forest hermitage, M. Fanjat saw
from a distance that the Baron was busy loading a pistol,
and knew that the lover had given up all hope. The
blood surged to the old doctor's heart; and if he overcame the dizzy sensation that seized on him, it was because he would rather see his niece live with a disordered
brain than lose her for ever. He hurried to the place.

'What are you doing?' he cried.

'That is for me,' the colonel answered, pointing to a
loaded pistol on the bench, 'and this is for her!' he
added, as he rammed down the wad into the pistol that
he held in his hands.

The Countess lay stretched out on the ground, playing with the balls.

'Then you do not know that last night, as she slept,
she murmured "Philip"'? said the doctor quietly, dis-
sembling his alarm.

'She called my name?' cried the Baron, letting his

weapon fall. Stéphanie picked it up, but he snatched it out of her hands, caught the other pistol from the bench, and fled.

'Poor little one!' exclaimed the doctor, rejoicing that his stratagem had succeeded so well. He held her tightly to his heart as he went on. 'He would have killed you, selfish that he is! He wants you to die because he is unhappy. He cannot learn to love you for your own sake, little one! We forgive him, do we not? He is senseless; you are only mad. Never mind; God alone shall take you to Himself. We look upon you as unhappy because you no longer share our miseries, fools that we are! . . . Why, she is happy,' he said, taking her on his knee; 'nothing troubles her; she lives like the birds, like the deer——'

Stéphanie sprang upon a young blackbird that was hopping about, caught it with a little shriek of glee, twisted its neck, looked at the dead bird, and dropped it at the foot of a tree without giving it another thought.

The next morning at daybreak the colonel went out into the garden to look for Stéphanie; hope was very strong in him. He did not see her, and whistled; and when she came, he took her arm, and for the first time they walked together along an alley beneath the trees, while the fresh morning wind shook down the dead leaves about them. The colonel sat down, and Stéphanie, of her own accord, lit upon his knee. Philip trembled with gladness.

'Love!' he cried, covering her hands with passionate kisses, 'I am Philip . . .'

She looked curiously at him.

'Come close,' he added, as he held her tightly. 'Do you feel the beating of my heart? It has beat for you, for you only. I love you always. Philip is not dead. He is here. You are sitting on his knee. You are my Stéphanie, I am your Philip!'

'Farewell!' she said, 'farewell!'

The colonel shivered. He thought that some vibration of his highly wrought feeling had surely reached his beloved; that the heartrending cry, drawn from him by hope, the utmost effort of a love that must last for ever, of passion in its ecstasy, striving to reach the soul of the woman he loved, must awaken her.

'Oh, Stéphanie! we shall be happy yet!'

A cry of satisfaction broke from her, a dim light of intelligence gleamed in her eyes.

'She knows me! . . . Stéphanie! . . .'

The colonel felt his heart swell, and tears gathered under his eyelids. But all at once the Countess held up a bit of sugar for him to see; she had discovered it by searching diligently for it while he spoke. What he had mistaken for a human thought was a degree of reason required for a monkey's mischievous trick!

Philip fainted. M. Fanjat found the Countess sitting on his prostrate body. She was nibbling her bit of sugar, giving expression to her enjoyment by little grimaces and gestures that would have been thought clever in a woman in full possession of her senses if she tried to mimic her paroquet or her cat.

'Oh, my friend!' cried Philip, when he came to himself. 'This is like death every moment of the day! I love her too much! I could bear anything if only through her madness she had kept some little trace of womanhood. But, day after day, to see her like a wild animal, not even a sense of modesty left, to see her——'

'So you must have a theatrical madness, must you?' said the doctor sharply, 'and your prejudices are stronger than your lover's devotion? What, monsieur! I resign to you the sad pleasure of giving my niece her food, and the enjoyment of her playtime; I have kept for myself nothing but the most burdensome cares. I watch over her while you are asleep, I—— Go, Monsieur, and give up the task. Leave this dreary hermitage; I can live with my little darling; I understand her disease; I study

Q

her movements; I know her secrets. Some day you shall thank me.'

The colonel left the Minorite convent, that he was destined to see only once again. The doctor was alarmed by the effect that his words made upon his guest; his niece's lover became as dear to him as his niece. If either of them deserved to be pitied, that one was certainly Philip; did he not bear alone the burden of an appalling sorrow?

The doctor made inquiries, and learned that the hapless colonel had retired to a country house of his near Saint-Germain. A dream had suggested to him a plan for restoring the Countess to reason, and the doctor did not know that he was spending the rest of the autumn in carrying out a vast scheme. A small stream ran through his park, and in winter time flooded a low-lying land, something like the plain on the eastern side of the Beresina. The village of Satout, on the slope of a ridge above it, bounded the horizon of a picture of desolation, something as Studzianka lay on the heights that shut in the swamp of the Beresina. The colonel set labourers to work to make a channel to resemble the greedy river that had swallowed up the treasures of France and Napoleon's army. By the help of his memories, Philip reconstructed on his own lands the bank where General Eblé had built his bridges. He drove in piles, and then set fire to them, so as to reproduce the charred and blackened balks of timber that on either side of the river told the stragglers that their retreat to France had been cut off. He had materials collected like the fragments out of which his comrades in misfortune had made the raft; his park was laid waste to complete the illusion on which his last hopes were founded. He ordered ragged uniforms and clothing for several hundred peasants. Huts and bivouacs and batteries were raised and burned down. In short, he omitted no device that could reproduce that most hideous of all scenes. He succeeded. When, in the earliest days of December, snow covered the earth with a thick white mantle, it seemed to him that he saw the Beresina itself. The mimic Russia was so startlingly real, that several of his old comrades recognised the scene of their past sufferings. M. de Sucy kept the secret of the drama to be enacted with this tragical background, but it was looked upon as a mad freak in several circles of society in Paris.

In the early days of the month of January 1820, the colonel drove over to the Forest of l'Isle-Adam in a carriage like the one in which M. and Mme. de Vandières had driven from Moscow to Studzianka. The horses closely resembled that other pair that he had risked his life to bring from the Russian lines. He himself wore the grotesque and soiled clothes, accoutrements, and cap that he had worn on the 29th of November 1812. He had even allowed his hair and beard to grow, and neglected his appearance, that no detail might be lacking to recall the scene in all its horror.

'I guessed what you meant to do,' cried M. Fanjat, when he saw the colonel dismount. 'If you mean your plan to succeed, do not let her see you in that carriage. This evening I will give my niece a little laudanum, and while she sleeps, we will dress her in such clothes as she wore at Studzianka, and put her in your travelling-carriage. I will follow you in a berline.'

Soon after two o'clock in the morning, the young Countess was lifted into the carriage, laid on the cushions, and wrapped in a coarse blanket. A few peasants held torches while this strange elopement was arranged.

A sudden cry rang through the silence of night, and Philip and the doctor, turning, saw Geneviève. She had come out half-dressed from the low room where she slept.

'Farewell, farewell; it is all over, farewell!' she called, crying bitterly.

'Why, Geneviève, what is it?' asked M. Fanjat.

Geneviève shook her head despairingly, raised her arm
to heaven, looked at the carriage, uttered a long snarling
sound, and with evident signs of profound terror, slunk
in again.

'"Tis a good omen,' cried the colonel. 'The girl is
sorry to lose her companion. Very likely she *sees* that
Stéphanie is about to recover her reason.'

'God grant it may be so!' answered M. Fanjat, who
seemed to be affected by this incident. Since insanity
had interested him, he had known several cases in which
a spirit of prophecy and the gift of second sight had been
accorded to a disordered brain—two faculties which
many travellers tell us are also found among savage tribes.

So it happened that, as the colonel had foreseen and
arranged, Stéphanie travelled across the mimic Beresina
about nine o'clock in the morning, and was awakened by an
explosion of rockets about a hundred paces from the scene
of action. It was a signal. Hundreds of peasants raised
a terrible clamour, like the despairing shouts that startled
the Russians when twenty thousand stragglers learned
that by their own fault they were delivered over to
death or to slavery.

When the Countess heard the report and the cries that
followed, she sprang out of the carriage, and rushed in
frenzied anguish over the snow-covered plain; she saw
the burned bivouacs and the fatal raft about to be
launched on a frozen Beresina. She saw Major Philip
brandishing his sabre among the crowd. The cry that
broke from Mme. de Vandières made the blood run
cold in the veins of all who heard it. She stood face to
face with the colonel, who watched her with a beating
heart. At first she stared blankly at the strange scene
about her, then she reflected. For an instant, brief as a
lightning flash, there was the same quick gaze and total
lack of comprehension that we see in the bright eyes of a
bird; then she passed her hand across her forehead with
the intelligent expression of a thinking being; she looked

round on the memories that had taken substantial form, into the past life that had been transported into her present; she turned her face to Philip—and saw him! An awed silence fell upon the crowd. The colonel breathed hard, but dared not speak; tears filled the doctor's eyes. A faint colour overspread Stéphanie's beautiful face, deepening slowly, till at last she glowed like a girl radiant with youth. Still the bright flush grew. Life and joy, kindled within her at the blaze of intelligence, swept through her like leaping flames. A convulsive tremor ran from her feet to her heart. But all these tokens, which flashed on the sight in a moment, gathered and gained consistence, as it were, when Stéphanie's eyes gleamed with heavenly radiance, the light of a soul within. She lived, she thought! She shuddered—was it with fear? God Himself unloosed a second time the tongue that had been bound by death, and set His fire anew in the extinguished soul. The electric torrent of the human will vivified the body whence it had so long been absent.

'Stéphanie!' the colonel cried.

'Oh! it is Philip!' said the poor Countess.

She fled to the trembling arms held out towards her, and the embrace of the two lovers frightened those who beheld it. Stéphanie burst into tears.

Suddenly the tears ceased to flow; she lay in his arms a dead weight, as if stricken by a thunderbolt, and said faintly—

'Farewell, Philip! . . . I love you . . . farewell!'

'She is dead!' cried the colonel, unclasping his arms.

The old doctor received the lifeless body of his niece in his arms as a young man might have done; he carried her to a stack of wood and set her down. He looked at her face, and laid a feeble hand, tremulous with agitation, upon her heart—it beat no longer.

'Can it really be so?' he said, looking from the colonel, who stood there motionless, to Stéphanie's face.

Death had invested it with a radiant beauty, a transient aureole, the pledge, it may be, of a glorious life to come.

'Yes, she is dead.'

'Oh, but that smile!' cried Philip; 'only see that smile. Is it possible?'

'She has grown cold already,' answered M. Fanjat.

M. de Sucy made a few strides to tear himself from the sight; then he stopped, and whistled the air that the mad Stéphanie had understood; and when he saw that she did not rise and hasten to him, he walked away, staggering like a drunken man, still whistling, but he did not turn again.

In society General de Sucy is looked upon as very agreeable, and above all things, as very lively and amusing. Not very long ago a lady complimented him upon his good humour and equable temper.

'Ah! madame,' he answered, 'I pay very dearly for my merriment in the evening if I am alone.'

'Then, you are never alone, I suppose.'

'No,' he answered, smiling.

If a keen observer of human nature could have seen the look that Sucy's face wore at that moment, he would, without doubt, have shuddered.

'Why do you not marry?' the lady asked (she had several daughters of her own at a boarding-school). 'You are wealthy; you belong to an old and noble house; you are clever; you have a future before you; everything smiles upon you.'

'Yes,' he answered; 'one smile is killing me——'

On the morrow the lady heard with amazement that M. de Sucy had shot himself through the head that night.

The fashionable world discussed the extraordinary news in divers ways, and each had a theory to account for it; play, love, ambition, irregularities in private life, according to the taste of the speaker, explained the last act of the tragedy begun in 1812. Two men alone, a magistrate and an old doctor, knew that Monsieur le Comte de Sucy was one of those souls unhappy in the strength God gives to them to enable them to triumph daily in a ghastly struggle with a mysterious horror. If for a moment God withdraws His sustaining hand, they succumb.

PARIS, *March* 1830.

THE CONSCRIPT

[The inner self] . . . *by a phenomenon of vision or of locomotion has been known at times to abolish Space in its two modes of Time and Distance—the one intellectual, the other physical.*
—History of Louis Lambert.

On a November evening in the year 1793 the principal citizens of Carentan were assembled in Mme. de Dey's drawing-room. Mme. de Dey held this *reception* every night of the week, but an unwonted interest attached to this evening's gathering, owing to certain circumstances which would have passed altogether unnoticed in a great city, though in a small country town they excited the greatest curiosity. For two days before Mme. de Dey had not been at home to her visitors, and on the previous evening her door had been shut, on the ground of indisposition. Two such events at any ordinary time would have produced in Carentan the same sensation that Paris knows on nights when there is no performance at the theatres—existence is in some sort incomplete ; but in those times when the least indiscretion on the part of an aristocrat might be a matter of life and death, this conduct of Mme. de Dey's was likely to bring about the most disastrous consequences for her. Her position in Carentan ought to be made clear, if the reader is to appreciate the expression of keen curiosity and cunning fanaticism on the countenances of these Norman citizens, and, what is of most importance, the part that the lady

248

played among them. Many a one during the days of the Revolution has doubtless passed through a crisis as difficult as hers at that moment, and the sympathies of more than one reader will fill in all the colouring of the picture.

Mme. de Dey was the widow of a Lieutenant-General, a Knight of the Orders of Saint Michael and of the Holy Ghost. She had left the Court when the Emigration began, and taken refuge in the neighbourhood of Carentan, where she had large estates, hoping that the influence of the Reign of Terror would be but little felt there. Her calculations, based on a thorough knowledge of the district, proved correct. The Revolution made little disturbance in Lower Normandy. Formerly, when Mme. de Dey had spent any time in the country, her circle of acquaintance had been confined to the noble families of the district; but now, from politic motives, she opened her house to the principal citizens and to the Revolutionary authorities of the town, endeavouring to touch and gratify their social pride without arousing either hatred or jealousy. Gracious and kindly, possessed of the indescribable charm that wins goodwill without loss of dignity or effort to pay court to any, she had succeeded in gaining universal esteem; the discreet warnings of exquisite tact enabled her to steer a difficult course among the exacting claims of this mixed society, without wounding the overweening self-love of parvenus on the one hand, or the susceptibilities of her old friends on the other.

She was about thirty-eight years of age, and still preserved, not the fresh, high-coloured beauty of the Basse-Normandes, but a fragile loveliness of what may be called an aristocratic type. Her figure was lissome and slender, her features delicate and clearly cut; the pale face seemed to light up and live when she spoke; but there was a quiet and devout look in the great dark eyes, for all their graciousness of expression—a look that seemed to say that the springs of her life lay without her own existence.

In her early girlhood she had been married to an elderly and jealous soldier. Her false position in the midst of a gay Court had doubtless done something to bring a veil of sadness over a face that must once have been bright with the charms of quick-pulsed life and love. She had been compelled to set constant restraint upon her frank impulses and emotions at an age when a woman feels rather than thinks, and the depths of passion in her heart had never been stirred. In this lay the secret of her greatest charm, a youthfulness of the inmost soul, betrayed at times by her face, and a certain tinge of innocent wistfulness in her ideas. She was reserved in her demeanour, but in her bearing and in the tones of her voice there was still something that told of girlish longings directed toward a vague future. Before very long the least susceptible fell in love with her, and yet stood somewhat in awe of her dignity and high-bred manner. Her great soul, strengthened by the cruel ordeals through which she had passed, seemed to set her too far above the ordinary level, and these men weighed themselves, and instinctively felt that they were found wanting. Such a nature demanded an exalted passion.

Moreover, Mme. de Dey's affections were concentrated in one sentiment—a mother's love for her son. All the happiness and joy that she had not known as a wife, she had found later in her boundless love for him. The coquetry of a mistress, the jealousy of a wife mingled with the pure and deep affection of a mother. She was miserable when they were apart, and nervous about him while he was away ; she could never see enough of him, and lived through and for him alone. Some idea of the strength of this tie may be conveyed to the masculine understanding by adding that this was not only Mme. de Dey's only son, but all she had of kith or kin in the world, the one human being on earth bound to her by all the fears and hopes and joys of her life.

The late Comte de Dey was the last of his race, and she, his wife, was the sole heiress and descendant of her house. So worldly ambitions and family considerations, as well as the noblest cravings of the soul, combined to heighten in the Countess a sentiment that is strong in every woman's heart. The child was all the dearer, because only with infinite care had she succeeded in rearing him to man's estate; medical science had predicted his death a score of times, but she had held fast to her presentiments and her hopes, and had known the inexpressible joy of watching him pass safely through the perils of infancy, of seeing his constitution strengthen in spite of the decrees of the Faculty.

Thanks to her constant care, the boy had grown up and developed so favourably, that at twenty years of age he was regarded as one of the most accomplished gentlemen at the Court of Versailles. One final happiness that does not always crown a mother's efforts was hers—her son worshipped her; and between these two there was the deep sympathy of kindred souls. If they had not been bound to each other already by a natural and sacred tie, they would instinctively have felt for each other a friendship that is rarely met with between two men.

At the age of eighteen, the young Count had received an appointment as sub-lieutenant in a regiment of dragoons, and had made it a point of honour to follow the emigrant Princes into exile.

Then Mme. de Dey faced the dangers of her cruel position. She was rich, noble, and the mother of an Emigrant. With the one desire to look after her son's great fortune, she had denied herself the happiness of being with him; and when she read the rigorous laws in virtue of which the Republic was daily confiscating the property of Emigrants at Carentan, she congratulated herself on the courageous course that she had taken.

Was she not keeping watch over the wealth of her son at the risk of her life? Later, when news came of the horrible executions ordered by the Convention, she slept, happy in the knowledge that her own treasure was in safety, out of reach of peril, far from the scaffolds of the Revolution. She loved to think that she had followed the best course, that she had saved her darling and her darling's fortunes; and to this secret thought she made such concessions as the misfortunes of the times demanded, without compromising her dignity or her aristocratic tenets, and enveloped her sorrows in reserve and mystery. She had foreseen the difficulties that would beset her at Carentan. Did she not tempt the scaffold by the very fact of going thither to take a prominent place? Yet, sustained by a mother's courage, she succeeded in winning the affection of the poor, ministering without distinction to every one in trouble; and made herself necessary to the well-to-do, by providing amusements for them.

The procureur of the commune might be seen at her house, the mayor, the president of the 'district,' and the public prosecutor, and even the judges of the Revolutionary tribunals went there. The four first named gentlemen were none of them married, and each paid court to her, in the hope that Mme. de Dey would take him for her husband, either from fear of making an enemy or from a desire to find a protector.

The public prosecutor, once an attorney at Caen, and the Countess's man of business, did what he could to inspire love by a system of devotion and generosity, a dangerous game of cunning! He was the most formidable of all her suitors. He alone knew the amount of the large fortune of his sometime client, and his fervour was inevitably increased by the cupidity of greed, and by the consciousness that he wielded an enormous power, the power of life and death in the district. He was still a young man, and, owing to the generosity of his behaviour,

Mme. de Dey was unable as yet to estimate him truly. But, in despite of the danger of matching herself against Norman cunning, she used all the craft and inventiveness that Nature has bestowed on women to play off the rival suitors one against another. She hoped, by gaining time, to emerge safe and sound from her difficulties at last; for at that time Royalists in the provinces flattered themselves with a hope, daily renewed, that the morrow would see the end of the Revolution—a conviction that proved fatal to many of them.

In spite of difficulties, the Countess had maintained her independence with considerable skill until the day, when, by an inexplicable want of prudence, she took occasion to close her salon. So deep and sincere was the interest that she inspired, that those who usually filled her drawing-room felt a lively anxiety when the news was spread; then, with the frank curiosity characteristic of provincial manners, they went to inquire into the misfortune, grief, or illness that had befallen Mme. de Dey.

To all these questions, Brigitte, the housekeeper, answered with the same formula: her mistress was keeping her room, and would see no one, not even her own servants. The almost claustral lives of dwellers in small towns fosters a habit of analysis and conjectural explanation of the business of everybody else; so strong is it, that when every one had exclaimed over poor Mme. de Dey (without knowing whether the lady was overcome by joy or sorrow), each one began to inquire into the causes of her sudden seclusion.

'If she were ill, she would have sent for the doctor,' said gossip number one; 'now the doctor has been playing chess in my house all day. He said to me, laughing, that in these days there is only one disease, and that, unluckily, it is incurable.'

The joke was hazarded discreetly. Women and men, elderly folk and young girls, forthwith betook themselves to the vast fields of conjecture. Every one imagined that there was some secret in it, and every head was busy with the secret. Next day the suspicions became malignant. Every one lives in public in a small town, and the women-kind were the first to find out that Brigitte had laid in an extra stock of provisions. The thing could not be disputed. Brigitte had been seen in the market-place betimes that morning, and, wonderful to relate, she had bought the one hare to be had. The whole town knew that Mme. de Dey did not care for game. The hare became a starting-point for endless conjectures.

Elderly gentlemen, taking their constitutional, noticed a sort of suppressed bustle in the Countess's house; the symptoms were the more apparent because the servants were at evident pains to conceal them. The man-servant was beating a carpet in the garden. Only yesterday no one would have remarked the fact, but to-day everybody began to build romances upon that harmless piece of household stuff. Every one had a version.

On the following day, that on which Mme. de Dey gave out that she was not well, the magnates of Carentan went to spend the evening at the mayor's brother's house. He was a retired merchant, a married man, a strictly honourable soul; every one respected him, and the Countess held him in high regard. There all the rich widow's suitors were fain to invent more or less probable fictions, each one thinking the while how to turn to his own advantage the secret that compelled her to com-promise herself in such a manner.

The public prosecutor spun out a whole drama to bring Mme. de Dey's son to her house of a night. The mayor had a belief in a priest who had refused the oath, a refugee from La Vendée; but this left him not a little embarrassed how to account for the purchase of a hare on a Friday. The president of the district had strong leanings towards a Chouan chief, or a Vendean leader hotly pursued. Others voted for a noble escaped from

the prisons of Paris.   In short, one and all suspected
that the Countess had been guilty of some piece of
generosity that the law of those days defined as a crime,
an offence that was like to bring her to the scaffold.
The public prosecutor, moreover, said, in a low voice,
that they must hush the matter up, and try to save the
unfortunate lady from the abyss towards which she was
hastening.

'If you spread reports about,' he added, 'I shall be
obliged to take cognisance of the matter, and to search
the house, and then ! . . .'

He said no more, but every one understood what was
left unsaid.

The Countess's real friends were so much alarmed for
her, that on the morning of the third day the *Procureur
Syndic* of the commune made his wife write a few lines
to persuade Mme. de Dey to hold her reception as usual
that evening.   The old merchant took a bolder step.
He called that morning upon the lady.   Strong in the
thought of the service he meant to do her, he insisted
that he must see Mme. de Dey, and was amazed beyond
expression to find her out in the garden, busy gathering
the last autumn flowers in her borders to fill the vases.

'She has given refuge to her lover, no doubt,' thought
the old man, struck with pity for the charming woman
before him.

The Countess's face wore a strange look, that con-
firmed his suspicions.   Deeply moved by the devotion so
natural to women, but that always touches us, because
all men are flattered by the sacrifices that any woman
makes for any one of them, the merchant told the
Countess of the gossip that was circulating in the town,
and showed her the danger that she was running.   He
wound up at last with saying that 'if there are some of
our public functionaries who are sufficiently ready to
pardon a piece of heroism on your part so long as it is
a priest that you wish to save, no one will show you any

mercy if it is discovered that you are sacrificing yourself to the dictates of your heart.'

At these words Mme. de Dey gazed at her visitor with a wild excitement in her manner that made him tremble, old though he was.

'Come in,' she said, taking him by the hand to bring him to her room, and as soon as she had assured herself that they were alone, she drew a soiled, torn letter from her bodice.—'Read it!' she cried, with a violent effort to pronounce the words.

She dropped as if exhausted into her armchair. While the old merchant looked for his spectacles and wiped them, she raised her eyes, and for the first time looked at him with curiosity; then, in an uncertain voice, 'I trust in you,' she said softly.

'Why did I come but to share in your crime?' the old merchant said simply.

She trembled. For the first time since she had come to the little town her soul found sympathy in another soul. A sudden light dawned meantime on the old merchant; he understood the Countess's joy and her prostration.

Her son had taken part in the Granville expedition; he wrote to his mother from his prison, and the letter brought her a sad, sweet hope. Feeling no doubts as to his means of escape, he wrote that within three days he was sure to reach her, disguised. The same letter that brought these weighty tidings was full of heartrending farewells in case the writer should not be in Carentan by the evening of the third day, and he implored his mother to send a considerable sum of money by the bearer, who had gone through dangers innumerable to deliver it. The paper shook in the old man's hands.

'And to-day is the third day!' cried Mme. de Dey. She sprang to her feet, took back the letter, and walked up and down.

'You have set to work imprudently,' the merchant

remarked, addressing her. 'Why did you buy provisions?'

'Why, he may come in dying of hunger, worn out with fatigue, and——' She broke off.

'I am sure of my brother,' the old merchant went on; 'I will engage him in your interests.'

The merchant in this crisis recovered his old business shrewdness, and the advice that he gave Mme. de Dey was full of prudence and wisdom. After the two had agreed together as to what they were to do and say, the old merchant went on various ingenious pretexts to pay visits to the principal houses of Carentan, announcing wherever he went that he had just been to see Mme. de Dey, and that, in spite of her indisposition, she would receive that evening. Matching his shrewdness against Norman wits in the cross-examination he underwent in every family as to the Countess's complaint, he succeeded in putting almost every one who took an interest in the mysterious affair upon the wrong scent.

His very first call worked wonders. He told, in the hearing of a gouty old lady, how that Mme. de Dey had all but died of an attack of gout in the stomach; how that the illustrious Tronchin had recommended her in such a case to put the skin from a live hare on her chest, to stop in bed, and keep perfectly still. The Countess, he said, had lain in danger of her life for the past two days; but after carefully following out Tronchin's singular prescription, she was now sufficiently recovered to receive visitors that evening.

This tale had an immense success in Carentan. The local doctor, a Royalist *in petto*, added to its effect by gravely discussing the specific. Suspicion, nevertheless, had taken too deep root in a few perverse or philosophical minds to be entirely dissipated; so it fell out that those who had the right of entry into Mme. de Dey's drawing-room hurried thither at an early hour, some to watch

R

her face, some out of friendship, but the more part attracted by the fame of the marvellous cure.

They found the Countess seated in a corner of the great chimneypiece in her room, which was almost as modestly furnished as similar apartments in Carentan; for she had given up the enjoyment of luxuries to which she had formerly been accustomed, for fear of offending the narrow prejudices of her guests, and she had made no changes in her house. The floor was not even polished. She had left the old sombre hangings on the walls, had kept the old-fashioned country furniture, burned tallow candles, had fallen in with the ways of the place and adopted provincial life without flinching before its cast-iron narrowness, its most disagreeable hardships; but knowing that her guests would forgive her for any prodigality that conduced to their comfort, she left nothing undone where their personal enjoyment was concerned; her dinners, for instance, were excellent. She even went so far as to affect avarice to recommend herself to these sordid natures; and had the ingenuity to make it appear that certain concessions to luxury had been made at the instance of others, to whom she had graciously yielded.

Towards seven o'clock that evening, therefore, the nearest approach to polite society that Carentan could boast was assembled in Mme. de Dey's drawing-room, in a wide circle, about the fire. The old merchant's sympathetic glances sustained the mistress of the house through this ordeal; with wonderful strength of mind, she underwent the curious scrutiny of her guests, and bore with their trivial prosings. Every time there was a knock at the door, at every sound of footsteps in the street, she hid her agitation by raising questions of absorbing interest to the countryside. She led the conversation on to the burning topic of the quality of various ciders, and was so well seconded by her friend who shared her secret, that her guests almost forgot to watch

her, and her face wore its wonted look ; her self-possession
was unshaken. The public prosecutor and one of the
judges of the Revolutionary Tribunal kept silence, however ; noting the slightest change that flickered over her
features, listening through the noisy talk to every sound
in the house. Several times they put awkward questions,
which the Countess answered with wonderful presence
of mind. So brave is a mother's heart !

Mme. de Dey had drawn her visitors into little groups,
had made parties of whist, boston, or reversis, and sat
talking with some of the young people ; she seemed to
be living completely in the present moment, and played
her part like a consummate actress. She elicited a suggestion of loto, and saying that no one else knew where
to find the game, she left the room.

'My good Brigitte, I cannot breathe down there !' she
cried, brushing away the tears that sprang to her eyes
that glittered with fever, sorrow, and impatience.—She
had gone up to her son's room, and was looking round
it. 'He does not come,' she said. 'Here I can breathe
and live. A few minutes more, and he will be here, for
he is alive, I am sure that he is alive ! my heart tells me
so. Do you hear nothing, Brigitte ?   Oh ! I would give
the rest of my life to know whether he is still in prison
or tramping across the country. I would rather not
think.'

Once more she looked to see that everything was in
order. A bright fire blazed on the hearth, the shutters
were carefully closed, the furniture shone with cleanli-
ness, the bed had been made after a fashion that showed
that Brigitte and the Countess had given their minds to
every trifling detail. It was impossible not to read her
hopes in the dainty and thoughtful preparations about
the room ; love and a mother's tenderest caresses seemed
to pervade the air in the scent of flowers. None but a
mother could have foreseen the requirements of a soldier
and arranged so completely for their satisfaction. A

dainty meal, the best of wine, clean linen, slippers—no necessary, no comfort, was lacking for the weary traveller, and all the delights of home heaped upon him should reveal his mother's love.

'Oh, Brigitte! . . .' cried the Countess, with a heart-rending inflexion in her voice. She drew a chair to the table as if to strengthen her illusions and realise her longings.

'Ah! madame, he is coming. He is not far off. . . . I haven't a doubt that he is living and on his way,' Brigitte answered. 'I put a key in the Bible and held it on my fingers while Cottin read the Gospel of St. John, and the key did not turn, madame.'

'Is that a certain sign?' the Countess asked.

'Why, yes, madame! everybody knows that. He is still alive; I would stake my salvation on it; God cannot be mistaken.'

'If only I could see him here in the house, in spite of the danger.'

'Poor Monsieur Auguste!' cried Brigitte; 'I expect he is tramping along the lanes!'

'And that is eight o'clock striking now!' cried the Countess in terror.

She was afraid that she had been too long in the room where she felt sure that her son was alive; all those preparations made for him meant that he was alive. She went down, but she lingered a moment in the peristyle for any sound that might waken the sleeping echoes of the town. She smiled at Brigitte's husband, who was standing there on guard; the man's eyes looked stupid with the strain of listening to the faint sounds of the night. She stared into the darkness, seeing her son in every shadow everywhere; but it was only for a moment. Then she went back to the drawing-room with an assumption of high spirits, and began to play at loto with the little girls. But from time to time she complained of feeling unwell, and went to sit in her great chair by the fireside. So things went in Mme. de Dey's house and in the minds of those beneath her roof.

Meanwhile, on the road from Paris to Cherbourg, a young man, dressed in the inevitable brown *carmagnole* of those days, was plodding his way towards Carentan. When the first levies were made, there was little or no discipline kept up. The exigencies of the moment scarcely admitted of soldiers being equipped at once, and it was no uncommon thing to see the roads thronged with conscripts in their ordinary clothes. The young fellows went ahead of their company to the next halting-place, or lagged behind it ; it depended upon their fitness to bear the fatigues of a long march. This particular wayfarer was some considerable way in advance of a company of conscripts on the way to Cherbourg, whom the mayor was expecting to arrive every hour, for it was his duty to distribute their billets. The young man's foot-steps were still firm as he trudged along, and his bearing seemed to indicate that he was no stranger to the rough life of a soldier. The moon shone on the pasture-land about Carentan, but he had noticed great masses of white cloud that were about to scatter showers of snow over the country, and doubtless the fear of being overtaken by a storm had quickened his pace in spite of his weariness.

The wallet on his back was almost empty, and he carried a stick in his hand, cut from one of the high, thick box-hedges that surround most of the farms in Lower Normandy. As the solitary wayfarer came into Carentan, the gleaming moonlit outlines of its towers stood out for a moment with ghostly effect against the sky. He met no one in the silent streets that rang with the echoes of his own footsteps, and was obliged to ask the way to the mayor's house of a weaver who was working late. The magistrate was not far to seek, and in a few minutes the conscript was sitting on a stone bench in the mayor's porch waiting for his billet. He was sent for, however, and confronted with that functionary, who scrutinised him closely. The foot-soldier was a good-looking young man, who appeared to be of gentle birth. There was something aristocratic in his bearing, and signs in his face of intelligence developed by a good education.

'What is your name?' asked the mayor, eyeing him shrewdly.

'Julien Jussieu,' answered the conscript.

'From?——' queried the official, and an incredulous smile stole over his features.

'From Paris.'

'Your comrades must be a good way behind?' remarked the Norman in sarcastic tones.

'I am three leagues ahead of the battalion.'

'Some sentiment attracts you to Carentan, of course, citizen-conscript,' said the mayor astutely. 'All right, all right!' he added, with a wave of the hand, seeing that the young man was about to speak. 'We know where to send you. There, off with you, *Citizen Jussieu*,' and he handed over the billet.

There was a tinge of irony in the stress the magistrate laid on the two last words while he held out a billet on Mme. de Dey. The conscript read the direction curiously.

'He knows quite well that he has not far to go, and when he gets outside he will very soon cross the market-place,' said the mayor to himself, as the other went out. 'He is uncommonly bold! God guide him! . . . He has an answer ready for everything. Yes, but if somebody else had asked to see his papers it would have been all up with him!'

The clocks in Carentan struck half-past nine as he spoke. Lanterns were being lit in Mme. de Dey's ante-chamber, servants were helping their masters and mistresses into sabots, greatcoats, and calashes. The card-players settled their accounts, and everybody went out together, after the fashion of all little country towns.

'It looks as if the prosecutor meant to stop,' said a lady, who noticed that that important personage was not in the group in the market-place, where they all took leave of one another before going their separate ways home. And, as a matter of fact, that redoubtable functionary was alone with the Countess, who waited trembling till he should go. There was something appalling in their long silence.

'Citoyenne,' said he at last, 'I am here to see that the laws of the Republic are carried out——'

Mme. de Dey shuddered.

'Have you nothing to tell me?'

'Nothing!' she answered, in amazement.

'Ah! madame,' cried the prosecutor, sitting down beside her and changing his tone. 'At this moment, for lack of a word, one of us—you or I—may carry our heads to the scaffold. I have watched your character, your soul, your manner, too closely to share the error into which you have managed to lead your visitors to-night. You are expecting your son, I could not doubt it.'

The Countess made an involuntary sign of denial, but her face had grown white and drawn with the struggle to maintain the composure that she did not feel, and no tremor was lost on the merciless prosecutor.

'Very well,' the Revolutionary official went on, 'receive him; but do not let him stay under your roof after seven o'clock to-morrow morning; for to-morrow, as soon as it is light, I shall come with a denunciation that I will have made out, and——'

She looked at him, and the dull misery in her eyes would have softened a tiger.

'I will make it clear that the denunciation was false by making a thorough search,' he went on in a gentle voice; 'my report shall be such that you will be safe

from any subsequent suspicion.   I shall make mention of
your patriotic gifts, your civism, and *all* of us will be
safe.'

Mme. de Dey, fearful of a trap, sat motionless, her face
afire, her tongue frozen.   A knock at the door rang
through the house.

'Oh ! . . .' cried the terrified mother, falling upon
her knees; 'save him ! save him !'

'Yes, let us save him !' returned the public prosecutor,
and his eyes grew bright as he looked at her, 'if it costs
us our lives !'

'Lost !' she wailed.   The prosecutor raised her
politely.

'Madam,' said he with a flourish of eloquence, 'to
your own free will alone would I owe——'

'Madame, he is——' cried Brigitte, thinking that her
mistress was alone.   At the sight of the public prosecutor,
the old servant's joy-flushed countenance became haggard
and impassive.

'Who is it, Brigitte ?' the prosecutor asked kindly, as
if he too were in the secret of the household.

'A conscript that the mayor has sent here for a night's
lodging,' the woman replied, holding out the billet.

'So it is,' said the prosecutor, when he had read the
slip of paper.   'A battalion is coming here to-night.'

And he went.

The Countess's need to believe in the faith of her
sometime attorney was so great, that she dared not
entertain any suspicion of him.   She fled upstairs ; she
felt scarcely strength enough to stand ; she opened the
door, and sprang, half-dead with fear, into her son's arms.

'Oh ! my child ! my child !' she sobbed, covering
him with almost frenzied kisses.

'Madame ! . . .' said a stranger's voice.

'Oh ! it is not he !' she cried, shrinking away in
terror, and she stood face to face with the conscript,
gazing at him with haggard eyes.

'*O saint bon Dieu!* how like he is!' cried Brigitte.

There was silence for a moment; even the stranger trembled at the sight of Mme. de Dey's face.

'Ah! monsieur,' she said, leaning on the arm of Brigitte's husband, feeling for the first time the full extent of a sorrow that had all but killed her at its first threatening; 'ah! monsieur, I cannot stay to see you any longer . . . permit my servants to supply my place, and to see that you have all that you want.'

She went down to her own room, Brigitte and the old serving-man half carrying her between them. The housekeeper set her mistress in a chair, and broke out—

'What, madame! is that man to sleep in Monsieur Auguste's bed, and wear Monsieur Auguste's slippers, and eat the pasty that I made for Monsieur Auguste? Why, if they were to guillotine me for it, I——'

'Brigitte!' cried Mme. de Dey.

Brigitte said no more.

'Hold your tongue, chatterbox,' said her husband, in a low voice; 'do you want to kill Madame?'

A sound came from the conscript's room as he drew his chair to the table.

'I shall not stay here,' cried Mme. de Dey; 'I shall go into the conservatory; I shall hear better there if any one passes in the night.'

She still wavered between the fear that she had lost her son and the hope of seeing him once more. That night was hideously silent. Once, for the Countess, there was an awful interval, when the battalion of conscripts entered the town, and the men went by, one by one, to their lodgings. Every footfall, every sound in the street, raised hopes to be disappointed; but it was not for long, the dreadful quiet succeeded again. Towards morning the Countess was forced to return to her room. Brigitte, ever keeping watch over her mistress's movements, did not see her come out again;

and when she went, she found the Countess lying there dead.

'I expect she heard that conscript,' cried Brigitte, 'walking about Monsieur Auguste's room, whistling that accursed *Marseillaise* of theirs while he dressed, as if he had been in a stable! That must have killed her.'

But it was a deeper and a more solemn emotion, and doubtless some dreadful vision, that had caused Mme. de Dey's death; for at the very hour when she died at Carentan, her son was shot in le Morbihan.

This tragical story may be added to all the instances on record of the workings of sympathies uncontrolled by the laws of time and space. These observations, collected with scientific curiosity by a few isolated individuals, will one day serve as documents on which to base the foundations of a new science which hitherto has lacked its man of genius.

Paris, *February* 1831.

A SEASIDE TRAGEDY [1]

*To Madame la Princesse Caroline Galitzin de
Genthod, née Comtesse Walewska, this souvenir
of the Author is respectfully dedicated.*

THE young for the most part delight to measure the
future with a pair of compasses of their own; when the
strength of the will equals the boldness of the angle that
they thus project, the whole world is theirs.

This phenomenon of mental existence takes place,
however, only at a certain age, and that age, without
exception, lies in the years between twenty-two and
eight-and-twenty. It is an age of first conceptions, because it is an age of vast longings, an age which is
doubtful of nothing; doubt at that time is a confession
of weakness; it passes as swiftly as the sowing time, and
is followed by the age of execution. There are in some
sort two periods of youth in every life—the youth of
confident hopes, and the youth of action; sometimes in
those whom Nature has favoured, the two ages coincide,
and then we have a Cæsar, a Newton, or a Bonaparte—
the greatest among great men.

I was measuring the space of time that a single
thought needs for its development, and (compass in
hand) stood on a crag a hundred fathoms above the sea,
surveying my future, and filling it with great works, like
an engineer who should survey an empty land, and cover
it with fortresses and palaces. The sea was calm, the

---

[1] A letter written by Louis Lambert.

267

waves toyed with the reefs of rock. I had just dressed after a swim, and was waiting for Pauline, my guardian angel, who was bathing in a granite basin floored with fine sand, the daintiest bathing-place of Nature's fashioning for the sea-fairies.

We were at the utmost extremity of Croisic-point, a tiny peninsula in Brittany; we were far from the haven itself, and in a part of the coast so inaccessible that the inland revenue department ignored it, and a coastguard scarcely ever passed that way. Ah! to dip in the winds of space, after a plunge in the sea! Who would not have launched forth into the future? Why did I think? Why does a trouble invade us?—Who knows? Ideas drift across heart and brain by no will of yours. No courtesan is more capricious, more imperious, than an artist's inspiration; you must seize her like Fortune, and grasp her by the hair—when she comes. Borne aloft by my thought, like Astolpho upon his hippogriff, I rode across my world, and arranged it all to my liking. Then when I was fain to find some augury in the things about me for these daring castles that a wild imagination bade me build, I heard a sweet cry above the murmur of the restless sea-fringe that marks the ebb and flow of the tide upon the shore, the sound of a woman's voice calling to me through the loneliness and silence, the glad cry of a woman fresh from the sea. It was as if a soul leapt forth in that cry, and it seemed to me as if I had seen the footprints of an angel on the bare rocks, an angel with outspread wings, who cried, 'You will succeed!' I came down, radiant and light of foot, by bounds, like a pebble flung down some steep slope. 'What is it?' she asked as soon as she saw me, and I did not answer; my eyes were full of tears.

Yesterday Pauline had felt my sorrow, as to-day she felt my joy, with the magical responsiveness of a harp that is sensitive to every change in the atmosphere.— Life has exquisite moments. We went in silence along the beach. The sky was cloudless; there was not a ripple on the sea; others might have seen nothing there but two vast blue steppes above and below; but as for us, who had no need of words to understand each other, who could conjure up illusions to feast the eyes of youth and fill the space between the zones of sea and sky—those swaddling-bands of the Infinite—we pressed each other's hands at the slightest change that passed over the fields of water or the fields of air, for in those fleeting signs we read the interpretation of our double thought. Who has not known, in the midst of pleasure, the moment of infinite joy when the soul slips its fetters of flesh, as it were, and returns to the world whence it came? And pleasure is not our only guide to those regions; are there not hours when feeling and thought intertwine with thought and feeling, and fare forth together as two children who take each other by the hand and run, without knowing why? We went thus.

The roofs of the town had come to be a faint grey line on the horizon by the time that we came upon a poor fisherman on his way back to Croisic. He was barefooted; his trousers, of linen cloth, were botched, and tattered, and fringed with rags; he wore a shirt of sailcloth, and a mere rag of a jacket. This wretchedness jarred upon us, as if it had been a discordant note in the midst of our harmony. We both looked at each other, regretting that we had not Abul Kasim's treasury to draw upon at that moment. The fisherman was swinging a splendid lobster and an adder-pike on a string in his right hand, while in the left he carried his fishing tackle. We called to him, with a view to buying his fish. The same idea that occurred to us both found expression in a smile, to which I replied by a light pressure of the arm that lay in mine as I drew it closer to my heart.

It was one of those nothings that memory afterwards weaves into poems, when by the fireside our thoughts

turn to the hour when that nothing so moved us, and
the place rises before us seen through a mirage which
as yet has not been investigated, a magical illusion that
often invests material things about us during those
moments when life flows swiftly and our hearts are
full.   The most beautiful places are only what we make
them.

What man is there, with something of a poet in him,
who does not find that some fragment of rock holds a
larger place in his memories than famous views in many
lands which he has made costly journeyings to see?
Beside that rock what thoughts surged through him!
There he lived through a whole life; there fears were
dissipated, and gleams of hope shone into the depths of
his soul.   At that moment the sun, as if sympathising
with those thoughts of love or of the future, cast a glow
of light and warmth over the tawny sides of the rock;
his eyes were drawn to a mountain flower here and
there on its sides, and the crannies and rifts grew larger
in the silence and peace; the mass, so dark in reality,
took the hue of his dreams; and then how beautiful
it was with its scanty plant life, its pungent-scented
camomile flowers, its velvet fronds of maiden-hair fern!
How splendidly decked for a prolonged festival of human
powers exultant in their strength!   Once already the
Lake of Bienne, seen from the island of Saint-Pierre,
had so spoken to me; perhaps the rock at Croisic will
be the last of these joys.   But, then, what will become
of Pauline?

'You have had a fine catch this morning, good man,'
I said to the fisherman.

'Yes, sir,' he answered, coming to a stand; and we
saw his face, swarthy with exposure to the sun's rays
that beat down on the surface of the sea.   The expression of his face told of the patient resignation and the
simple manners of fisher folk.   There was no roughness
in the man's voice; he had a kindly mouth, and there

was an indefinable something about him—ambitionless,
starved, and stunted.   We should have been disappointed
if he had looked otherwise.

'Where will you sell the fish ? '

'In the town.'

'What will they give you for the lobster ? '

'Fifteen sous.'

'And for the adder-pike ? '

'Twenty sous.'

'Why does it cost so much more than the lobster ? '

'Oh ! the adder-pike' (he called it an *etter*-pike) 'is
much more delicate, sir !   And then they are as spiteful
as monkeys, and very hard to catch.'

'Will you let us have them both for five francs?'
asked Pauline.   The man stood stock-still with astonishment.

'You shall not have them !' I cried, laughing.   'I
bid ten francs for them.   Emotions should be paid for at
a proper rate.'

'Quite right,' returned she; 'but I mean to have them.
I bid ten francs two sous for them.'

'Ten sous.'

'Twelve francs.'

'Fifteen francs.'

'Fifteen francs fifty centimes,' said she.

'A hundred francs.'

'A hundred and fifty.'

I bowed.   We were not rich enough just then to bid
against each other any longer.   Our poor fisherman was
mystified, not knowing whether to be annoyed or to give
himself up to joy; but we helped him out of his difficulty
by telling him where we lodged, and bidding him take
the lobster and the adder-pike to our landlady.

'Is that how you make a living ?' I asked, wondering
how he came to be so poor.

'It is about all I can do, and it is a very hard life,' he
said.   'Shore fishing is a chancy trade when you have

neither boat nor nets and must do it with hooks and
tackle.   You have to wait for the tide, you see,
for the fish or the shell-fish, while those who do
things on a large scale put out to sea.   It is so hard to
make a living at it, that I am the only shore-fisher in
these parts.   For whole days together I get nothing at
all.   For if you are to catch anything, an adder-pike
must fall asleep and get left by the tide, like this one
here, or a lobster must be fool enough to stick to the
rocks.   Sometimes some basse come up with a high tide,
and then I get hold of them.'

'And, after all, taking one thing with another, what
do you make each day?'

'Eleven or twelve sous.   I could get on if I had no
one but myself, but I have my father to keep, and the
old man can't help me; he is blind.'

The words came from him quite simply; Pauline and
I looked at each other in silence.

'Have you a wife or a sweetheart?'

He glanced at us with one of the most piteous
expressions that I have ever seen on a human face, and
answered, 'If I had a wife, I should have to turn my old
father adrift; I could not keep him and keep a wife and
children too.'

'But, my good fellow, why don't you try to earn more
by carrying salt in the haven, or by working in the salt
pits?'

'Ah! sir, I could not stand the work for three months.
I am not strong enough, and if anything happened to me
my father would have to beg.   The only sort of work
for me is something that wants a little skill and a lot of
patience.'

'But how can two people live on twelve sous a-day?'

'Oh, sir, we live on buckwheat bannocks and the
barnacles I break off the rocks.'

'How old are you?'

'Thirty-seven.'

'Have you always stopped here?'

'I once went to Guérande to be drawn for the army, and once to Savenay to be examined by some gentlemen who measured me. If I had been an inch taller, they would have made me into a soldier. The first long march would have put an end to me, and my poor father would have been begging his bread this day.'

I have imagined many tragedies, and Pauline, who passes her life by the side of a man who suffers as I do, is used to strong emotion, yet neither of us had ever heard words so touching as these of the fisherman. We walked on for several steps in silence, fathoming the dumb depths of this stranger's life, admiring the nobleness of a sacrifice made unconsciously; the strength of his weakness made us marvel, his reckless generosity humbled us. A vision of the life of this poor creature rose before me, a life of pure instinct, a being chained to his rock like a convict fettered to a cannon ball, seeking for shell-fish to gain a livelihood, and upheld in that long patience of twenty years by a single feeling! How many hopes disappointed by a squall, or a change in the weather! And while he was hanging over the edge of a block of granite with arms outstretched like a Hindoo fakir, his old father, crouching on his stool in the dark, silent hut, was waiting for the coarsest of the shell-fish, and bread, if the sea should please.

'Do you drink wine now and then?' I asked.

'Three or four times a year.'

'Very well, you shall drink wine to-day, you and your father; and we will send you a white loaf.'

'You are very kind, sir.'

'We will give you the wherewithal for dinner, if you care to show us the way along the shore to Batz, where we shall see the tower that gives you a view of the harbour and the shore between Batz and Croisic.'

'With pleasure,' said he. 'Go straight on, follow the road you are in; I will overtake you again when I have got rid of my tackle.'

s

We both made the same sign of assent, and he rushed off towards the town in great spirits. We were still as we had been before, but the meeting had dimmed our joyousness.

'Poor man!' Pauline exclaimed, in the tone that takes from a woman's compassion any trace of the something that wounds us in pity, 'it makes one ashamed to feel happy when he is so miserable, doesn't it?'

''There is nothing more bitter than helpless wishing,' I answered. 'The two poor creatures, this father and son, could no more understand how keen our sympathy has been than the world could understand the beauty in that life of theirs, for they are laying up treasures in heaven.'

'Poor country!' she said, pointing out to me the heaps of cow-dung spread along a field under a wall of unhewn stones. 'I asked why they did that, and a peasant woman who was spreading it said that she was "making firewood." Just imagine, dear, that when the cow-dung is dry, the poor people heap it up and light fires with it. During the winter they sell it, like blocks of bark fuel. And, finally, how much do you think the best-paid sempstresses earn?—Five sous a day and their board,' she went on after a pause.

'Look,' I said, 'the sea-winds blight or uproot everything; there are no trees. Those who can afford it burn the drift-wood and broken-up boats; it costs too dear, I expect, to bring firewood from other parts of Brittany where there is so much timber. It is a country without beauty, save for great souls, and those who have no hearts could not live here—it is a land for poets and barnacles, and nothing between. It was only when the salt warehouses were built on the cliff that people came to live here. There is nothing here but the sand, the sea beyond it, and above us—space.'

We had already passed the town, and were crossing the waste between Croisic and the market town of Batz.

Imagine, dear uncle, two leagues of waste covered with gleaming sand. Here and there a few rocks raised their heads; you might almost think that extinct monsters were crouching among the dunes. The waves broke over the low ridges along the margin of the sea, till they looked like large white roses floating on the surface of the water and drifted up upon the beach. I looked across this savanna that lay between the ocean on the right and the great lagoon on the left, made by the encroaching sea between Croisic and the sandy heights of Guérande, with the barren salt marshes at their feet; then I looked at Pauline, and asked if she felt able to walk across the sands in the burning sun.

'I have laced boots on; let us go over there,' she said, looking towards the Tower of Batz, which caught the eye by its great mass, erected there like a pyramid in the desert, a slender spindle-shaped pyramid however, a pyramid so picturesquely ornate that one could imagine it to be an outlying sentinel ruin of some great Eastern town laid desolate.

We went a few paces further to reach a fragment of rock to sit in the shade that it still cast, but it was eleven o'clock in the morning, and the shadows which crept closer and closer to our feet swiftly disappeared altogether.

'How beautiful the silence is,' she said; 'and how the murmur of the sea beating steadily against the beach deepens it!'

'If you surrender your mind to the three immensities around us—the air, the sea, and the sands,' I answered, 'and heed nothing but the monotonous sound of the ebb and flow, you would find its speech intolerable, for you would think that it bore the burden of a thought that would overwhelm you. Yesterday, at sunset, I felt that sensation; it crushed me.'

'Oh yes, let us talk,' she said after a long pause. 'No speaker is more terrible. I imagine that I am discovering the causes of the harmonies about us,' she went on. 'This landscape that has but three contrasting colours—the gleaming yellow of the sand, the blue heaven, and the changeless green of the sea—is great without anything savage in its grandeur, vast but not desolate, monotonous but not dreary; it is made up of three elements; it has variety.'

'Women alone can render their impressions like that,' I said; 'you would be the despair of a poet, dear soul that I have read so well.'

'These three expressions of the Infinite glow like a burning flame in the noonday heat,' Pauline said, laughing. 'Here I can imagine the poetry and passions of the East.'

'And I, a vision of Despair.'

'Yes,' she said; 'the dune is a sublime cloister.'

We heard our guide hurrying after us; he wore his holiday clothes. We asked him a few insignificant questions; he thought he saw that our mood had changed, and, with the self-repression that misfortune teaches, he was silent; and we also—though from time to time each pressed the hand of the other to communicate thoughts and impressions—walked for half an hour in silence, either because the shimmering heat above the sands lay heavily upon us, or because the difficulty of walking absorbed our attention. We walked hand in hand like two children; we should not have gone a dozen paces if we had walked arm in arm.

The way that led to Batz was little more than a track; the first high wind effaced the ruts or the dints left by horses' hoofs; but the experienced eyes of our guide discerned traces of cattle and sheep dung on this way, which sometimes wound towards the sea, sometimes towards the land, to avoid the cliffs on the one hand and the rocks on the other. It was noon, and we were only half-way.

'We will rest there,' I said, pointing to a headland where the rocks rose high enough to make it probable that we might find a cave among them. The fisherman, following the direction of my finger, jerked his head.

'There is some one there! Any one coming from market at Batz to Croisic, or from Croisic to Batz, always goes round some way so as not to pass near the place.'

He spoke in a low voice that suggested a mystery.

'Then is there a robber there, a murderer?'

Our guide's only answer was a deep breath that left us twice as curious as before.

'If we go past, will any harm come to us?'

'Oh no!'

'Will you go with us?'

'No, sir!'

'Then we shall go, if you will assure us that there is no danger for us.'

'I do not say that,' the fisherman answered quickly; 'I only say that the one who is there will say nothing to you, and will do you no harm. Oh, good heavens! he will not so much as stir from his place.'

'Then who is it.'

'A man!'

Never were two syllables uttered in such a tragical fashion.

At that moment we were some twenty paces away from the ridge about which the sea was lapping. Our guide took the way that avoided the rocks, and we held straight on for them, but Pauline took my arm. Our guide quickened his pace so as to reach the spot where the two ways met again at the same time as ourselves. He thought, no doubt, that when we had seen 'the man,' we should hurry from the place. This kindled our curiosity; it became so strong that our hearts beat fast, as if a feeling of terror possessed us both. In spite of the heat of the day and a certain weariness after our walk over the sands, our souls were steeped in the ineffable languid calm of an ecstasy that possessed us both, brimming with pure joy, that can only be compared with the delight of hearing exquisite music—music like the *Andiamo mio ben* of Mozart.   When two souls are blended in one pure thought, are they not like two sweet voices singing together?   Before you can appreciate the emotion that thrilled us both, you must likewise share in the half-voluptuous mood in which the morning's experiences had steeped us.

If you had watched for a while some daintily coloured wood-dove on a swaying branch, above a spring, you would utter a cry of distress if you saw a hawk pounce down, bury claws of steel in its heart, and bear it away with the murderous speed with which powder wings a bullet.   We had scarcely set foot in the space before the cavern, a sort of esplanade some hundred feet above the sea, protected from the surge by the steep rocks that sloped to the water's edge, when we were conscious of an electric thrill, something like the shock of a sudden awakening by some noise in a silent night.   Both of us had seen a man sitting there on a block of granite, and he had looked at us.

That glance, from two bloodshot eyes, was like the flash of fire from a cannon, and his stoical immobility could only be compared to the changeless aspect of the granite slabs that lay about him.   Slowly his eyes turned towards us; his body as rigid and motionless as if he had been turned to stone; then after that glance, that made such a powerful impression upon our minds, his eyes turned to gaze steadily over the vast stretch of sea, in spite of the glare reflected from it, as the eagle, it is said, gazes at the sun without lowering his eyelids, nor did he look up again from the waves.

Try to call up before you, dear uncle, some gnarled oak stump, with all its branches lately lopped away, rearing its head, like a strange apparition, by the side of a lonely road, and you will have a clear idea of this man that we saw.   The form of an age-worn Hercules the face of Olympian Jove bearing marks of the ravages of time, of a life of rough toil upon the sea, of sorrow within, of coarse food, and darkened as if blasted by lightning. I saw the muscles, like a framework of iron, standing out upon his hard shaggy hands, and all things else about him indicated a vigorous constitution. In a corner of the cavern I noticed a fairly large heap of moss, and on a rough slab of granite, that did duty as a table, a piece of a round loaf lay over the mouth of a stone-ware pitcher.

Never among my visions of the life led in the desert by early Christian anchorites had I pictured a face more awe-inspiring, more grand and terrible in repentance than this. And even you, dear uncle, in your experience of the confessional, have, perhaps, never seen a penitence so grand; for this remorse seemed to be drowned in a sea of prayers, of prayers that flowed for ever from a dumb despair. This fisherman, this rough Breton sailor, was sublime through a thought hidden within him. Had those eyes shed tears? Had the hand of that rough-hewn statue ever struck a blow? A fierce honesty was stamped upon a rugged forehead where force of character had still left some traces of the gentleness that is the prerogative of all true strength. Was that brow, so scored and furrowed with wrinkles, compatible with a great heart? How came this man to abide with the granite? How had the granite entered into him? Where did the granite end and the man begin? A whole crowd of thoughts passed through our minds; and, as our guide had expected, we went by quickly and in silence. When he saw us again, we were either perturbed with a sense of dread, or overcome by the strangeness of this thing, but he did not remind us that his prediction had come true.

'Did you see him?' he asked.

'What is the man?'

'They call him the "man under a vow."'

You can readily imagine how we both turned to our fisherman at these words. He was a simple-minded fellow; he understood our mute inquiry; and this is the story which I have tried to tell, as far as possible, in the homely language in which he told it.

'The Croisic folk and the people at Batz think that he has been guilty of something, madame, and that he is doing a penance laid upon him by a famous *recteur*, to whom he went to confess, beyond Nantes. There are some who think that Cambremer (that is his name) is unlucky, and that it brings bad luck to pass through the air he breathes, so a good many of them before going round the rocks will stop to see which way the wind blows. If it blows from the nor'-west,' he said, pointing in that direction with his finger, 'they would not go on if they had set out to seek a bit of the True Cross; they turn back again; they are afraid. Other folk, rich people in Croisic, say that Cambremer once made a vow, and that is why he is called "the man under a vow." He never leaves the place; he is there night and day.

'There is some show of reason for these tales,' he added, turning round to point out to us something that had escaped our notice. 'You see that wooden cross that he has set up there on the left; that is to show that he has put himself under the protection of God and the Holy Virgin and the Saints. He would not be respected as he is, if it were not that the terror people have of him makes him as safe as if he had a guard of soldiers.

'He has not said a word since he went into prison in the open air. He lives on bread and water that his brother's little girl brings him every morning, a little slip of a thing twelve years old; he has left all he has to her, and a pretty child she is, as gentle as a lamb, and full of fun, a dear little pet. She has blue eyes as long as *that*,' he went on, holding out his thumb, 'and hair like a cherub's. When you begin—"I say, Pérotte"—(that is what we say for *Pierrette*,' he said, interrupting himself; 'Saint Pierre is her patron saint, Cambremer's name is Pierre, and he was her godfather)—"I say, Pérotte, what does your uncle say to you?"—"He says nothing," says she, "nothing whatever, nothing at all." —"Well, then, what does he do when you go?"—"He kisses me on the forehead of a Sunday."—"Aren't you afraid of him?"—"Not a bit," says she; "he is my god-father."—He will not have any one else bring his food. Pérotte says that he smiles when she comes; but you might as well say that the sun shone in a fog, for he is as gloomy as a sea mist, they say.'

'But you are exciting our curiosity without satisfying it,' I broke in. 'Do you know what brought him there? Was it trouble, or remorse, or crime, or is he mad, or what?'

'Eh! sir, there is hardly a soul save my father and me that knows the rights of the matter. My mother that's gone was in service in the house of the justice that Cambremer went to. The priest told him to go to a justice, and only gave him absolution on that condition, if the tale is true that they tell in the haven. My poor mother overheard Cambremer without meaning to do so, because the kitchen was alongside the sitting-room in the justice's house. So she heard. She is dead, and the justice has gone too. My mother made us promise, my father and me, never to let on to the people round about; and I can tell *you* this, every hair bristled up on my head that night when my mother told us the story——'

'Well, then, tell it to us; we will not repeat it.'

The fisherman looked at us both—then he went on, something after this fashion—

'Pierre Cambremer, whom you saw yonder, is the oldest of the family. The Cambremers have been sea-men from father to son; you see, their name means that the sea has always bent under them. The one you saw had a fishing-boat, several fishing-boats, and the sardine-fishery was his trade, though he did deep-sea fishing as

well for the dealers.   He would have fitted out a bigger
vessel, and gone to the cod-fishing, if he had not been so
fond of his wife ; a fine woman she was, a Brouin from
Guérande, a strapping girl with a warm heart.   She was
so fond of Cambremer that she would never let her man
go away from her for longer than for the sardine-fishing.
They lived down yonder, there!' said our fisherman,
standing on a hillock to point out to us an islet in the
little inland sea between the dunes where we were walking and the salt marshes at Guérande.   ' Do you see the
house ?   It belonged to him.

'Jacquette Brouin and Cambremer had but one child,
a boy, whom they loved like—what shall I say?—like an
only child; they were crazy over him.   Their little
Jacques might have done something (asking your pardon)
into the soup, and they would have thought it sweetened
it.   Times and times again we used to see them, buying the finest toys at the fair for him !   There was
no sense in it—everybody told them so.   Little Cambremer found out that he could do as he liked with them,
and he grew as wilful as a red donkey.   If any one told
his father, " Your boy has all but killed little So-and-so,'
Cambremer used to laugh and say, " Bah ! he will be a
mettlesome sailor !   He will command the king's ships."
Another would say, "Pierre Cambremer, do you know
that your lad put out Pougaud's little girl's eye ? "—" He
will be one for the girls," Pierre would say.   It was all
right in his eyes.   By the time the little rascal was ten
years old he knocked everybody about, and twisted the
fowls' necks for fun, and ripped open the pigs ; he was
as bloodthirsty as a weasel.   " He will make a famous
soldier ! " said Cambremer ; " he has a liking for blood-
shed."

'You see, I myself remember all this,' said our fisherman ; 'and so does Cambremer,' he added, after a
pause.

'Jacques Cambremer grew up to be fifteen or sixteen,

and he was—well, a bully. He would go off and amuse himself at Guérande, and cut a figure at Savenay. He must have money for that. So he began robbing his mother, and she did not dare to tell her husband. Cambremer was so honest that if any one had overpaid him twopence on an account, he would have gone twenty leagues to pay it back. At last one day the mother had nothing left. While the father was away at the fishing, Jacques made off with the dresser, the plenishing, and the sheets and the linen, and left nothing but the four walls; he had sold all the things in the house to pay for his carryings-on at Nantes. The poor woman cried about it day and night. She would have to tell his father when he came back, and she was afraid of the father; not for herself though, not she! So when Pierre Cambremer came back and saw his house furnished with things the neighbours had lent her, he asked—

'"What does this mean?"

'And the poor thing, more dead than alive, answered, "We have been robbed."

'"What has become of Jacques?"

'"Jacques is away on a spree!"

'Nobody knew where the rogue had gone.

'"He is too fond of his fun," said Pierre.

'Six months afterwards the poor father heard that Jacques had got into trouble at Nantes. He goes over on foot—it is quicker than going by sea—puts his hand on his son's shoulder, and fetches him home. He did not ask him, "What have you been doing?"

'"If you don't keep steady here for a couple of years with your mother and me," he said, "and help with the fishing, and behave yourself like a decent fellow, you will have me to reckon with!"

'The harebrained youngster, counting on the weakness his father and mother had for him, made a grimace at his father, and thereupon Pierre fetched him a slap in the face that laid up Jacques for six months afterwards.

'The poor mother was breaking her heart all the time.
One night she was lying quietly asleep by her husband's
side, when she heard a noise and sat up, and got a stab in
the arm from a knife. She shrieked; and when they
had struck a light, Pierre Cambremer found that his wife
was wounded. He thought it was a robber, as if there
were any robbers in our part of the world, when you can
carry ten thousand francs in gold from Croisic to Saint
Nazaire, and no one would so much as ask you what you
had under your arm. Pierre looked about for Jacques,
and could not find him anywhere. In the morning the
unnatural wretch had the face to come back and say that
he had been at Batz.

'I should tell you that the mother did not know
where to hide her money. Cambremer himself used to
leave his with M. Dupotet at Croisic. Their son's wild
ways had eaten up crowns and francs and gold louis;
they were ruined, as you may say, and it was hard on
folk who had about twelve thousand livres, including
their little island. Nobody knew how much Cambremer
had paid down at Nantes to have his son back. Their
luck went from bad to worse. One of Cambremer's
brothers was unfortunate, and wanted help. Pierre told
him, to comfort him, that Jacques and Pérotte (the
younger brother's girl) should be married some day.
Then, to put him in the way of earning his bread, he
took him to help in the fishing; for Joseph Cambremer
was obliged to work with his own hands. His wife had
died of the fever, and he had to pay some one else to
nurse Pérotte till she was weaned. Pierre Cambremer's
wife owed as much as a hundred francs to different people
on the baby's account for linen and things, and two or
three months to big Frelu, who had a child by Simon
Gaudry, and nursed Pérotte. La Cambremer, too, had
sewn a Spanish doubloon into the flock of her mattress,
and written on it "For Pérotte." You see, she had had
a good education, and could write like a clerk; she

had taught her son to read too—that was the ruin of him.

'Nobody knew how it came about, but that scoundrel Jacques got wind of the gold and took it, and went off to get drunk at Croisic. Old Cambremer, just as if it had happened on purpose, came in with his boat; and as he came up to the house he saw a scrap of paper floating about. He picked it up and took it in to his wife; and she dropped down, for she knew her own handwriting. Cambremer said not a word. He went over to Croisic, and heard there that his son was in the billiard-room. Then he sent for the good woman who kept the café, and said to her—

'"I told Jacques not to change a piece of gold that he will pay his score with: let me have it; I will wait at the door, and you shall have silver for it."

'The woman of the house brought him out the gold piece. Cambremer took it.

'"Good!" said he, and he went away home.

'All the town knew that. But this I know, and the rest of them have only a sort of general guess at how it was. He told his wife to set their room to rights; it is on the ground floor. He kindled a fire on the hearth, he lighted two candles, and put two chairs on one side of the fireplace, and a three-legged stool on the other. Then he bade his wife put out the suit he was married in, and to put on her wedding gown. He dressed himself; and then when he was dressed, he went out for his brother, and told him to keep watch outside the house, and give warning if he heard any sound on either beach, here by the sea or yonder on the salt marshes at Guérande. When he thought his wife must be dressed, he went in again; he loaded a gun, and hid it in the chimney corner.

'Back comes Jacques to the house. It was late when he came; he had been drinking and gambling up to ten o'clock; he had got some one to ferry him over at

Carnouf point.   His uncle heard him hail the boat, and went to look for him along the side of the salt marshes, and passed him without saying anything.

'When Jacques came in, his father spoke.

'"Sit you down there," he said, pointing to the stool. "You are before your father and mother; you have sinned against them, and they are your judges."

'Jacques began to bellow, for Cambremer's face twitched strangely.   The mother sat there, stiff as an oar.

'"If you make any noise, if you stir, if you don't sit straight up like a mast on your stool," said Pierre, pointing his gun at him, "I will shoot you like a dog."

'Cambremer's son grew mute as a fish, and all this time the mother said not a word.

'"Here is a bit of paper that wrapped up a Spanish gold coin.   That coin was in your mother's mattress. No one knew where it was except your mother.   I found the bit of paper floating on the water when I came in. Only this evening you changed the piece of Spanish gold at Mother Fleurant's, and your mother cannot find the coin in her mattress.—Explain yourself."

'Jacques said that he had not taken his mother's money, and that he had had the coin at Nantes.

'"So much the better," said Pierre. 'How can you prove it?"

'"I did have it."

'"You did not take your mother's coin?"

'"No."

'"Can you swear it on your salvation?"

'He was just going to swear, when his mother looked up and said—

'"Jacques, my child, take care; do not swear if it is not true. . . . You can repent and mend; there is still time," and she cried at that.

'"You are a So-and-so," said he; "you have always tried to ruin me."

'Cambremer turned white, and said, "What you have

just said to your mother goes to swell your account. Now, come to the point! Will you swear?"

'"Yes."

'"Stop a bit," said Pierre, "was there a cross on your coin like the mark the sardine merchant put on the coin he paid me?"

'Jacques grew sober at that, and began to cry.

'"That is enough talk," said Pierre. "I say nothing of what you have done before—I have no mind that a Cambremer should die in the market-place at Croisic. Say your prayers, and let us be quick! A priest is coming to hear your confession."

'The mother had gone out of the room that she might not hear her son's doom. As soon as she went out, Joseph Cambremer, the uncle, came in with the *recteur* from Piriac. To him Jacques would not open his mouth. He was shrewd; he knew his father well enough to feel sure that he would not kill him till he had confessed.

'"Thanks. Pardon us, sir," Cambremer said to the priest when Jacques continued obstinate. "I meant to give my son a lesson, and I beg you to say nothing about it.—As for you," he went on, turning to Jacques, "if you do not mend your ways, next time you go wrong shall be the last, and shrift or no shrift, I will make an end of it."

'He sent him off to bed. The young fellow believed him, and fancied that he could make things right with his father. He slept. His father sat up. When he saw his son fast asleep, he covered the young fellow's mouth with hemp, bound it tightly round with a strip of sail-cloth; then he tied him hand and foot. He writhed, he "shed tears of blood," so Cambremer told the justice. What would you have! His mother flung herself at the father's feet.

'"He is doomed," said Cambremer; "you will help me to put him into the boat."

'She would not help him, and Cambremer did it alone; he fastened him down in the bottom of the boat, and tied a stone round his neck, put out of the bay, reached the sea, and came out as far as the rock where he sits now. Then the poor mother, who had made her brother-in-law take her over, cried out in vain for mercy; it was like throwing a stone at a wolf. By the moonlight she saw the father take the son, towards whom her heart still yearned, and fling him into the water; and as there was not a breath of air stirring, she heard the gurgling sound, and then *nothing*—not an eddy, not a ripple; the sea is a famous keeper of secrets, that it is! When Cambremer reached the place to silence her moans, he found her lying like one dead. The two brothers could not carry her, so they had to put her in the boat that had carried her son, and they took her round home by way of the Croisic channel.

'Ah, well! *la belle Brouin,* as they called her, did not live the week out. She died, asking her husband to burn the accursed boat. Oh! he did it; yes, he did it. He himself was queer after that; he did not know what ailed him; he reeled about like a man who cannot carry his wine. Then he went off somewhere for ten days, and came back again to put himself where you saw him; and since he has been there, he has not said a word.'

The fisherman told us the story in a few minutes, in words even more simple than those that I have used. Working people make little comment on what they tell; they give you the facts that strike them, and interpret them by their own feelings. His language was as keenly incisive as the stroke of a hatchet.

'I shall not go to Batz,' said Pauline, when we reached the outer rim of the lake.

We went back to Croisic by way of the salt marshes, the fisherman guiding us through the labyrinth. He also had grown silent. Our mood had changed. Both

of us were deep in melancholy musings, and saddened by
the mournful story which explained the swift presentiment that we had felt at the sight of Cambremer.   We
had each of us sufficient knowledge of human nature to
fill in the outlines of the three lives that our guide had
sketched for us.   The tragedy of these three human
beings rose up before us as if we saw scene after scene of a
drama crowned by the father's expiation of an inevitable
crime.   We did not dare to look at the rocks where he
sat, the fate-bound soul who struck terror into a whole
country-side.   A few clouds overcast the sky.   The mist
rose on the horizon of the sea.   We were walking
through the most acrid dreariness that I have ever seen ;
the earth beneath our feet seemed sick and unwholesome
in these salt marshes which, with good reason, might be
called a cutaneous eruption on the face of the earth.
The ground is scored over in rough squares, with high
banks of grey earth about them ; each is full of brackish
water ; the salt rises to the surface.   These artificial
hollows are intersected by raised pathways, on which
the workmen stand to skim the surface of the pools
with long scrapers ; and the salt, when collected, is
deposited to drain on circular platforms set at even
distances, till it is fit to lay up in heaps.   For two hours
we skirted this dreary chessboard, where the salt stops
the growth of any green thing ; occasionally, at long
intervals, we came upon one or two *paludiers*, so they call
the men who work among the salt marshes.   These
workers, or it should rather be said, this race apart among
the Bretons, wears a special costume, a white jacket
rather like those that brewers wear.   They marry only
among themselves ; a girl belonging to this tribe has
never been known to marry any one but a *paludier*.
The hideous desolation of those swamps where the boggy
soil is scraped up into symmetrical heaps, the greyness of
the soil, from which every Breton flower shrinks in
disgust, was in keeping with the sadness within us.

T

We reached the spot where you cross an arm of the sea, the channel doubtless through which the salt water breaks in upon the low-lying land and leaves its deposits on the soil, and we were glad to see the scanty plant-life growing along the edge of the sand. As we crossed it, we saw the island in the lagoon where the Cambremers once lived, and turned our heads away.

When we reached our inn we noticed a billiard-table in the room on the ground floor, and when we learned that it was the only public billiard-table in Croisic, we made our preparations for departure that night, and on the morrow we went to Guérande.

Pauline was still depressed, and I myself felt a return of the burning sensation that scorches my brain. I was so grievously haunted by the visions of those three lives that I had conjured up, that Pauline said, 'Write the story, Louis, and the fever may take a turn.'

So, dear uncle, I have written the story for you; but our adventure has already undone the good effects of repose, the result of our stay here and at the Baths.

PARIS, *November* 20, 1834.

THE RED HOUSE

To Monsieur le Marquis de Custine.

ONCE upon a time (I forget the exact year) a Parisian banker, who had very extensive business relations with Germany, gave a dinner party in honour of one of the friends that merchants make in this place and that by correspondence, a sort of friendship that subsists for a long while between men who have never met. The friend, the senior partner of some considerable firm in Nuremberg, was a stout, good-natured German, a man of learning and of taste, more particularly in the matter of tobacco pipes. He was a typical Nuremberger, with a pleasant, broad countenance and a massive, square forehead, with a few stray fair hairs here and there ; a typical German, a son of the stainless and noble Fatherland, so fertile in honourable characters, preserving its manners uncorrupted even after seven invasions. The stranger laughed simply, listened attentively, and drank with marked enjoyment, seeming to like champagne perhaps as well as the pale red wines of the Johannisberg. Like nearly every German in nearly every book, he was named Hermann ; and in the quality of a man who does nothing with levity, he was comfortably seated at the banker's table, eating his way through the dinner with the Teutonic appetite renowned all over Europe, and thorough indeed was his manner of bidding adieu to all the works of the great Carême.

The master of the house had invited several intimate friends to do honour to his guest. These were for the most part capitalists or merchants, interspersed with a few pretty and agreeable women, whose light, graceful talk and frank manner harmonised with German open-heartedness. And, indeed, if you could have seen, as I had the pleasure of seeing, this blithe gathering of folk who had sheathed the active claws employed in raking-in wealth, that they might make the best of an opportunity of enjoying the pleasures of life, you would scarcely have found it in your heart to grudge high rates of interest or to revile defaulters. A man cannot always be in mischief. Even in the society of pirates, for instance, there must surely be a pleasant hour now and then when you may feel at your ease beneath the black flag.

'Oh, I do hope that before M. Hermann goes he will tell us another dreadful, thrilling German story!'

The words were uttered over the dessert by a pale, fair-haired young lady, who had doubtless been reading Hoffmann's tales and Sir Walter Scott's novels. She was the banker's only daughter, an irresistibly charming girl, whose education was being finished at the Gymnase; she was wild about the plays given there. The dinner party had just reached the period of lazy content and serene disinclination to talk that succeeds an excellent dinner in the course of which somewhat heavy demands have been made upon the digestion; when the guests lean back in their chairs and play idly with the gilded knife-blades, while their wrists repose lightly on the table edge; the period of decline when some torment apple pips, or knead a crumb of bread between thumb and finger, when the sentimental write illegible initials among the *débris* of the dessert, and the penurious count the stones on their plates, and arrange them round the edge, as a playwright marshals the supernumeraries at the back of the stage. These are minor gastronomical pleasures which Brillat-Savarin has passed over unnoticed, exhaustively as he has treated his subject in other respects.

The servants had disappeared. The dessert, like a squadron after an action, was quite disorganised, disarrayed, forlorn. In spite of persistent efforts on the part of the mistress of the house, the various dishes strayed about the table. People fixed their eyes on the Swiss views that adorned the grey walls of the dining-room. No one felt it tedious. The man has yet to be found who can mope while he digests a good dinner. At that time we like to sit steeped in an indescribable calm, a sort of golden mean between the two extremes of the thinker's musings and the sleek content of the ruminating brute, which should be termed the physical melancholy of gastronomy.

So the party turned spontaneously towards the worthy German, all of them delighted to listen to a tale, even if it should be a dull one. During this beatific pause, the mere sound of the voice of the one who tells the story is soothing to our languid senses; it is one more aid to passive enjoyment. As an amateur of pictures, I watched the faces, bright with smiles, lit up by the light of the tapers and flushed with good cheer; the different expressions produced piquant effects among the sconces, the porcelain baskets of fruit, and the crystal glasses.

One face, exactly opposite, particularly struck my imagination. It belonged to a middle-sized man, tolerably stout and jovial-looking; who from his manner and appearance seemed to be a stockbroker, and, so far as one could see, gifted with no extraordinary amount of brains. Hitherto I had not noticed him, but at that moment his face, obscured, to be sure, by a bad light, seemed to me to undergo a total change; it took a cadaverous hue, veined with purple streaks. You might have taken it for the ghastly countenance of a man in the death agony. Impassive as a painted figure in a diorama, he was staring stupidly at the facets of a crystal decanter-stopper, but he certainly took no heed of them ; he seemed to be deep in some visionary contemplation of the future or of the past. A long scrutiny of this dubious-looking face made me think.

'Is he ill?' I asked myself. 'Has he taken too much wine? Is he ruined by the fall of the funds? Is he thinking how to cheat his creditors?—Look!' I said to the lady who sat next to me, calling her attention to the stranger's face, 'that is a budding bankruptcy, is it not?'

'Oh!' she answered, 'if it were, he would be in better spirits.' Then, with a graceful toss of her head, she added : 'If that individual ever ruins himself, I will take the news to Pekin myself. He is a rather eccentric old gentleman worth a million in real estate ; he used to be a contractor to the Imperial armies. He married again, as a business speculation, but he makes his wife very happy for all that. He has a pretty daughter, whom for a very long time he would not recognise ; but when his son died by a sad accident in a duel, he was obliged to take her home, for he was not likely to have any more children. So all at once the poor girl became one of the richest heiresses in Paris. The loss of his only son threw the poor dear man into great grief, and he still shows signs of it at times.'

As she spoke the army contractor looked up, and our eyes met ; his expression made me shudder, it was so gloomy and so sad. Assuredly a whole life was summed up in that glance. Then in a moment he looked cheerful. He took up the glass stopper, put it unthinkingly into the mouth of the water decanter that stood on the table in front of him, and turned smilingly towards M. Hermann. The man was positively beaming with full-fed content, and had, no doubt, not two ideas in his head ; he had been thinking of nothing! I was in some sort ashamed to have thrown away my powers of divination *in animâ vili*, to have taken this thick-skulled capitalist as a subject. But while I was making my phrenological observations in pure waste, the good-natured German had flicked a few grains of snuff off his face and begun his story.

It would be a passably difficult matter to give it in the same words, with his not infrequent interruptions and wordy digressions ; so I have written it after my own fashion, omitting these defects of the Nuremberger's narrative, and helping myself to such elements of poetry and interest as it may possess, emulating the modesty of other writers who omit the formula *translated from the German* from their title-pages.

I.

THE IDEA AND THE DEED

'Towards the end of Vendémiaire, in the year VII. of the Republican era (a date that corresponds to the 20th of October, present style), two young men were making their way towards Andernach, a little town on the left bank of the Rhine, a few leagues from Coblentz. The travellers had set out from Bonn that morning, and now the day was drawing to a close. At that particular time a French army under command of General Augereau was keeping in check the Austrians on the right bank of the river. The headquarters of the Republican division were at Coblentz, and one of the demi-brigades belonging to Augereau's corps was quartered in Andernach.

'The two wayfarers were Frenchmen. At first sight of their blue and white uniforms, with red velvet facings, their sabres, and, above all, their caps covered with green oilcloth and adorned with a tricolour cockade, the German peasants themselves might have known them for a pair of army surgeons, men of science and of sterling worth, popular for the most part not only in the army, but also in the countries occupied by French troops. At that time many young men of good family, torn from their medical studies by General Jourdan's conscription law, not unnaturally preferred to continue their studies on the battlefield to compulsory service in the ranks, a life ill suited to their antecedents and unwarlike ambitions. Men of this stamp, studious, serviceable, peaceably inclined, did some good among so many evils, and found congenial spirits among the learned of the various countries invaded by the ruthless affranchisement of the Republic.

'These two, provided with a route of the road, and with assistant-surgeons' commissions signed by La Coste and Bernadotte, were on their way to join the demibrigade to which they were attached. Both belonged to well-to-do middle families in Beauvais, and traditions of gentle breeding and of provincial integrity had been a part of their inheritance. A curiosity quite natural in youth had brought them to the seat of war before the time fixed for entrance on active service, and they had come by the *diligence* as far as Strasbourg. Maternal prudence had suffered them to leave home with a very scanty supply of money, but they felt rich in the possession of a few louis ; and, indeed, at a time when assignats had reached the lowest point of depreciation, those few louis meant wealth, for gold was at a high premium.

'The two assistant-surgeons, aged twenty years at most, gave themselves up to the romance of their situation with all the enthusiasm of youth. They had traversed the Palatinate from Strasbourg to Bonn in the quality of artists, philosophers, and observers. When we have a scientific career before us, there are, in truth, at that age many natures within us ; and even while making love or travelling about, an assistant-surgeon should be laying the foundations of his future fame and fortune.

Accordingly, the pair had been carried away by the profound admiration that every well-read man must feel at the sight of the scenery of Swabia and the banks of the Rhine between Mayence and Cologne. They saw a vigorous and fertile country, an undulating green landscape full of strong contrasts and of memories of feudal times, and everywhere scarred by fire and sword. Louis XIV. and Turenne once before laid that fair land in ashes; heaps of ruins bear witness to the pride, or, it may be, to the prudence of the monarch of Versailles, who rased the wonderful castles which once were the glory of this part of Germany. You arrive at some conception of the German mind; you understand its dreaminess and its mysticism from this wonderful forest-land of theirs, full of remains of the Middle Ages, picturesque, albeit in ruins.

'The two friends had made some stay in Bonn with two objects in view—scientific knowledge and pleasure. The grand hospital of the Gallo-Batavian army and of Augereau's division had been established in the Electoral palace itself, and thither the two novices had gone to see their comrades, to deliver letters of recommendation to their chiefs, and to make their first acquaintance with the life of army surgeons. But with the new impressions, there as elsewhere, they parted with some of their national prejudices, and discovered that France had no monopoly of beautiful public buildings and landscapes. The marble columns that adorn the Electoral palace took them by surprise; they admired the magnificence of German architecture and found fresh treasures of ancient and modern art at every step.

'Now and again in the course of their wanderings toward Andernach their way led them over some higher peak among the granite hills. Through a clear space in the forest, or a chasm in the rocks, they caught a glimpse of the Rhine, a picture framed in the grey stone, or in some setting of luxuriant trails of green leaves.

Every valley, field-path, and forest was filled with autumn scents that conduce to musings and with signs of the aging of the year; the tree-tops were turning golden, taking warmer hues and shades of brown; the leaves were falling, but the sky was blue and cloudless overhead; the roads were dry, and shone like threads of gold across the country in the late afternoon sunlight.

'Half a league from Andernach the country through which the two friends were travelling lay in a silence as deep as if there were no war laying waste the beautiful land. They were following a goat track among the steep crags of bluish granite that rise like walls above the eddying Rhine, and before very long were descending the sloping sides of the ravine above the little town, nestling coyly at its foot on the river bank, its picturesque quay for the Rhine boatmen.

'"Germany is a very beautiful country!" cried one of the two, Prosper Magnan by name, as he caught sight of the painted houses of Andernach lying close together like eggs in a basket, among the trees and flower-gardens.

'For a few minutes they looked at the high-pitched roofs with their projecting beams, at the balconies and wooden staircases of all those peaceful dwellings, and at the boats swaying in the current by the quay.'

When M. Hermann mentioned the name of Prosper Magnan, my opposite neighbour, the army contractor, snatched up the decanter, poured himself out a glass of water, and drank it down at a gulp. This proceeding recalled my attention to him; I thought I saw a slight quiver in his hands and a trace of perspiration on his forehead.

'What is the army contractor's name?' I inquired of my gracious neighbour.

'His name is Taillefer,' said she.

'Are you feeling unwell?' I exclaimed, as this unaccountable being turned pale.

'Not at all, not at all,' he said, with a courteous gesture of acknowledgment. 'I am listening,' he said, with a nod to the rest of the party, for all eyes were turned at once upon him.

'I forget the other young man's name,' said M. Hermann. 'But, at any rate, from Prosper Magnan's confidences I learned that his friend was dark, lively, and rather thin. If you have no objection, I will call him Wilhelm for the sake of clearness in the story.' And the good German took up his tale again, after baptizing a French assistant surgeon with a German name, totally regardless of local colour and of the demands of Romanticism.

'So by the time these two young fellows reached Andernach night had fallen ; and they, fancying that it was too late to report themselves to their chiefs, make themselves known and obtain billets in a place already full of soldiers, made up their minds to spend their last night of freedom in an inn, about a hundred paces outside the town. They had seen it from the crags above, and had admired the warm colours of the house, heightened by the glow of the sunset. The whole building was painted red, and produced a piquant effect in the landscape, whether it was seen against the crowd of houses in the town, or as a mass of bright colour against a background of forest trees, or a patch of scarlet by the grey water's edge. Doubtless the inn owed its external decoration, and consequently its name, to the whim of the builder in some forgotten time. The colour had come to be literally a matter of custom to successive owners, for the inn had a name among the Rhine boatmen who frequented it. The sound of horses' hoofs brought the landlord of the Red House to the threshold.

'"*Pardieu !* gentlemen," cried he, "a little later you would have had to sleep out of doors like most of your countrymen bivouacking yonder at the other end of

Andernach.   The house is full.   If you positively must have a bed to sleep in, I have only my own room to offer you.   As for the horses, I can lay down some litter in a corner of the yard for them ; my stables are full of christened men this day.—The gentlemen will be from France ? " he went on after a brief pause.

'" From Bonn," cried Prosper, "and we have had nothing to eat since morning."

'" Oh ! as to victuals," said the landlord, jerking his head, "people come to the Red House for ten leagues round for wedding feasts.   You shall have a banquet fit for a prince, fish from the Rhine !   That tells you everything."

'When they had given over their tired beasts into the host's care, they left him to shout in vain for the stable folk, and went into the public room of the inn.   It was so full of dense white clouds blown from the pipes of a room-full of smokers, that at first they could not make out what kind of company they had fallen among ; but after they had sat for a while at a table, and put in practice the patience of travelled philosophers who know when it is useless to make a fuss, they gradually made out the inevitable accessories of a German inn.   The stove, the clock, the tables, pots of beer and long pipes, loomed out through the tobacco smoke ; so did the faces of the motley crew, Jews, Germans, and what not, with one or two rough boatmen thrown in.

'The epaulettes of a few French officers shone through the thick mist, and spurs and sabres clanked incessantly upon the flagstones.   Some were playing at cards, the rest quarrelled among themselves, or were silent, ate, or drank, and came or went.   A stout little woman, who wore the black velvet cap, blue stomacher embroidered with silver, the pincushion, bunch of keys, silver clasps, and plaited hair of the typical German landlady (a costume made so familiar in all its details by a host of prints that it is too well known to need description), came to the two friends and soothed their impatience, while she stimulated their interest in their supper with very remarkable skill.

'Gradually the noise diminished, the travellers went off one by one, the clouds of tobacco smoke cleared away. By the time that the table was set for the assistant surgeons, and the classic carp from the Rhine appeared, it was eleven o'clock, and the room was empty. Through the stillness of the night it was possible to hear faint noises of horses stamping or crunching their provender, the ripple of the Rhine, the vague indefinable sounds in an inn full of people when every one has retired to rest. Doors and windows opened or shut ; there was an inarticulate murmur of voices, or a name was called out in some room overhead. During this time of silence and of commotion, while the two Frenchmen were eating their supper and the landlord engaged in extolling Andernach, the meal, his Rhine wine, his wife, and the Republican army, for the benefit of his guests, the three heard, with a certain degree of interest, the hoarse shouts of boatmen and the rattling sound of a boat being moored alongside the quay. The innkeeper, doubtless accustomed to be hailed by the guttural cries of the boatmen, hurried out, and soon came in again with a short, stout man, a couple of the boat's crew following them with a heavy valise and several packages. As soon as the baggage was deposited in the room, the short man picked up his valise and seated himself without ceremony at the table opposite the two surgeons.

' " You can sleep on board," said he to the boatmen, "as the inn is full. All things considered, that will be the best way."

' " All the provisions I have in the house are here before you, sir," said the landlord, and he indicated the Frenchmen's supper. " I have not a crust of bread, and not so much as a bone——"

' " And no sauerkraut ? "

' " Not so much as would fill my wife's thimble ! As I had the honour of telling you just now, you can have no bed but the chair you are sitting on, and this is the only unoccupied room."

'At these words the short personage glanced at the landlord, at the room, and at the two Frenchmen, caution and alarm equally visible in the expression of his countenance.

'At this point,' said M. Hermann, interrupting himself, 'I should tell you that we never knew this stranger's real name, nor his history; we found out from his papers that he came from Aix-la-Chapelle, that he had assumed the name of Walhenfer, and owned a rather large pin-factory somewhere near Neuwied—that was all.

'He wore, like other manufacturers in that part of the world, an ordinary cloth overcoat, waistcoat and breeches of dark-green velvet, high boots, and a broad leather belt. His face was perfectly round, his manners frank and hearty, and during the evening he found it very difficult to disguise some inward apprehensions, or, it may be, cruel anxieties. The innkeeper always said that the German merchant was flying the country, and I learned later on that his factory had been burned down through one of the unlucky accidents so frequent in time of war. But in spite of the uneasy look that his face generally wore, its natural expression denoted good-humour and good-nature. He had good features, and a particularly noticeable personal trait was a thick neck, so white in contrast with a black cravat, that Wilhelm jokingly pointed it out to Prosper——'

Here M. Taillefer drank another glass of water.

'Prosper courteously invited the merchant to share their supper, and Walhenfer fell to without more ado, like a man who is conscious that he can repay a piece of civility. He set down his valise on the floor, put his feet upon it, took off his hat, drew his chair to the table, and laid down his gloves beside him, together with a pair of pistols, which he carried in his belt. The landlord quickly laid a cover for him, and the three began to satisfy their hunger silently enough.

'The room was so close and the flies so troublesome, that Prosper besought the landlord to open the window that looked out upon the quay to let in fresh air. This window was fastened by an iron bar that dropped into a socket on either side of the window frame, and for greater security, a nut fastened to each of the shutters received a bolt. It so happened that Prosper watched the landlord unfasten the window.

'But since I am going into these particulars,' M. Hermann remarked, 'I ought to describe the internal arrangements of the house; for the whole interest of the story depends on an accurate knowledge of the place.

'There were two entrance doors in the room where these three personages were sitting. One opened on to the road that followed the river bank to Andernach, and, as might be expected, just opposite the inn, there was a little jetty where the boat which the merchant had hired for his voyage was moored at that moment. The other door gave admittance to the inn-yard, a court shut in by very high walls, and at the moment full of horses and cattle, for human beings occupied the stables.

'The house door had been so carefully bolted and barred that, to save time, the landlord had opened the street door of the sitting-room to admit the merchant and the boatmen, and now, when he had opened the window at Prosper Magnan's instance, he set to work to shut this door, slipping the bolts and screwing the nuts.

'The landlord's bedroom, where the friends were to sleep, was next to the public room of the inn, and only separated from the kitchen, where the host and hostess were probably to pass the night, by a sufficiently thin partition wall. The maid-servant had just gone out to find a nook in some manger, or in the corner of a hay

loft somewhere or other. It will be readily understood
that the public room, the landlord's bedroom, and the
kitchen were in a manner apart from the rest of the
inn. The deep barking of two great dogs in the yard
indicated that the house had vigilant and wakeful
guardians.

' "How quiet it is, and what a glorious night!" said
Wilhelm, looking out at the sky when the landlord had
bolted the door. There was not a sound to be heard at
the moment save the rippling of the water.

' "Gentlemen," said the merchant, addressing the
Frenchmen, "allow me to offer you a bottle or two of
wine to wash down your carp. A glass will refresh us
after a tiring day. By the look of you and the condition
of your clothes, I can see that, like myself, you have come
a good way."

' The two friends accepted the proposal, and the landlord
went out through the kitchen to the cellar, doubtless
situated beneath that part of the establishment. About
the time that five venerable bottles appeared upon the
table, the landlord's wife had finished serving the supper.
She gave a housewife's glance over the dishes and round
the room, assured herself that the travellers had everything they were likely to want, and went back to the
kitchen. The four boon companions, for the host was
asked to join the party, did not hear her go off to bed;
but before long, in the pauses of the chat over the wine,
there came an occasional very distinct sound of snoring
from the loft above the kitchen where she was sleeping,
a sound rendered still more resonant by reason of the
thin plank floor. This made the guests smile, and the
landlord smiled still more.

' Towards midnight, when there was nothing left on
the table but cheese and biscuits, dried fruit, and good
wine, the whole party, and the young Frenchmen more
particularly, grew communicative. They talked about
their country, their studies, and the war. After a while

the conversation grew lively. Prosper Magnan drew
tears to the merchant's eyes when, with a Picard's frankness and the simplicity of a kindly and affectionate
nature, he began to imagine what his mother would be
doing while he, her son, was here on the bank of the
Rhine.

'"It is just as if I can see her," he said ; " she is reading
the evening prayer, the last thing at night ! She will
not forget me I know ; she is sure to say, 'Where is
my poor Prosper, I wonder ?' Then if she has won a
few sous at cards—of *your* mother perhaps," he added,
jogging Wilhelm's elbow—" she will be putting them in
the big red jar, where she keeps the money she is saving
up to buy those thirty acres that lie within her own
little bit of land at Lescheville. The thirty acres will
be worth something like sixty thousand francs. Good
meadow land it is ! Ah ! if I were to have it some day,
I would live all the rest of my life at Lescheville, and
want nothing better ! How often my father wanted
those thirty acres and the nice little stream that winds
along through the fields ! And, after all, he died and could
not buy the land. . . . I have played there many and
many a time !"

'" M. Walhenfer, haven't you also your *hoc erat in
votis* ? " asked Wilhelm.

'" Yes, sir, yes ! But it all came to me as it was,
and now . . ." the good man stopped short and said no
more.

'" For my own part," said the landlord, whose countenance was slightly flushed, " I bought a bit of meadow
last year that I had set my mind on these ten years past."

'So they chatted on, as folk will talk when wine has
unloosed their tongues, and struck up one of those
travellers' friendships that we are little chary of making
on a journey, in such a sort that when they rose to go to
their room Wilhelm offered his bed to the merchant.

'" You can take the offer without hesitation," he said,

U

"for Prosper and I can sleep together. It will not be the first time nor the last either, I expect. You are the oldest among us, and we ought to honour old age."

' "Pooh!" said the landlord, "there are several mattresses on our bed, one can be laid on the floor for you," and he went to shut the window with the usual clatter caused by this precaution.

' "I accept your offer," said the merchant, addressing Wilhelm. "I confess," he added, lowering his voice, and looking at the friends, "that I wanted you to make it. I feel that I cannot trust my boatmen; and I am not sorry to find myself in the company of two decent young fellows, two French military men, moreover, for the night. I have a hundred thousand francs in gold and diamonds in that valise."

' The two younger men received this incautious communication with a discreet friendliness that reassured the worthy German. The landlord helped his guests to shift one of the mattresses, and, when things had been arranged as comfortably as possible, wished them a good night and went off to bed. The merchant and the surgeons joked each other about their pillows. Prosper put Wilhelm's case of surgical instruments, as well as his own, under the mattress, to raise the end and supply the place of a bolster, just as Walhenfer, in an access of extreme caution, bestowed his valise under his bolster.

' "We are both going to sleep on our fortunes—you on your money, and I on my case of instruments! It remains to be seen whether my case will bring me in as much money as you have made."

' "You may hope so," said the merchant. " Honest work will accomplish most things, but you must have patience."

' Before very long Walhenfer and Wilhelm fell asleep. But whether it was because his bed was too hard, or he himself was over-tired and wakeful, or through some

unlucky mood of mind, Prosper Magnan lay broad
awake.   Imperceptibly his thoughts took an ill turn.
He could think of nothing but that hundred thousand
francs beneath the merchant's pillow.   For him a
hundred thousand francs was a vast fortune ready
made.   He began by laying out the money in endless
ways, building castles in the air, as we are all apt to do
with so much enjoyment just before we drop off to
sleep, when indistinct and hazy ideas arise in our minds,
and not seldom night and silence give a magical vivid-
ness to our thoughts.

'In these visions Prosper Magnan overtopped his
mother's ambitions; he bought the thirty acres of
meadow, and married a young lady in Beauvais, to
whose hand he could not aspire at present owing to
inequality of fortune.   With this wealth he planned
out a whole pleasant lifetime, saw himself the prosperous
father of a family, rich, looked up to in the neighbourhood, possibly even Mayor of Beauvais.   The Picard head
was on fire; he cast about for the means of realising
these dreams of his.   With extraordinary warmth of
imagination he set himself to plan out a crime, and gold
and diamonds were the most vivid and distinct portion
of a vision of the merchant's death; the glitter dazzled
him.   His heart beat fast.   He had committed a crime,
no doubt, by harbouring such thoughts as these.   The
spell of the gold was upon him; his moral nature was
intoxicated by insidious reasonings.   He asked himself
whether there was any reason why the poor German
should live, and imagined how it would have been if he
had never existed.   To put it briefly, he plotted out a
way to do the deed with complete impunity.

'The Austrians held the other bank of the Rhine; a
boat lay there under the windows; there were boatmen
there; he could cut the man's throat, fling him into the
Rhine, escape with the valise through a casement, bribe
the boatmen, and go over to the Austrian side.   He even

went so far as to count upon his surgeon's dexterity with the knife; he knew of a way of decapitating his victim before the sleeper could utter a single shriek . . .'

M. Taillefer wiped his forehead at this point, and again he drank a little water.

'Then Prosper Magnan rose—slowly and noiselessly. He assured himself that he had awakened nobody, dressed and went into the public room. Then, with the fatal lucidity of mind that suddenly comes at certain crises, with the heightened power of intuition and strength of will that is never lacking to criminals or to prisoners in the execution of their designs, he unscrewed the iron bars, and drew them from their sockets, and set them against the wall without the slightest sound, hanging with all his weight on to the shutters lest they should creak as they turned on their hinges. In the pale moonlight he could dimly see the objects in the room where Wilhelm and Walhenfer were sleeping.

'Then, he told me, he stopped short for a moment. His heart beat so hard and so heavily, that the sound seemed to ring through the room, and he stood like one dismayed as he heard it. He began to fear for his coolness; his hands shook, he felt as if he were standing on burning coals. But so fair a prospect depended upon the execution of his design, that he saw something like a providence in this dispensation of fate that had brought the merchant thither. He opened the window, went back to his room, took up his case, and looked through it for an instrument best adapted to his purpose.

'"And when I stood by the bed" (he told me this), "I asked God for His protection, unthinkingly."

'He had just raised his arm, and was summoning all his strength for the blow, when something like a voice cried within him, and he thought he saw a light. He flung down the surgical instrument on his bed, fled into the next room, and stood at the window. A profound horror of himself came over him, and feeling how

little he could trust himself, fearing to yield to the
fascination that held him, he sprang quickly out of
the window and walked along by the Rhine, acting as
sentinel, as it were, before the inn.   Again and again
he walked restlessly to and from Andernach, often also
his wanderings led him to the slope of the ravine which
they had descended that afternoon to reach the inn; but so
deep was the silence of the night, and so strong his dread
of arousing the watch-dogs, that he kept away from the
Red House, and lost sight altogether more than once of
the window that he had left open.   He tried to weary
himself out, and so to induce sleep.   Yet, as he walked
to and fro under the cloudless sky, watching the brilliant
stars, it may be that the pure night air and the melancholy
lapping of the water wrought upon him, and restored him
by degrees to moral sanity.   Sober reason completed the
work and dispelled that short-lived madness.   His education, the precepts of religion, and, above all things (so he
told me), visions of the homely life that he had led beneath
his father's roof, got the better of his evil thoughts.   He
thought and pondered for long, his elbow resting on a
boulder by the side of the Rhine; and when he turned to
go in again, he could not only have slept, so he said, but
have watched over millions of gold.

'When his honesty emerged strengthened and triumphant from that ordeal, he knelt in joy and ecstasy to
thank God; he felt as happy, light-hearted, and content
as on the day when he took the sacrament for the first
time, and felt not unworthy of the angels because he had
spent the day without sin in word, or thought, or deed.

'He went back again to the inn, shut the window
without care to move noiselessly, and went to bed at
once.   Mind and body were utterly exhausted, and sleep
overcame him.   He had scarcely laid his head on the
mattress before the dreamy drowsiness that precedes sound
slumber crept over him; when the senses grow torpid,
conscious life ebbs away, thought grows fragmentary,

and the last communications of sense to the brain are like the impressions of a dream.

'"How close the air is!" said Prosper to himself. "It is just as if I were breathing a damp mist . . ."

'Dimly he sought to account for this state of things by attributing it to the difference between the outside temperature in the pure country air and the closed room; but before long he heard a constantly recurring sound, very much like the slow drip of water from a leaking tap. On an impulse of panic terror, he thought of rising and calling the landlord, or the merchant, or Wilhelm; but, for his misfortune, he bethought himself of the wooden clock in the next room, fancied that the sound was the beat of the pendulum, and dropped off to sleep with this dim and confused idea in his head.'

'Do you want some water, M. Taillefer?' asked the master of the house, seeing the banker take up the empty decanter mechanically.

M. Hermann went on with his story after the slight interruption of the banker's reply.

'The next morning,' he went on, 'Prosper Magnan was awakened by a great noise. It seemed to him that he had heard shrill cries, and he felt that violent nervous tremor which we experience when we wake to a painful sensation that began during slumber. The thing that takes place in us when we "wake with a start," to use the common expression, has been insufficiently investigated, though it presents interesting problems to physiological science. The terrible shock, caused it may be by the too sudden reunion of the two natures in us that are almost always apart while we sleep, is usually momentary, but it was not so for the unlucky young surgeon. The horror grew, and his hair bristled hideously all at once, when he saw a pool of blood between his own mattress and Walhenfer's bedstead. The unfortunate German's head was lying on the floor, the body was still on the bed, all this blood had drained from the neck. Prosper Magnan saw Walhenfer's eyes unclosed and staring, saw red on the sheets that he had slept in, and even on his own hands, saw his own surgeon's knife on the bed, and fainted away on the blood-stained floor.

'"I was punished already for my thoughts," he said to me afterwards.

'When he came to himself again, he was sitting in a chair in the public room of the inn, a group of French soldiers round about him, and an inquisitive and interested crowd. He stared in dull bewilderment at a Republican officer who was busy taking down the depositions of several witnesses and drawing up an official report; he recognised the landlord and his wife, the two boatmen, and the maid-servant. The surgical instrument used by the murderer——'

Here M. Taillefer coughed, drew out his pocket-hand-kerchief, and wiped his forehead. His movements were so natural, that I alone noticed them; indeed, all eyes were fixed on M. Hermann with a kind of greedy interest. The army-contractor leant his elbow on the table, propped his head on his right hand, and looked fixedly at Hermann. From that time forward I saw no involuntary signs of agitation nor of interest in the tale, but his face was grave and corpse-like; he looked just as he had done while he was playing with the decanter-stopper.

'The surgical instrument used by the murderer lay on the table, beside the case with Prosper's pocket-book and papers. The crowd looked by turns at the young surgeon and at these convincing proofs of his guilt; he himself appeared to be dying; his dull eyes seemed to have no power of sight in them. A confused murmur outside made it evident that a crowd had gathered about the inn, attracted by the news of the murder, and perhaps by a wish to catch a sight of the criminal. The tramp of the sentries posted under the windows and the clanking of their weapons rose over the whispered talk of the populace. The inn itself was shut up, the courtyard was silent and deserted.

'The gaze of the officer who was drawing up the report was intolerable; Prosper Magnan felt some one grasp his hand; looked up to see who it was that stood by him among that unfriendly crowd, and recognised, by the uniform that he wore, the senior surgeon of the demi-brigade quartered in Andernach. So keen and merciless were those eyes, that the poor young fellow shuddered, and his head dropped on to the back of the chair. One of the men held vinegar for him to inhale, and Prosper regained consciousness at once; but his haggard eyes were so destitute of life and intelligence, that the senior surgeon felt his pulse, and spoke to the officer.

'"Captain," he said, "it is impossible to examine the man just now——"

'"Very well. Take him away," returned the captain, cutting the surgeon short, and speaking to a corporal who stood behind the junior's chair.

'"Confounded scoundrel!" the man muttered; "try at least to hold up your head before these German beggars, to save the honour of the Republic."

'Thus adjured, Prosper Magnan came to his senses, rose, and went forward a few paces; but when the door opened, when he felt the outer air, and saw the people crowding up, all his strength failed him, his knees bent under him, he tottered.

'"The confounded sawbones deserves to be put an end to twice over!—March, can't you!" said the two men on either side of him, on whom he leant.

'"Oh, the coward! the coward! Here he comes! here he comes! . . . There he is!"

'The words were uttered as by one voice, the clamorous voice of the mob who hemmed him in, insulting and reviling him at every step. During the time that it took to go from the inn to the prison, the trampling feet of the crowd and the soldiers who guarded him, the muttered talk of those about him, the sky above, the morning air, the streets of Andernach, the rippling murmur of the current of the Rhine, all reached him as dull, vague impressions, confused and dim, like all his experiences since his awakening. At times he thought that he had ceased to exist, so he told me afterwards.

'I myself was in prison just then,' said M. Hermann, interrupting himself. 'We are all enthusiasts at twenty. I was on fire to defend my country, and commanded a volunteer troop raised in and about Andernach. A short time previously, I managed to fall in one night with a French detachment of eight hundred men. There were two hundred of us at the most; my scouts had betrayed me. I was thrown into the prison at Andernach while they debated whether or no to have me shot by way of a warning to the country. The French, moreover, talked of reprisals, but the murder for which they had a mind to avenge themselves on me turned out to have been committed outside the Electorate. My father had obtained a reprieve of three days, to make application for my pardon to General Augereau, who granted it.

'So I saw Prosper Magnan as soon as he came into the prison at Andernach, and the first sight of him filled me with the deepest pity for him. Haggard, exhausted, and blood-stained though he was, there was a certain frankness in his face that convinced me of his innocence, and made a deep impression upon me. It was as if Germany stood there visibly before me—the prisoner with the long, fair hair and blue eyes, was for my imagination the very personification of the prostrate Fatherland,—this was no murderer, but a victim. As he went past my window, a sad, bitter smile lit up his face for a moment, as if a transitory gleam of sanity crossed a disordered brain. Such a smile would surely not be seen on a murderer's lips. When I next saw the turnkey, I asked him about his new prisoner.

'"He hasn't said a word since he went into his cell. He sits there with his head on his hands, and sleeps or thinks about his trouble. From what I hear the French-men saying, they will settle his case to-morrow, and he will be shot within twenty-four hours."

'That evening I lingered a little under his windows during the short time allowed for exercise in the prison yard. We talked together, and he told me very simply the story of his ill-luck, giving sufficiently straightforward answers to my different questions. After that conversa-tion I no longer doubted his innocence. I asked and obtained the favour of spending a few hours in his com-pany, and saw him in this way several times. The poor boy let me into the secret of his thoughts without reserve. In his own opinion, he was at once innocent and guilty. He remembered the hideous temptation which he had found strength to resist, and was afraid that he had committed the murder planned while he was awake in an access of somnambulism.

'"But how about your companion?" said I.

'"Oh, Wilhelm is incapable!——" he cried vehemently. He did not even finish the sentence. I grasped his hand at the warm-hearted outburst, so fraught with youth and virtue.

'"I expect he was frightened when he woke," he said; "he must have lost his presence of mind and fled——"

'"Without waking you?" I asked. "Why, in that case your defence is soon made, for Walhenfer's valise will not have been stolen."

'All at once he burst into tears.

'"Oh, yes, yes!" he cried; "I am not guilty. I can-not have killed him. I remember the dreams I had. I was at school, playing at prisoners-base. I could not have cut his throat while I was dreaming of running about."

'But in spite of the gleams of hope that quieted his mind somewhat at times, he still felt crushed by the weight of remorse. There was no blinking the fact he had raised his arm to strike the blow. He condemned himself, and considered that he was morally guilty after committing the crime in imagination.

'"And yet, I am not a bad fellow," he cried. "Oh, poor mother! Perhaps just now she is happily playing at cards with her friends in the little tapestried room at home. If she knew that I had so much as raised my hand to take another man's life—Oh! it would kill her! And I am in prison, and accused of murder! If I did not kill the man, I shall certainly be the death of my mother!"

'He shed no tears as he spoke. In a wild fit of frenzy, not uncommon among Picards, he sprang up, and if I had not forcibly restrained him, would have dashed his head against the wall.

'"Wait until you have been tried," I said. "You will be acquitted; you are innocent. And your mother——"

'"My mother," he cried wildly; "my mother will hear that I have been accused of murder, that is the main point. You always hear things like that in little places, and my poor mother will die of grief. Besides, I am not innocent. Do you care to know the whole truth! I feel that I have lost the virginity of my conscience."

'With those terrible words, he sat down, folded his arms across his chest, bowed his head, and fixed his eyes gloomily on the floor. Just then the turnkey came to bid me return to my cell; but loth to leave my companion when his discouragement seemed at its blackest, I clasped him in a friendly embrace. "Be patient," I said, "perhaps it will all come right. If an honest man's opinion can silence your doubts, I tell you this—that I esteem you and love you. Accept my friendship, and repose on my heart, if you cannot feel at peace with your own."

'On the following day, about nine o'clock, a corporal and four fusiliers came for the assistant surgeon. I heard the sound of the soldiers' footsteps, and went to the window;

our eyes met as he crossed the court. Never shall I
forget the glance fraught with so many thoughts and
forebodings, nor the resignation and indescribably sad
and melancholy sweetness in his expression. In that
dumb swift transference of thought, my friend conveyed
his testament to me; he left his lost life to the one friend
who was beside him at the last.

'That night must have been very hard to live through,
a very lonely night for him; but perhaps the pallor that
overspread his face was a sign of a newly acquired
stoicism, based on a new view of himself. Perhaps he
felt purified by remorse, and thought to expiate his sin
in this anguish and shame. He walked with a firm step;
and I noticed that he had removed the accidental stains
of blood that soiled his clothing the night before.

'"Unluckily I stained my hands while I was asleep;
I always was an uneasy sleeper," he had said, a dreadful
despair in the tones of his voice.

'I was told that he was about to be tried by a court-
martial. The division was to go forward in two days'
time, and the commandant of the demi-brigade meant to
try the criminal on the spot before leaving Andernach.

'While that court-martial was sitting, I was in an
agony of suspense. It was noon before they brought
Prosper Magnan back to prison. I was taking my prescribed exercise when he came; he saw me, and rushed
into my arms.

'"I am lost!" he said. "Lost beyond hope! Every
one here must look on me as a murderer——"

Then he raised his head proudly. "This injustice
has completely given me back my innocence," he said.
"If I had lived, my life must always have been troubled,
but my death shall be without reproach. But is there
anything beyond?"

'The whole eighteenth century spoke in that sudden
questioning. He was absorbed in thought.

'"But what did you tell them? What did they ask

you?" I cried. "Did you not tell them the simple truth as you told it to me?"

'He gazed at me for a minute, then after the brief, dreadful pause, he answered with a feverish readiness of speech—

'"First of all they asked me—'Did you go out of the inn during the night?'—'Yes,' I told them.—'How did you get out?'—I turned red, and answered, 'Through the window.'—'Then you must have opened it?'—'Yes,' I said.—'You set about it very cautiously; the landlord heard nothing!'—I was like one stupefied all the time. The boatmen swore that they had seen me walking, sometimes towards Andernach, sometimes towards the forest. I went to and fro many times, they said. I had buried the gold and diamonds. As a matter of fact the valise has not been found. Then, the whole time, I myself was struggling against remorse. Whenever I opened my mouth to speak, a merciless voice seemed to cry, '*You meant to do it!*' Everything was against me, even myself! . . . They wanted to know about my comrade, and I completely exonerated *him*. Then they said, 'One of you four must be guilty—you or your comrade, the innkeeper or his wife. All the doors and windows were shut fast this morning!' When they said that," he went on, "I had no voice, no strength, no spirit left in me. I was more sure of my friend than of myself; I saw very well that they thought us both equally guilty of the murder, and I was the clumsier one of the two. I tried to explain the thing by somnambulism; I tried to clear my friend; then I got muddled, and it was all over with me. I read my sentence in the judges' eyes. Incredulous smiles stole across their faces. That is all. The suspense is over. I am to be shot to-morrow—— I do not think of myself now," he said, "but of my poor mother."

'He stopped short and looked up to heaven. He shed no tears; his eyes were dry and contracted with pain.

'Frédéric ! . . .

'Ah ! I remember now ! The other one was called Frédéric . . . Frédéric ! Yes, I am sure that was the name,' M. Hermann exclaimed triumphantly.

I felt the pressure of my fair neighbour's foot; she made a sign to me, and looked across at M. Taillefer. The sometime army-contractor's hand drooped carelessly over his eyes, but through the fingers we thought we saw a smouldering blaze in them.

'Eh ?' she said in my ear, 'and now suppose that his name is Frédéric ?'

I gave the lady a side glance of entreaty to be silent. Hermann went on with his tale.

'"It is cowardly of Frédéric to leave me to my fate. He must have been afraid.   Perhaps he is hiding in the inn, for both our horses were there in the yard that morning.—What an inexplicable mystery it is !" he added, after a pause.   "Somnambulism, somnambulism ! I never walked in my sleep but once in my life, and then I was not six years old.   And I am to go out of this," he went on, striking his foot against the earth, "and take with me all the friendship that there is in the world !   Must I die twice over, doubting the friendship that began when we were five years old, and lasted through our school life and our student days !   Where is Frédéric ?"

'The tears filled his eyes.   We cling more closely to a sentiment than to our life, it seems !

'"Let us go in again," he said ; "I would rather be in my cell.   I don't mean them to see me crying.   I shall go bravely to my death, but I cannot play the hero in season and out of season, and I confess that I am sorry to leave my life, my fair life, and my youth.   I did not sleep last night ; I remembered places about my home when I was a child ; I saw myself running about in the meadows, perhaps it was the memories of those fields that led to my ruin.—I had a future before me" (he interrupted himself). " A dozen men, a sub-lieutenant who will cry, ' Ready ! present ! fire !' a roll of drums, and disgrace ! that is my future now ! Ah ! there is a God, there is a God, or all this would be too non-sensical."

' Then he grasped my arm, put his arms about me, and held me tightly to him.

' " Ah ! you are the last human soul to whom I can pour out my soul. *You* will be free again ! You will see your mother ! I do not know whether you are rich or poor, but no matter for that, you are all the world for me. . . . They cannot keep the fighting up for ever. Well and good then, when they make peace, go to Beauvais. If my mother survives the disastrous news of my death, you will find her out and tell her ' He was innocent,' to comfort her. " She will believe you," he went on. " I shall write to her as well, but you will carry my last look to her ; you shall tell her how that you were the last friend whom I embraced before I died. Ah ! how she will love you, my poor mother, you who have stood my friend at the last ! He was silent for a moment or two, the burden of his memories seemed too heavy for him to bear. " Here they are all strangers to me," he said, " the other surgeons and the men, and they all shrink from me in horror. But for you, my innocence must remain a secret between me and Heaven."

' I vowed to fulfil his last wishes as a sacred charge. He felt that·my heart went out to him, and was touched by my words. A little later the soldiers came back to take him before the court-martial again. He was doomed.

' I know nothing of the formalities or circumstances that attend a sentence of this kind ; I do not know whether there is any appeal, nor whether the young surgeon's defence was made according to rule and precedent, but he prepared to go to his death early on the morrow, and spent that night in writing to his mother.

'"We shall both be set free to-day," he said, smiling, when I went the next day to see him. "The general has signed your pardon, I hear."

'I said nothing, and gazed at him to engrave his features on my memory.

'A look of loathing crossed his face, and he said, "I have been a miserable coward! All night long I have been praying the very walls for mercy," and he looked round his cell. "Yes, yes," he went on, "I howled with despair, I rebelled against this, I have been through the most fearful inward conflict. . . . I was alone! . . . Now I am thinking of what others will say of me— Courage is like a garment that we put on. I must go decently to my death. . . . And so . . ."'

II.

A DOUBLE RETRIBUTION

'Oh! do not tell us any more!' cried the girl who had asked for the story, cuttin short the Nuremberger. 'I want to live in suspense, and to believe that he was saved. If I were to know to-night that they shot him, I should not sleep. You must tell me the rest to-morrow.'

We rose. M. Hermann offered his arm to my fair neighbour, who asked as she took it, 'They shot him, did they not?'

'Yes. I was there.'

'What, Monsieur, you could——'

'He wished it, Madame. It is something very ghastly to attend the funeral of a living man, your own friend who is not guilty of the crime laid to his charge. The poor young fellow never took his eyes off me. He seemed to have no life but mine left. "He wished," he said, "that I should bear his last sigh to his mother."'

'Well, and did you see her?'

'After the Peace of Amiens I went to France to take the glad tidings "He was innocent!" That pilgrimage was like a sacred duty laid upon me. But Mme. Magnan was dead, I found; she had died of consumption. I burned the letter I had brought for her, not without deep emotion. Perhaps you will laugh at my German high-flown sentimentality; but for me there was a tragedy most sublimely sad in the eternal silence which was about to swallow up those farewells uttered in vain from one grave to another grave, and heard by none, like the cry of some traveller in the desert surprised by a beast of prey.'

Here I broke in with a 'How if some one were to bring you face to face with one of the men in this drawing-room, and say, "There is the murderer!" would not that be another tragedy? And what would you do?'

M. Hermann took up his hat and went.

'You are acting like a young man, and very thought-lessly,' said the lady. 'Just look at Taillefer; there he sits in a low chair by the fire, Mademoiselle Fanny is handing him a cup of coffee; he is smiling. How could a murderer display such quiet self-possession as that, after a story that must have been torture to him. He looks quite patriarchal, does he not?'

'Yes; but just ask him if he has been with the army in Germany!' I exclaimed.

'Why not?' and with the audacity rarely lacking in womankind when occasion tempts, or curiosity gets the better of her, my fair neighbour went across to the army-contractor.

'Have you been in Germany, M. Taillefer?' quoth she.

Taillefer all but dropped his saucer.

'I, Madame?—No, never.'

x

'Why, what is that you are saying, Taillefer ?' protested the banker, chiming in. 'You were in the Wagram campaign, were you not—on the victualling establishment ?'

'Oh yes!' answered Taillefer; 'I was there, that once.'

'You are wrong about him; he is a good sort of man,' decided the lady when she came back to me.

'Very well,' said I to myself, 'before this evening is over I will drive the murderer out of the mire in which he is hiding.'

There is a phenomenon of consciousness that takes place daily beneath our eyes, so commonplace that no one notices it, and yet there are astounding depths beneath it. Two men meet in a drawing-room who have some cause to disdain or to hate each other; perhaps one of them knows something which is not to the credit of the other; perhaps it is a condition of things that is kept a secret; perhaps one of them is meditating a revenge; but both of them are conscious of the gulf that divides them, or that ought to divide them. Before they know it, they are watching each other and absorbed in each other; some subtle emanation of their thought seems to distil from every look and gesture; they have a magnetic influence. Nor can I tell which has the more power of attraction—revenge or crime, hatred or contempt. Like some priest who cannot consecrate the house where an evil spirit abides, the two are ill at ease and suspicious; one of them, it is hard to say which, is polite, and the other sullen; one of them turns pale or red, and the other trembles, and it often happens that the avenger is quite as cowardly as the victim. For very few of us have the nerve to cause pain, even if it is necessary pain, and many a man passes over a matter or forgives from sheer hatred of fuss or dread of making a tragical scene.

With this inter-susceptibility of minds, and apprehensiveness of thought and feeling, there began a mysterious struggle between the army-contractor and me. Ever since my interruption of M. Hermann's story he had shunned my eyes. Perhaps in like manner he looked none of the party in the face. He was chatting now with the inexperienced Fanny, the banker's daughter; probably, like all criminals, he felt a longing to take shelter with innocence, as if the mere proximity of innocence might bring him peace for a little. But though I stood on the other side of the room, I still listened to all that he said; my direct gaze fascinated him. When he thought he could glance at me in turn, unnoticed, our eyes met, and his eyelids fell directly. Taillefer found this torture intolerable, and hastened to put a stop to it by betaking himself to a card-table. I backed his opponent, hoping to lose my money. It fell out as I had wished. The other player left the table, I cut in, and the guilty man and I were now face to face.

'Monsieur,' I said, as he dealt the cards, 'will you be so good as to begin a fresh score?' He swept his counters from right to left somewhat hastily. The lady, my neighbour at dinner, passed by; I gave her a significant glance.

'M. Frédéric Taillefer,' I asked, addressing my opponent, 'are you related to a family in Beauvais with whom I am well acquainted?'

'Yes, sir.' He let the cards fall, turned pale, hid his face in his hands, begged one of his backers to finish the game for him, and rose.

'It is too warm here,' he gasped; 'I am afraid . . .'

He did not finish his sentence. An expression of horrible anguish suddenly crossed his face, and he hurried out of the room; the master of the house following him with what appeared to be keen anxiety. My neighbour and I looked at each other, but her face was

overcast by indescribable sadness; there was a tinge
of bitterness in it.

'Is your behaviour very merciful?' she asked, as I
rose from the card-table, where I had been playing and
losing. She drew me into the embrasure of the window
as she spoke. 'Would you be willing to accept the
power of reading all hearts if you could have it? Why
interfere with man's justice or God's? We may
escape the one; we shall never escape the other. Is
the prerogative of a President of a Court of Assize so
enviable? And you have all but done the executioner's
office as well——'

'After sharing and stimulating my curiosity,' I said,
'you are lecturing me!'

'You have made me think,' she answered.

'So it is to be peace to scoundrels, and woe to the
unfortunate, is it? Let us down on our knees and
worship gold! But shall we change the subject?' I
said with a laugh. 'Please look at the young lady who
is just coming into the room.'

'Well?'

'I met her three days ago at a ball at the Neapolitan
embassy, and fell desperately in love. For pity's sake,
tell me who she is. No one could tell me ···'

'That is Mlle. Victorine Taillefer!'

Everything swam before my eyes; I could scarcely
hear the tones of the speaker's voice.

'Her stepmother brought her home only a while ago
from the convent where she has been finishing her education somewhat late. . . . For a long time her father
would not recognise her. She comes here to-day for the
first time. She is very handsome—and very rich!'

A sardonic smile went with the words. Just as she
spoke, we heard loud cries that seemed to come from an
adjoining room; stifled though they were, they echoed
faintly through the garden.

'Is not that M. Taillefer's voice?' I asked. We

both listened intently to the sounds, and fearful groans reached our ears.   Just then our hostess hurried towards us and closed the window.

'Let us avoid scenes,' she said to us.   'If Mlle. Taillefer were to hear her father, it would be quite enough to send her into a fit of hysterics.'

The banker came back to the drawing-room, looked for Victorine, and spoke a few low words in her ear. The girl sprang at once towards the door with an exclamation, and vanished.   This produced a great sensation.   The card-parties broke up ; every one asked his neighbour what had happened.   The buzz of talk grew louder, and groups were formed.

'Has M. Taillefer ——— ?' I began.

'Killed himself ?' put in my sarcastic friend.   'You would wear mourning for him with a light heart, I can see.'

'But what can have happened to him ? '

'Poor man !' (it was the lady of the house who spoke) 'he suffers from a complaint—I cannot recollect the name of it, though M. Brousson has told me about it often enough—and he has just had a seizure.'

'What kind of complaint is it ?' asked an examining magistrate suddenly.

'Oh, it is something dreadful,' she answered ; 'and the doctors can do nothing for him.   The agony must be terrible.   Taillefer had a seizure, I remember, once, poor man, when he was staying with us in the country; I was obliged to go to a neighbour's house so as not to hear him ; his shrieks are fearful ; he tries to kill himself; his daughter had to have him put into a strait waistcoat and tied down to his bed.   Poor man ! he says there are live creatures in his head gnawing his brain ; it is a horrible, sawing, shooting pain that throbs through every nerve.   He suffers so fearfully with his head that he did not feel the blisters that they used to apply at one time to draw the inflammation ; but M.

Brousson, his present doctor, forbade this ; he says that
it is nervous inflammation, and puts leeches on the
throat, and applies laudanum to the head ; and, indeed,
since they began this treatment the attacks have been
less frequent ; he seldom has them oftener than once
a year, in the late autumn. When he gets over one
of these seizures, Taillefer always says that he would
rather be broken on the wheel than endure such agony
again.'

'That looks as if he suffered considerably ! ' said a
stockbroker, the wit of the party.

'Oh ! last year he very nearly died,' the lady went
on. 'He went alone to his country-house on some
urgent business ; there was no one at hand perhaps, for
he lay stiff and stark, like one dead, for twenty-two
hours. They only saved his life by a scalding hot
bath.'

'Then is it some kind of tetanus ? ' asked the stockbroker.

'I do not know,' returned she. 'He has had the
complaint nearly thirty years ; it began while he was
with the army. He says that he had a fall on a boat,
and a splinter got into his head, but Brousson hopes to
cure him. People say that in England they have found
out a way of treating it with prussic acid, and that you
run no risks——'

A shrill cry, louder than any of the preceding ones,
rang through the house. The blood ran cold in our
veins.

'There !' the banker's wife went on, 'that is just
what I was expecting every moment. It makes me
start on my chair and creep through every nerve. But—
it is an extraordinary thing !—poor Taillefer, suffering
such unspeakable pain as he does, never runs any risk of
his life ! He eats and drinks as usual whenever he has
a little respite from that ghastly torture. . . . Nature
has such strange freaks. Some German doctor once told

him that it was a kind of gout in the head ; and Brousson's opinion was pretty much the same.'

I left the little group about our hostess and went out with Mlle. Taillefer. A servant had come for her. She was crying.

' *Oh, mon Dieu, mon Dieu !* ' she sobbed ; ' how can my father have offended heaven to deserve such suffering as this ? . . . So kind as he is.'

I went downstairs with her, and saw her into the carriage ; her father was lying doubled up inside it. Mlle. Taillefer tried to smother the sound of her father's moaning by covering his mouth with a handkerchief. Unluckily, he saw me, and his drawn face seemed further distorted, a scream of agony rent the air, he gave me a dreadful look, and the carriage started.

That dinner party and the evening that followed it was to exercise a painful influence on my life and on my views. Honour and my own scruples forbade me to connect myself with a murderer, no matter how good a husband and father he might be, and so I must needs fall in love with Mlle. Taillefer. It was well-nigh incredible how often chance drew me to visit at houses where I knew I might meet Victorine. Again and again, when I had pledged myself to renounce her society, the evening would find me hovering about her. The pleasures of this life were immense. It gave the colour of an illicit passion to this unforbidden love, and a chimerical remorse filled up the measure of my bliss. I scorned myself when I greeted Taillefer, if by accident he was with his daughter ; but, after all, I bowed to him.

Unluckily, in fact, Victorine, being something more than a pretty girl, was well read, charming, and gifted in no small degree, without being in the least a blue stocking, without the slightest taint of affectation. There is a certain reserve in her light talk, and a pensive

graciousness about her that no one could resist. She
liked me, or, at any rate, she allowed me to think so ;
there was a certain smile that she kept for me ; for me the
tones of her voice grew sweeter still. Oh ! she cared
about me, but she worshipped her father ; she would
praise his kindness to me, his gentleness, his various
perfections, and all her praises were like so many daggers
thrust into my heart.

At length I all but became an accessory after the
fact, an accomplice in the crime which had laid the
foundation of the wealth of the Taillefers. I was fain
to ask for Victorine's hand. I fled. I travelled abroad.
I went to Germany and to Andernach. But I came
back again, and Victorine was looking thinner and paler
than her wont. If she had been well and in good spirits,
I should have been safe ; but now the old feeling for her
was rekindled with extraordinary violence.

Fearing lest my scruples were degenerating into
monomania, I resolved to convene a Sanhedrim of
consciences that should not have been tampered with,
and so to obtain some light on this problem of the
higher morality and philosophy. The question had only
become more complex since my return.

So the day before yesterday I assembled those among
my friends whom I looked upon as notably honest,
scrupulous, and honourable. I asked two Englishmen,
a secretary to the Embassy and a Puritan ; a retired
Minister, in the character of matured worldly wisdom ;
a few young men still under the illusions of inexperiences ;
a priest, an elderly man ; my old guardian, a simple-
hearted being, who gave me the best account of his
management of my property that ever trustee has been
known to give in the annals of the Palais ; an advocate, a
notary, and a judge,—in short, all social opinions were
represented, and all practical wisdom. We had begun by
a good dinner, good talk, and a deal of mirth ; and over
the dessert I told my story plainly and simply (suppress-

ing the name of my lady-love), and asked for sound counsel.

'Give me your advice,' I said to my friends as I came to an end. 'Go thoroughly into the question as if it were a point of law. I will have an urn and billiard-balls brought round, and you shall vote for or against my marriage, the secrecy of the ballot shall be scrupulously observed.'

Deep silence prevailed all at once. Then the notary declined to act.

'There is a contract to draw up,' he alleged.

Wine had had a quietening effect on my guardian; indeed, it clearly behoved me to find a guardian for *him* if he was to reach his home in safety.

'I see how it is!' I said to myself. 'A man who does not give me an opinion is telling me pretty forcibly what I ought to do.'

There was a general movement round the table. A landowner, who had subscribed to a fund for putting a headstone to General Foy's grave and providing for his family, exclaimed—

'"Even, as virtue, crime hath its degrees."'

'The babbler,' said the Minister in a low voice, as he nudged my elbow.

'Where is the difficulty?' asked a duke, whose property consisted of lands confiscated from Protestants after the Revocation of the Edict of Nantes.

The advocate rose to his feet.

'In law,' opined the mouthpiece of Justice, 'the case before us presents no difficulty whatever. Monsieur le Duc is right! Is there not a statute of limitations? Begin to inquire into the origins of a fortune, and where should we all of us be? This is a matter of conscience, and not of law. If you must drag the case before some tribunal, the confessional is the proper place in which to hear it.'

And the Code incarnate, having said his say, sat down

and drank a glass of champagne. The man intrusted with the interpretation of the Gospel, the good priest, spoke next.

'God has made us weak,' he said with decision. 'If you love the criminal's heiress, marry her; but content yourself with her mother's property, and give her father's money to the poor.'

'Why, in all likelihood the father only made a great match because he had made money first,' cried one of the pitiless quibblers that you meet with everywhere. 'And it is just the same with every little bit of good fortune—it all came of his crime!'

'The fact that the matter can be discussed is enough to decide it! There are some things which a man cannot weigh and ponder,' cried my guardian, thinking to enlighten the assembly by this piece of drunken gravity.

'True!' said the secretary to the Embassy.

'True!' exclaimed the priest, each meaning quite differently.

A doctrinaire, who escaped being elected by a bare hundred and fifty votes out of a hundred and fifty-five, rose next.

'Gentlemen,' said he, 'this phenomenal manifestation of the intellectual nature is one of the most strongly marked instances of an exception to the normal condition of things, the rules which society obeys. The decision, therefore, on an abnormal case should be an extemporaneous effort of the conscience, a sudden conception, a delicate discrimination of the inner consciousness, not unlike the flashes of insight that constitute perception in matters of taste. . . . Let us put it to the vote.'

'Yes, let us put it to the vote,' cried the rest of the party.

Each was provided with two billiard-balls—one white, the other red. White, the colour of virginity, was to proscribe marriage; red to count in favour of it. My scruples prevented me from voting. My friends being seventeen in number, nine made a decisive majority. We grew excited and curious as each dropped his ball into the narrow-mouthed wicker basket, which holds the numbered balls when players draw for their places at pool, for there was a certain novelty in this process of voting by ballot on a nice point of conduct. When the basket was turned out there were nine white balls. To me this did not come as a surprise; but it occurred to me to count up the young men of my own age among this Court of Appeal. There were exactly nine of these casuists; one thought had been in all their minds.

'Aha!' I said to myself, 'there was a unanimous feeling against the marriage in their minds, and a no less unanimous verdict in favour of it among the rest! Here is a fix, and how am I to get out of it?'

'Where does the father-in-law live?' one of my school-fellows, less crafty than the rest, asked carelessly.

'There is no longer a father-in-law in the case!' I exclaimed. 'A while ago my conscience spoke sufficiently plainly to make your verdict superfluous. And if it speaks more uncertainly to-day, here are the inducements that led me to waver. Here is the tempter—this letter that I received two months ago; and I drew a card from my pocket-book and held it up.

'*You are requested to be present,*' so it ran, '*at the funeral and burial service of*

M. JEAN-FRÉDÉRIC TAILLEFER

of the firm of Taillefer and Company, sometime contractor of provisions to the Army, late Chevalier of the Legion of Honour and of the Order of the Golden Spur, Captain of the First Company of Grenadiers of the National Guard, Paris: who died on May 1st, at his house in the Rue Joubert. The interment will take place,' and so forth, and so forth.

'*On behalf of,*' and so forth.

'What am I to do now?' I continued. 'I will just put the question roughly before you. There is unquestionably a pool of blood on Mlle. Taillefer's estates. Her father's property is one vast *Aceldama*. . . . Granted! But, then, Prosper Magnan has no representatives, and I could not find any traces of the family of the pin-maker who was murdered that night at Andernach. To whom should the fortune be returned? And ought it all to be returned? Have I any right to betray a secret discovered by accident, to add a severed human head to an innocent girl's marriage portion, to give her ugly dreams, to destroy her pleasant illusions, to kill the father she loved a second time, by telling her that there is a dark stain on all her wealth?

'I have borrowed a *Dictionary of Cases of Conscience* from an old ecclesiastic, and found therein no solution whatever of my doubts. Can you make a religious foundation for the souls of Prosper Magnan and Walhenfer and Taillefer now midway through this nineteenth century of ours? And as for endowing a charitable institution or awarding periodic prizes to virtue—most of our charitable institutions appear to me to be harbouring scoundrels, and the prize of virtue would fall to the greatest rogues.

'And not only so. Would these investments, more or less gratifying to vanity, be any reparation? And is it my place to make any? Then I am in love, passionately in love. My love has come to be my life. If, without any apparent reason, I propose that a young girl, accustomed to splendour and elegance, and a life abundant in all the luxuries art can devise, a girl who indolently enjoys Rossini's music at the Bouffons,—if to her I should propose that she should rob herself of fifteen hundred thousand francs for the benefit of aged imbeciles and problematical scrofula patients, she would laugh and turn her back upon me, or her confidante would take me for a wag who makes jokes in poor taste. If in an ecstasy of love I extol the charms of humble life in a cottage by the Loire, if I ask her to give up, for my sake, her life in Paris, it would be a virtuous lie to begin with, and probably would end in a sad experience for me, for I should lose the girl's heart; she is passionately fond of dancing and of pretty dresses, and, for the time being, of me. Enter some smart stripling of an officer with a nicely curled moustache, who shall play the piano, rave about Byron, and mount a horse gracefully, and I shall be supplanted. What is to be done? Gentlemen, advise me, for pity's sake?'

Then one of the party, who hitherto had not breathed a word, the Englishman with a Puritanical cast of face, not unlike the father of Jeanie Deans, shrugged his shoulders.

'Idiot that you were,' he said. 'What made you ask him if he came from Beauvais?'

PARIS, *May* 1831.

THE ELIXIR OF LIFE

To the Reader

AT the very outset of the writer's literary career, a friend, long since dead, gave him the subject of this Study. Later on he found the same story in a collection published about the beginning of the present century. To the best of his belief, it is some stray fancy of the brain of Hoffmann of Berlin; probably it appeared in some German almanack, and was omitted in the published editions of his collected works. The *Comédie Humaine* is sufficiently rich in original creations for the author to own to this innocent piece of plagiarism; when, like the worthy La Fontaine, he has told unwittingly, and after his own fashion, a tale already related by another. This is not one of the hoaxes in vogue in the year 1830, when every author wrote his 'tale of horror' for the amusement of young ladies. When you have read the account of Don Juan's decorous parricide, try to picture to yourself the part which would be played under very similar circumstances by honest folk who, in this nineteenth century, will take a man's money and undertake to pay him a life annuity on the faith of a chill, or let a house to an ancient lady for the term of her natural life? Would they be for resuscitating their clients? I should dearly like a connoisseur in consciences to consider how far there is a resemblance between a Don Juan and fathers who marry their children to great expectations. Does humanity, which, according to certain philosophers, is making progress, look on the art of waiting for dead men's shoes as a step in the right direction? To this art we owe several honourable professions, which open up ways of living on death. There are people who rely entirely on an expected

334

demise ; who brood over it, crouching each morning upon a corpse, that serves again for their pillow at night. To this class belong bishops' coadjutors, cardinals' supernumeraries, *tontiniers*, and the like. Add to the list many delicately scrupulous persons eager to buy landed property beyond their means, who calculate with dry logic and in cold blood the probable duration of the life of a father or of a stepmother, some old man or woman of eighty or ninety, saying to themselves, 'I shall be sure to come in for it in three years' time, and then——' A murderer is less loathsome to us than a spy. The murderer may have acted on a sudden mad impulse ; he may be penitent and amend ; but a spy is always a spy, night and day, in bed, at table, as he walks abroad ; his vileness pervades every moment of his life. Then what must it be to live when every moment of your life is tainted with murder ? And have we not just admitted that a host of human creatures in our midst are led by our laws, customs, and usages to dwell without ceasing on a fellow-creature's death. There are men who put the weight of a coffin into their deliberations as they bargain for Cashmere shawls for their wives, as they go up the staircase of a theatre, or think of going to the Bouffons, or of setting up a carriage ; who are murderers in thought when dear ones, with the irresistible charm of innocence, hold up childish foreheads to be kissed with a ' Good-night, father ! ' Hourly they meet the gaze of eyes that they would fain close for ever, eyes that still open each morning to the light, like Belvidero's in this Study. God alone knows the number of those who are parricides in thought. Picture to yourself the state of mind of a man who must pay a life annuity to some old woman whom he scarcely knows ; both live in the country with a brook between them, both sides are free to hate cordially, without offending against the social conventions that require two brothers to wear a mask if the older will succeed to the entail, and the other to the fortune of a younger son. The whole civilisation of Europe turns upon the principle of hereditary succession as upon a pivot ; it would be madness to subvert the principle ; but could we not, in an age that prides itself upon its mechanical inventions, perfect this essential portion of the social machinery ?

If the author has preserved the old-fashioned style of address *To the Reader* before a work wherein he endeavours to represent all literary forms, it is for the purpose of making a remark that applies to several of the Studies, and very specially to this. Every one of his compositions has been based upon ideas more or less novel, which, as it seemed to him, needed literary expression; he can claim priority for certain forms and for certain ideas which have since passed into the domain of literature, and have there, in some instances, become common property; so that the date of the first publication of each Study cannot be a matter of indifference to those of his readers who would fain do him justice.

Reading brings us unknown friends, and what friend is like a reader! We have friends in our own circle who read nothing of ours. The author hopes to pay his debt, by dedicating this work *Diis ignotis*.

———

ONE winter evening, in a princely palace at Ferrara, Don Juan Belvidero was giving a banquet to a prince of the house of Este. A banquet in those times was a marvellous spectacle which only royal wealth or the power of a mighty lord could furnish forth. Seated about a table lit up with perfumed tapers, seven laughter-loving women were interchanging sweet talk. The white marble of the noble works of art about them stood out against the red stucco walls, and made strong contrasts with the rich Turkey carpets. Clad in satin, glittering with gold, and covered with gems less brilliant than their eyes, each told a tale of energetic passions as diverse as their styles of beauty. They differed neither in their ideas nor in their language; but the expression of their eyes, their glances, occasional gestures, or the tones of their voices supplied a commentary, dissolute, wanton, melancholy, or satirical, to their words.

One seemed to be saying—'The frozen heart of age might kindle at my beauty.'

Another—'I love to lounge upon cushions, and think with rapture of my adorers.'

A third, a neophyte at these banquets, was inclined to blush. 'I feel remorse in the depths of my heart! I am a Catholic, and afraid of hell. But I love you, I love you so that I can sacrifice my hereafter to you.'

The fourth drained a cup of Chian wine. 'Give me a joyous life!' she cried; 'I begin life afresh each day with the dawn. Forgetful of the past, with the intoxication of yesterday's rapture still upon me, I drink deep of life—a whole lifetime of pleasure and of love!'

The woman who sat next to Juan Belvidero looked at him with a feverish glitter in her eyes. She was silent. Then—'I should need no hired bravo to kill my lover if he forsook me!' she cried at last, and laughed, but the marvellously wrought gold comfit box in her fingers was crushed by her convulsive clutch.

'When are you to be Grand Duke?' asked the sixth. There was the frenzy of a Bacchante in her eyes, and her teeth gleamed between the lips parted with a smile of cruel glee.

'Yes, when is that father of yours going to die?' asked the seventh, throwing her bouquet at Don Juan with bewitching playfulness. It was a childish girl who spoke, and the speaker was wont to make sport of sacred things.

'Oh! don't talk about it,' cried Don Juan, the young and handsome giver of the banquet. 'There is but one eternal father, and, as ill luck will have it, he is mine.'

The seven Ferrarese, Don Juan's friends, the Prince himself, gave a cry of horror. Two hundred years later, in the days of Louis xv., people of taste would have laughed at this witticism. Or was it, perhaps, that at the outset of an orgy there is a certain unwonted lucidity of mind? Despite the taper light, the clamour of the senses, the gleam of gold and silver, the fumes of wine, and the exquisite beauty of the women, there may perhaps have been in the depths of the revellers' hearts some struggling glimmer of reverence for things divine and

Y

human, until it was drowned in glowing floods of wine ! Yet even then the flowers had been crushed, eyes were growing dull, and drunkenness, in Rabelais' phrase, had 'taken possession of them down to their sandals.'

During that brief pause a door opened ; and as once the Divine presence was revealed at Belshazzar's feast, so now it seemed to be manifest in the apparition of an old white-haired servant, who tottered in, and looked sadly from under knitted brows at the revellers. He gave a withering glance at the garlands, the golden cups, the pyramids of fruit, the dazzling lights of the banquet, the flushed scared faces, the hues of the cushions pressed by the white arms of the women.

'My Lord, your father is dying ! ' he said ; and at those solemn words, uttered in hollow tones, a veil of crape seemed to be drawn over the wild mirth.

Don Juan rose to his feet with a gesture to his guests that might be rendered by, ' Excuse me ; this kind of thing does not happen every day.'

Does it so seldom happen that a father's death sur-prises youth in the full-blown splendour of life, in the midst of the mad riot of an orgy ? Death is as unex-pected in his caprice as a courtesan in her disdain ; but Death is truer—Death has never forsaken any man.

Don Juan closed the door of the banqueting-hall ; and as he went down the long gallery, through the cold and darkness, he strove to assume an expression in keep-ing with the part he had to play ; he had thrown off his mirthful mood, as he had thrown down his table napkin, at the first thought of this *rôle*. The night was dark. The mute servitor, his guide to the chamber where the dying man lay, lighted the way so dimly, that Death, aided by cold, silence, and darkness, and it may be by a reaction of drunkenness, could send some sober thoughts through the spendthrift's soul. He examined his life, and became thoughtful, like a man involved in a lawsuit on his way to the Court.

Bartolommeo Belvidero, Don Juan's father, was an old man of ninety, who had devoted the greatest part of his life to business pursuits. He had acquired vast wealth in many a journey in magical Eastern lands, and knowledge, so it was said, more valuable than the gold and diamonds, which had almost ceased to have any value for him.

' I would give more to have a tooth in my head than for a ruby,' he would say at times with a smile. The indulgent father loved to hear Don Juan's story of this and that wild freak of youth. 'So long as these follies amuse you, dear boy—' he would say laughingly, as he lavished money on his son. Age never took such pleasure in the sight of youth ; the fond father did not remember his own decaying powers while he looked on that brilliant young life.

Bartolommeo Belvidero, at the age of sixty, had fallen in love with an angel of peace and beauty. Don Juan had been the sole fruit of this late and short-lived love. For fifteen years the widower had mourned the loss of his beloved Juana ; and to this sorrow of age, his son and his numerous household had attributed the strange habits that he had contracted. He had shut himself up in the least comfortable wing of his palace, and very seldom left his apartments ; even Don Juan himself must first ask permission before seeing his father. If this hermit, unbound by vows, came or went in his palace or in the streets of Ferrara, he walked as if he were in a dream, wholly engrossed, like a man at strife with a memory, or a wrestler with some thought.

The young Don Juan might give princely banquets, the palace might echo with clamorous mirth, horses pawed the ground in the courtyards, pages quarrelled and flung dice upon the stairs, but Bartolommeo ate his seven ounces of bread daily and drank water. A fowl was occasionally dressed for him, simply that the black poodle, his faithful companion, might have the bones. Bartolommeo never complained of the noise. If huntsmen's horns and baying dogs disturbed his sleep during his illness, he only said, 'Ah ! Don Juan has come back again.' Never on earth has there been a father so little exacting and so indulgent ; and, in consequence, young Belvidero, accustomed to treat his father unceremoniously, had all the faults of a spoiled child. He treated old Bartolommeo as a wilful courtesan treats an elderly adorer ; buying indemnity for insolence with a smile, selling good-humour, submitting to be loved.

Don Juan, beholding scene after scene of his younger years, saw that it would be a difficult task to find his father's indulgence at fault. Some new-born remorse stirred the depths of his heart ; he felt almost ready to forgive this father now about to die for having lived so long. He had an accession of filial piety, like a thief's return in thought to honesty at the prospect of a million adroitly stolen.

Before long Don Juan had crossed the lofty chilly suite of rooms in which his father lived ; the penetrating influences of the damp close air, the mustiness diffused by old tapestries and presses thickly covered with dust had passed into him, and now he stood in the old man's antiquated room, in the repulsive presence of the death-bed, beside a dying fire. A flickering lamp on a Gothic table sent broad uncertain shafts of light, fainter or brighter, across the bed, so that the dying man's face seemed to wear a different look at every moment. The bitter wind whistled through the crannies of the ill-fitting casements ; there was a smothered sound of snow lashing the windows. The harsh contrast of these sights and sounds with the scenes which Don Juan had just quitted was so sudden, that he could not help shuddering. He turned cold as he came towards the bed ; the lamp flared in a sudden vehement gust of wind and lighted up his father's face ; the features were wasted and distorted ; the skin that cleaved to their bony outlines had taken wan livid hues, all the more ghastly by force of contrast with the white pillows on which he lay. The muscles about the toothless mouth had contracted with pain and drawn apart the lips ; the moans that issued between them with appalling energy found an accompaniment in the howling of the storm without.

In spite of every sign of coming dissolution, the most striking thing about the dying face was its incredible power. It was no ordinary spirit that wrestled there with Death. The eyes glared with strange fixity of gaze from the cavernous sockets hollowed by disease. It seemed as if Bartolommeo sought to kill some enemy sitting at the foot of his bed by the intent gaze of dying eyes. That steady remorseless look was the more appalling because the head that lay upon the pillow was passive and motionless as a skull upon a doctor's table. The outlines of the body, revealed by the coverlet, were no less rigid and stiff ; he lay there as one dead, save for those eyes. There was something automatic about the moaning sounds that came from the mouth. Don Juan felt something like shame that he must be brought thus to his father's bedside, wearing a courtesan's bouquet, redolent of the fragrance of the banqueting-chamber and the fumes of wine.

'You were enjoying yourself!' the old man cried as he saw his son.

Even as he spoke the pure high notes of a woman's voice, sustained by the sound of the viol on which she accompanied her song, rose above the rattle of the storm against the casements, and floated up to the chamber of death. Don Juan stopped his ears against the barbarous answer to his father's speech.

'I bear you no grudge, my child,' Bartolommeo went on.

The words were full of kindness, but they hurt Don Juan ; he could not pardon this heart-searching goodness on his father's part.

'What a remorseful memory for me!' he cried, hypo-critically.

'Poor Juanino,' the dying man went on, in a smothered voice, 'I have always been so kind to you, that you could not surely desire my death?'

'Oh, if it were only possible to keep you here by giving up a part of my own life!' cried Don Juan.

('We can always *say* this sort of thing,' the spendthrift thought; 'it is as if I laid the whole world at my mistress's feet.')

The thought had scarcely crossed his mind when the old poodle barked. Don Juan shivered; the response was so intelligent that he fancied the dog must have understood him.

'I was sure that I could count upon you, my son!' cried the dying man. 'I shall live. So be it; you shall be satisfied. I shall live, but without depriving you of a single day of your life.'

'He is raving,' thought Don Juan. Aloud he added, 'Yes, dearest father, yes; you shall live, of course, as long as I live, for your image will be for ever in my heart.'

'It is not that kind of life that I mean,' said the old noble, summoning all his strength to sit up in bed; for a thrill of doubt ran through him, one of those suspicions that come into being under a dying man's pillow. 'Listen, my son,' he went on, in a voice grown weak with that last effort, 'I have no more wish to give up life than you to give up wine and mistresses, horses and hounds, and hawks and gold——'

'I can well believe it,' thought the son; and he knelt down by the bed and kissed Bartolommeo's cold hands. 'But, father, my dear father,' he added aloud, 'we must submit to the will of God.'

'I am God!' muttered the dying man.

'Do not blaspheme!' cried the other, as he saw the menacing expression on his father's face. 'Beware what you say; you have received extreme unction, and I should be inconsolable if you were to die before my eyes in mortal sin.'

'Will you listen to me?' cried Bartolommeo, and his mouth twitched.

Don Juan held his peace; an ugly silence prevailed. Yet above the muffled sound of the beating of the snow against the windows rose the sounds of the beautiful voice and the viol in unison, far off and faint as the dawn. The dying man smiled.

'Thank you,' he said, 'for bringing those singing voices and the music, a banquet, young and lovely women with fair faces and dark tresses, all the pleasures of life! Bid them wait for me; for I am about to begin life anew.'

'The delirium is at its height,' said Don Juan to himself.

'I have found out a way of coming to life again,' the speaker went on. 'There, just look in that table drawer, press the spring hidden by the griffin, and it will fly open.'

'I have found it, father.'

'Well, then, now take out a little phial of rock crystal.'

'I have it.'

'I have spent twenty years in——' but even as he spoke the old man felt how very near the end had come, and summoned all his dying strength to say, 'As soon as the breath is out of me, rub me all over with that liquid, and I shall come to life again.'

'There is very little of it,' his son remarked.

Though Bartolommeo could no longer speak, he could still hear and see. When those words dropped from Don Juan, his head turned with appalling quickness, his neck was twisted like the throat of some marble statue which the sculptor has condemned to remain stretched out for ever, the wide eyes had come to have a ghastly fixity.

He was dead, and in death he lost his last and sole illusion.

He had sought a shelter in his son's heart, and it had proved to be a sepulchre, a pit deeper than men dig for their dead. The hair on his head had risen and stiffened with horror, his agonised glance still spoke. He was a father rising in just anger from his tomb, to demand vengeance at the throne of God.

'There! it is all over with the old man!' cried Don Juan.

He had been so interested in holding the mysterious phial to the lamp, as a drinker holds up the wine-bottle at the end of a meal, that he had not seen his father's eyes fade. The cowering poodle looked from his master to the elixir, just as Don Juan himself glanced again and again from his father to the flask. The lamplight flickered. There was a deep silence; the viol was mute. Juan Belvidero thought that he saw his father stir, and trembled. The changeless gaze of those accusing eyes frightened him; he closed them hastily, as he would have closed a loose shutter swayed by the wind of an autumn night. He stood there motionless, lost in a world of thought.

Suddenly the silence was broken by a shrill sound like the creaking of a rusty spring. It startled Don Juan; he all but dropped the phial. A sweat, colder than the blade of a dagger, issued through every pore. It was only a piece of clockwork, a wooden cock that sprang out and crowed three times, an ingenious contrivance by which the learned of that epoch were wont to be awakened at the appointed hour to begin the labours of the day. Through the windows there came already a flush of dawn. The thing, composed of wood, and cords, and wheels, and pulleys, was more faithful in its service than he in his duty to Bartolommeo—he, a man with that peculiar piece of human mechanism within him that we call a heart.

Don Juan the sceptic shut the flask again in the secret drawer in the Gothic table—he meant to run no more risks of losing the mysterious liquid.

Even at that solemn moment he heard the murmur of a crowd in the gallery, a confused sound of voices, of stifled laughter and light footfalls, and the rustling of silks—the sounds of a band of revellers struggling for gravity. The door opened, and in came the Prince and Don Juan's friends, the seven courtesans, and the singers, dishevelled and wild like dancers surprised by the dawn, when the tapers that have burned through the night struggle with the sunlight.

They had come to offer the customary condolence to the young heir.

'Oho! is poor Don Juan really taking this seriously?' said the Prince in Brambilla's ear.

'Well, his father was very good,' she returned.

But Don Juan's night-thoughts had left such unmistakable traces on his features, that the crew was awed into silence. The men stood motionless. The women, with wine-parched lips and cheeks marbled with kisses, knelt down and began a prayer. Don Juan could scarce help trembling when he saw splendour and mirth and laughter and song and youth and beauty and power bowed in reverence before Death. But in those times, in that adorable Italy of the sixteenth century, religion and revelry went hand in hand ; and religious excess became a sort of debauch, and a debauch a religious rite !

The Prince grasped Don Juan's hand affectionately, then when all faces had simultaneously put on the same grimace — half-gloomy, half-indifferent — the whole masque disappeared, and left the chamber of death empty. It was like an allegory of life.

As they went down the staircase, the Prince spoke to Rivabarella : 'Now, who would have taken Don Juan's impiety for a boast ? He loves his father.'

'Did you see that black dog ?' asked La Brambilla.

'He is enormously rich now,' sighed Bianca Cavatolino.

'What is that to me?' cried the proud Veronese (she who had crushed the comfit-box).

'What does it matter to you, forsooth?' cried the Duke. 'With his money he is as much a prince as I am.'

At first Don Juan was swayed hither and thither by countless thoughts, and wavered between two decisions. He took counsel with the gold heaped up by his father, and returned in the evening to the chamber of death, his whole soul brimming over with hideous selfishness. He found all his household busy there. 'His lordship' was to lie in state to-morrow; all Ferrara would flock to behold the wonderful spectacle; and the servants were busy decking the room and the couch on which the dead man lay. At a sign from Don Juan all his people stopped, dumbfounded and trembling.

'Leave me alone here,' he said, and his voice was changed, 'and do not return until I leave the room.'

When the footsteps of the old servitor, who was the last to go, echoed but faintly along the paved gallery, Don Juan hastily locked the door, and, sure that he was quite alone, 'Let us try,' he said to himself.

Bartolommeo's body was stretched on a long table. The embalmers had laid a sheet over it, to hide from all eyes the dreadful spectacle of a corpse so wasted and shrunken that it seemed like a skeleton, and only the face was uncovered. This mummy-like form lay in the middle of the room. The limp clinging linen lent itself to the outlines it shrouded—so sharp, bony, and thin. Large violet patches had already begun to spread over the face; the embalmer's work had not been finished too soon.

Don Juan, strong as he was in his scepticism, felt a tremor as he opened the magic crystal flask. When he stood over that face, he was trembling so violently, that he was actually obliged to wait for a moment. But Don

Juan had acquired an early familiarity with evil; his morals had been corrupted by a licentious court, a reflection worthy of the Duke of Urbino crossed his mind, and it was a keen sense of curiosity that goaded him into boldness. The devil himself might have whispered the words that were echoing through his brain, *Moisten one of the eyes with the liquid!* He took up a linen cloth, moistened it sparingly with the precious fluid, and passed it lightly over the right eyelid of the corpse. The eye unclosed. . . .

'Aha!' said Don Juan. He gripped the flask tightly, as we clutch in dreams the branch from which we hang suspended over a precipice.

For the eye was full of life. It was a young child's eye set in a death's head; the light quivered in the depths of its youthful liquid brightness. Shaded by the long dark lashes, it sparkled like the strange lights that travellers see in lonely places in winter nights. That eye seemed as if it would fain dart fire at Don Juan; he saw it thinking, upbraiding, condemning, uttering accusations, threatening doom; it cried aloud, and gnashed upon him. All anguish that shakes human souls was gathered there; supplications the most tender, the wrath of kings, the love in a girl's heart pleading with the headsman; then, and after all these, the deeply searching glance a man turns on his fellows as he mounts the last step of the scaffold. Life so dilated in this fragment of life that Don Juan shrank back; he walked up and down the room, he dared not meet that gaze, but he saw nothing else. The ceiling and the hangings, the whole room was sown with living points of fire and intelligence. Everywhere those gleaming eyes haunted him.

'He might very likely have lived another hundred years!' he cried involuntarily. Some diabolical influence had drawn him to his father, and again he gazed at that luminous spark. The eyelid closed and opened again abruptly; it was like a woman's sign of assent. It was an intelligent movement.   If a voice had cried 'Yes!' Don Juan could not have been more startled.

'What is to be done?' he thought.

He nerved himself to try to close the white eyelid. In vain.

'Kill it?   That would perhaps be parricide,' he debated with himself.

'Yes,' the eye said, with a strange sardonic quiver of the lid.

'Aha!' said Don Juan to himself, 'here is witchcraft at work!'   And he went closer to crush the thing.   A great tear trickled over the hollow cheeks, and fell on Don Juan's hand.

'It is scalding!' he cried.   He sat down.   This struggle exhausted him; it was as if, like Jacob of old, he was wrestling with an angel.

At last he rose.   'So long as there is no blood——' he muttered.

Then, summoning all the courage needed for a coward's crime, he extinguished the eye, pressing it with the linen cloth, turning his head away.   A terrible groan startled him.   It was the poor poodle, who died with a long-drawn howl.

'Could the brute have been in the secret?' thought Don Juan, looking down at the faithful creature.

Don Juan Belvidero was looked upon as a dutiful son. He reared a white marble monument on his father's tomb, and employed the greatest sculptors of the time upon it.   He did not recover perfect ease of mind till the day when his father knelt in marble before Religion, and the heavy weight of the stone had sealed the mouth of the grave in which he had laid the one feeling of remorse that sometimes flitted through his soul in moments of physical weariness.

He had drawn up a list of the wealth heaped up by the old merchant in the East, and he became a miser : had

he not to provide for a second lifetime ?   His views of
life were the more profound and penetrating ; he grasped
its significance, as a whole, the better, because he saw it
across a grave.   All men, all things, he analysed once and
for all ; he summed up the Past, represented by its records ;
the Present in the law, its crystallised form ; the Future,
revealed by religion.   He took spirit and matter, and
flung them into his crucible, and found — Nothing.
Thenceforward he became ·Don Juan.

At the outset of his life, in the prime of youth and the
beauty of youth, he knew the illusions of life for what
they were ; he despised the world, and made the utmost
of the world.   His felicity could not have been of the
bourgeois kind, rejoicing in periodically recurrent *bouilli*,
in the comforts of a warming-pan, a lamp of a night,
and a new pair of slippers once a quarter.   Nay, rather
he seized upon existence as a monkey snatches a nut,
and after no long toying with it, proceeds deftly to strip
off the mere husks to reach the savoury kernel within.

Poetry and the sublime transports of passion scarcely
reached ankle-depth with him now.   He in nowise fell into
the error of strong natures who flatter themselves now and
again that little souls will believe in a great soul, and are
willing to barter their own lofty thoughts of the future
for the small change of our life-annuity ideas.   He, even
as they, had he chosen, might well have walked with his
feet on the earth and his head in the skies ; but he liked
better to sit on earth, to wither the soft, fresh, fragrant
lips of a woman with kisses, for, like Death, he devoured
everything without scruple as he passed ; he would have
full fruition ; he was an Oriental lover, seeking prolonged pleasures easily obtained.   He sought nothing
but a woman in women, and cultivated cynicism, until
it became with him a habit of mind.   When his mistress,
from the couch on which she lay, soared and was lost in
regions of ecstatic bliss, Don Juan followed suit, earnest,
expansive, serious as any German student.   But he said

I, while she, in the transports of intoxication, said We. He understood to admiration the art of abandoning himself to the influence of a woman; he was always clever enough to make her believe that he trembled like some boy fresh from college before his first partner at a dance, when he asks her, 'Do you like dancing?' But, no less, he could be terrible at need, could unsheath a formidable sword and make short work of Commandants. Banter lurked beneath his simplicity, mocking laughter behind his tears—for he had tears at need, like any woman nowadays who says to her husband, 'Give me a carriage, or I shall go into a consumption.'

For a merchant the world is a bale of goods or a mass of circulating bills; for most young men it is a woman, and for a woman here and there it is a man; for a certain order of mind it is a salon, a coterie, a quarter of the town, or some single city; but Don Juan found his world in himself.

This model of grace and dignity, this captivating wit, moored his bark by every shore; but wherever he was led he was never carried away, and was only steered in a course of his own choosing. The more he saw, the more he doubted. He watched men narrowly, and saw how, beneath the surface, courage was often rashness; and prudence, cowardice; generosity, a clever piece of calculation; justice, a wrong; delicacy, pusillanimity; honesty, a *modus vivendi*; and by some strange dispensation of fate, he must see that those who at heart were really honest, scrupulous, just, generous, prudent, or brave were held cheaply by their fellow-men.

'What a cold-blooded jest!' said he to himself. 'It was not devised by a God.'

From that time forth he renounced a better world, and never uncovered himself when a Name was pronounced, and for him the carven saints in the churches became works of art. He understood the mechanism of society too well to clash wantonly with its prejudices;

for, after all, he was not as powerful as the executioner, but he evaded social laws with the wit and grace so well rendered in the scene with M. Dimanche. He was, in fact, Molière's Don Juan, Goethe's Faust, Byron's Manfred, Mathurin's Melmoth—great allegorical figures drawn by the greatest men of genius in Europe, to which Mozart's harmonies, perhaps, do no more justice than Rossini's lyre. Terrible allegorical figures that shall endure as long as the principle of evil existing in the heart of man shall produce a few copies from century to century. Sometimes the type becomes half-human when incarnate as a Mirabeau, sometimes it is an inarticulate force in a Bonaparte, sometimes it overwhelms the universe with irony as a Rabelais; or, yet again, it appears when a Maréchal de Richelieu elects to laugh at human beings instead of scoffing at things, or when one of the most famous of our ambassadors goes a step further and scoffs at both men and things. But the profound genius of Juan Belvidero anticipated and resumed all these. All things were a jest to him. His was the life of a mocking spirit. All men, all institutions, all realities, all ideas were within its scope. As for eternity, after half an hour of familiar conversation with Pope Julius II. he had said, laughing—

'If it is absolutely necessary to make a choice, I would rather believe in God than in the Devil; power combined with goodness always offers more resources than the spirit of Evil can boast.'

'Yes; still God requires repentance in this present world——'

'So you always think of your indulgences,' returned Don Juan Belvidero. 'Well, well, I have another life in reserve in which to repent of the sins of my previous existence.'

'Oh, if you regard old age in that light,' cried the Pope, 'you are in danger of canonisation——'

'After your elevation to the Papacy nothing is

incredible.' And they went to watch the workmen who were building the huge basilica dedicated to Saint Peter.

'Saint Peter, as the man of genius who laid the foundation of our double power,' the Pope said to Don Juan, 'deserves this monument. Sometimes, though, at night, I think that a deluge will wipe all this out as with a sponge, and it will be all to begin over again.'

Don Juan and the Pope began to laugh; they understood each other. A fool would have gone on the morrow to amuse himself with Julius II. in Raphael's studio or at the delicious Villa Madama; not so Belvidero. He went to see the Pope as pontiff, to be convinced of any doubts that he (Don Juan) entertained. Over his cups the Rovere would have been capable of denying his own infallibility and of commenting on the Apocalypse.

Nevertheless, this legend has not been undertaken to furnish materials for future biographies of Don Juan; it is intended to prove to honest folk that Belvidero did not die in a duel with stone, as some lithographers would have us believe.

When Don Juan Belvidero reached the age of sixty he settled in Spain, and there in his old age he married a young and charming Andalusian wife. But of set purpose he was neither a good husband nor a good father. He had observed that we are never so tenderly loved as by women to whom we scarcely give a thought. Doña Elvira had been devoutly brought up by an old aunt in a castle a few leagues from San Lucar in a remote part of Andalusia. She was a model of devotion and grace. Don Juan foresaw that this would be a woman who would struggle long against a passion before yielding, and therefore hoped to keep her virtuous until his death. It was a jest undertaken in earnest, a game of chess which he meant to reserve till his old age. Don Juan had learned wisdom from the mistakes made by his father Bartolommeo; he determined that the least details of his life in old age should be subordinated to one object—the success of the drama which was to be played out upon his deathbed.

For the same reason the largest part of his wealth was buried in the cellars of his palace at Ferrara, whither he seldom went. As for the rest of his fortune, it was invested in a life annuity, with a view to give his wife and children an interest in keeping him alive; but this Machiavellian piece of foresight was scarcely necessary. His son, young Felipe Belvidero, grew up as a Spaniard as religiously conscientious as his father was irreligious, in virtue, perhaps, of the old rule, 'A miser has a spend-thrift son.' The Abbot of San-Lucar was chosen by Don Juan to be the director of the consciences of the Duchess of Belvidero and her son Felipe. The ecclesiastic was a holy man, well shaped, and admirably well proportioned. He had fine dark eyes, a head like that of Tiberius, worn with fasting, bleached by an ascetic life, and, like all dwellers in the wilderness, was daily tempted. The noble lord had hopes, it may be, of despatching yet another monk before his term of life was out.

But whether because the Abbot was every whit as clever as Don Juan himself, or Doña Elvira possessed more discretion or more virtue than Spanish wives are usually credited with, Don Juan was compelled to spend his declining years beneath his own roof, with no more scandal under it than if he had been an ancient country parson. Occasionally he would take wife and son to task for negligence in the duties of religion, peremptorily insisting that they should carry out to the letter the obligations imposed upon the flock by the Court of Rome. Indeed, he was never so well pleased as when he had set the courtly Abbot discussing some case of conscience with Doña Elvira and Felipe.

At length, however, despite the prodigious care that

the great magnifico, Don Juan Belvidero, took of himself, the days of decrepitude came upon him, and with those days the constant importunity of physical feebleness, an importunity all the more distressing by contrast with the wealth of memories of his impetuous youth and the sensual pleasures of middle age.   The unbeliever who in the height of his cynical humour had been wont to persuade others to believe, in laws and principles at which he scoffed, must repose nightly upon a *perhaps*.   The great Duke, the pattern of good breeding, the champion of many a carouse, the proud ornament of Courts, the man of genius, the graceful winner of hearts that he had wrung as carelessly as a peasant twists an osier withe, was now the victim of a cough, of a ruthless sciatica, of an unmannerly gout.   His teeth gradually deserted him, as at the end of an evening the fairest and best-dressed women take their leave one by one till the room is left empty and desolate.   The active hands became palsy-stricken, the shapely legs tottered as he walked.   At last, one night, a stroke of apoplexy caught him by the throat in its icy clutch.   After that fatal day he grew morose and stern.

He would reproach his wife and son with their devotion, casting it in their teeth that the affecting and thoughtful care that they lavished so tenderly upon him was bestowed because they knew that his money was invested in a life annuity.   Then Elvira and Felipe would shed bitter tears and redouble their caresses, and the wicked old man's insinuating voice would take an affectionate tone—'Ah, you will forgive me, will you not, dear friends, dear wife?   I am rather a nuisance.   Alas, Lord in heaven, how canst Thou use me as the instrument by which Thou provest these two angelic creatures?   I who should be the joy of their lives am become their scourge . . .'

In this manner he kept them tethered to his pillow, blotting out the memory of whole months of fretfulness and unkindness in one short hour when he chose to display for them the ever-new treasures of his pinchbeck tenderness and charm of manner—a system of paternity that yielded him an infinitely better return than his own father's indulgence had formerly gained. At length his bodily infirmities reached a point when the task of laying him in bed became as difficult as the navigation of a felucca in the perils of an intricate channel. Then came the day of his death; and this brilliant sceptic, whose mental faculties alone had survived the most dreadful of all destructions, found himself between his two special antipathies—the doctor and the confessor. But he was jovial with them. Did he not see a light gleaming in the future beyond the veil? The pall that is like lead for other men was thin and translucent for him; the light-footed, irresistible delights of youth danced beyond it like shadows.

It was on a beautiful summer evening that Don Juan felt the near approach of death. The sky of Spain was serene and cloudless; the air was full of the scent of orange-blossom; the stars shed clear, pure gleams of light; nature without seemed to give the dying man assurance of resurrection; a dutiful and obedient son sat there watching him with loving and respectful eyes. Towards eleven o'clock he desired to be left alone with this single-hearted being.

'Felipe,' said the father, in tones so soft and affectionate that the young man trembled, and tears of gladness came to his eyes; never had that stern father spoken his name in such a tone. 'Listen, my son,' the dying man went on. 'I am a great sinner. All my life long, however, I have thought of my death. I was once the friend of the great Pope Julius II.; and that illustrious Pontiff, fearing lest the excessive excitability of my senses should entangle me in mortal sin between the moment of my death and the time of my anointing with

the holy oil, gave me a flask that contains a little of the
holy water that once issued from the rock in the wilderness.   I have kept the secret of this squandering of
a treasure belonging to Holy Church, but I am per-
mitted to reveal the mystery *in articulo mortis* to my son.
You will find the flask in a drawer in that Gothic table
that always stands by the head of the bed. . . . The
precious little crystal flask may be of use yet again for
you, dearest Felipe.   Will you swear to me, by your
salvation, to carry out my instructions faithfully ? '

Felipe looked at his father, and Don Juan was too
deeply learned in the lore of the human countenance
not to die in peace with that look as his warrant, as his
own father had died in despair at meeting the expression
in his son's eyes.

'You deserved to have a better father,' Don Juan
went on.   'I dare to confess, my child, that while the
reverend Abbot of San-Lucar was administering the
Viaticum I was thinking of the incompatibility of the
co-existence of two powers so infinite as God and the
Devil——'

'Oh, father ! '

'And I said to myself, when Satan makes his peace
he ought surely to stipulate for the pardon of his fol-
lowers, or he will be the veriest scoundrel.   The thought
haunted me ; so I shall go to hell, my son, unless you
carry out my wishes.'

'Oh, quick ; tell me quickly, father.'

'As soon as I have closed my eyes,' Don Juan went
on, 'and that may be in a few minutes, you must take
my body before it grows cold and lay it on a table in
this room.   Then put out the lamp ; the light of the
stars should be sufficient.   Take off my clothes, reciting
Aves and *Paters* the while, raising your soul to God in
prayer, and carefully anoint my lips and eyes with this
holy water ; begin with the face, and proceed suc-
cessively to my limbs and the rest of my body ; my

dear son, the power of God is so great that you must be astonished at nothing.'

Don Juan felt death so near, that he added in a terrible voice, 'Be careful not to drop the flask.'

Then he breathed his last gently in the arms of his son, and his son's tears fell fast over his sardonic, haggard features.

It was almost midnight when Don Felipe Belvidero laid his father's body upon the table. He kissed the sinister brow and the grey hair ; then he put out the lamp.

By the soft moonlight that lit strange gleams across the country without, Felipe could dimly see his father's body, a vague white thing among the shadows. The dutiful son moistened a linen cloth with the liquid, and, absorbed in prayer, he anointed the revered face. A deep silence reigned. Felipe heard faint, indescribable rustlings ; it was the breeze in the tree-tops, he thought. But when he had moistened the right arm, he felt himself caught by the throat, a young strong hand held him in a tight grip—it was his father's hand ! He shrieked aloud ; the flask dropped from his hand and broke in pieces. The liquid evaporated ; the whole household hurried into the room, holding torches aloft. That shriek had startled them, and filled them with as much terror as if the Trumpet of the Angel sounding on the Last Day had rung through earth and sky. The room was full of people, and a horror-stricken crowd beheld the fainting Felipe upheld by the strong arm of his father, who clutched him by the throat. They saw another thing, an unearthly spectacle—Don Juan's face grown young and beautiful as Antinoüs, with its dark hair and brilliant eyes and red lips, a head that made horrible efforts, but could not move the dead, wasted body.

An old servitor cried, 'A miracle ! a miracle !' and all the Spaniards echoed, 'A miracle ! a miracle !'

Doña Elvira, too pious to attribute this to magic, sent for the Abbot of San-Lucar; and the Prior beholding the miracle with his own eyes, being a clever man, and withal an Abbot desirous of augmenting his revenues, determined to turn the occasion to profit. He immediately gave out that Don Juan would certainly be canonised; he appointed a day for the celebration of the apotheosis in his convent, which thenceforward, he said, should be called the convent of San Juan of Lucar. At these words a sufficiently facetious grimace passed over the features of the late Duke.

The taste of the Spanish people for ecclesiastical solemnities is so well known, that it should not be difficult to imagine the religious pantomime by which the Convent of San-Lucar celebrated the translation of the *blessed Don Juan Belvidero* to the abbey-church. The tale of the partial resurrection had spread so quickly from village to village, that a day or two after the death of the illustrious nobleman the report had reached every place within fifty miles of San-Lucar, and it was as good as a play to see the roads covered already with crowds flocking in on all sides, their curiosity whetted still further by the prospect of a *Te Deum* sung by torchlight. The old abbey-church of San-Lucar, a marvellous building erected by the Moors, a mosque of Allah, which for three centuries had heard the name of Christ, could not hold the throng that poured in to see the ceremony. Hidalgos in their velvet mantles, with their good swords at their sides, swarmed like ants, and were so tightly packed in among the pillars that they had not room to bend the knees, which never bent save to God. Charming peasant girls, in the basquina that defines the luxuriant outlines of their figures, lent an arm to white-haired old men. Young men, with eyes of fire, walked beside aged crones in holiday array. Then came couples tremulous with joy, young lovers led thither by curiosity, newly wedded folk; children timidly clasping each other by the hand. This throng, so rich in colouring, in vivid contrasts, laden with flowers, enamelled like a meadow, sent up a soft murmur through the quiet night. Then the great doors of the church opened.

Late comers who remained without saw afar, through the three great open doorways, a scene of which the theatrical illusions of modern opera can give but a faint idea. The vast church was lighted up by thousands of candles, offered by saints and sinners alike eager to win the favour of this new candidate for canonisation, and these self-commending illuminations turned the great building into an enchanted fairyland. The black archways, the shafts and capitals, the recessed chapels with gold and silver gleaming in their depths, the galleries, the Arab traceries, all the most delicate outlines of that delicate sculpture, burned in the excess of light like the fantastic figures in the red heart of a brazier. At the further end of the church, above that blazing sea, rose the high altar like a splendid dawn. All the glories of the golden lamps and silver candlesticks, of banners and tassels, of the shrines of the saints and votive offerings, paled before the gorgeous brightness of the reliquary in which Don Juan lay. The blasphemer's body sparkled with gems, and flowers, and crystal, with diamonds and gold, and plumes white as the wings of seraphim ; they had set it up on the altar, where the picture of Christ had stood. All about him blazed a host of tall candles ; the air quivered in the radiant light. The worthy Abbot of San-Lucar, in pontifical robes, with his mitre set with precious stones, his rochet and golden crosier, sat enthroned in imperial state among his clergy in the choir. Rows of impassive aged faces, silver-haired old men clad in fine linen albs, were grouped about him, as the saints who confessed Christ on earth are set by painters, each in his place, about the throne of God in heaven. The precentor and the dignitaries of the chapter, adorned with the gorgeous insignia of ecclesiastical vanity, came and went

through the clouds of incense, like stars upon their
courses in the firmament.

When the hour of triumph arrived, the bells awoke the
echoes far and wide, and the whole vast crowd raised to
God the first cry of praise that begins the *Te Deum*. A
sublime cry ! High, pure notes, the voices of women in
ecstasy, mingled in it with the sterner and deeper voices
of men ; thousands of voices sent up a volume of sound
so mighty, that the straining, groaning organ-pipes could
not dominate that harmony.   But the shrill sound of
children's singing among the choristers, the reverberation
of deep bass notes, awakened gracious associations, visions
of childhood, and of man in his strength, and rose above
that entrancing harmony of human voices blended in one
sentiment of love.

Te Deum laudamus!

The chant went up from the black masses of men and
women kneeling in the cathedral, like a sudden breaking
out of light in darkness, and the silence was shattered as by
a peal of thunder. The voices floated up with the clouds
of incense that had begun to cast thin bluish veils over the
fanciful marvels of the architecture, and the aisles were
filled with splendour and perfume and light and melody.
Even at the moment when that music of love and thanks-
giving soared up to the altar, Don Juan, too well bred
not to express his acknowledgments, too witty not to
understand how to take a jest, bridled up in his reliquary,
and responded with an appalling burst of laughter. Then
the Devil having put him in mind of the risk he was
running of being taken for an ordinary man, a saint, a
Boniface, a Pantaleone, he interrupted the melody of love
by a yell; the thousand voices of hell joined in it. Earth
blessed, Heaven banned. The church was shaken to its
ancient foundations.

Te Deum laudamus ! cried the many voices.

'Go to the devil, brute beasts that you are ! *Dios !
Dios ! Carajos demonios !* Idiots ! What fools you are

with your dotard-God!' and a torrent of imprecations poured forth like a stream of red-hot lava from the mouth of Vesuvius.

'*Deus Sabaoth!* . . . *Sabaoth!*' cried the believers.

'You are insulting the majesty of Hell,' shouted Don Juan, gnashing his teeth. In another moment the living arm struggled out of the reliquary, and was brandished over the assembly in mockery and despair.

'The saint is blessing us,' cried the old women, children, lovers, and the credulous among the crowd.

And note how often we are deceived in the homage we pay; the great man scoffs at those who praise him, and pays compliments now and again to those whom he laughs at in the depths of his heart.

Just as the Abbot, prostrate before the altar, was chanting '*Sancte Johannes, ora pro nobis!*' he heard a voice exclaim sufficiently distinctly: '*O coglione!*'

'What can be going on up there?' cried the Sub-prior, as he saw the reliquary move.

'The saint is playing the devil,' replied the Abbot.

Even as he spoke, the living head tore itself away from the lifeless body, and dropped upon the sallow cranium of the officiating priest.

'Remember Doña Elvira!' cried the thing, with its teeth set fast in the Abbot's head.

The Abbot's horror-stricken shriek disturbed the ceremony; all the ecclesiastics hurried up and crowded about their chief.

'Idiot, tell us now if there is a God!' the voice cried, as the Abbot, bitten through the brain, drew his last breath.

PARIS, *October* 1830.

2 A

Printed by T. and A. CONSTABLE, Printers to Her Majesty
at the Edinburgh University Press

The Two Babylons
Alexander Hislop
You may be surprised to learn that many traditions of Roman Catholicism in fact don't come from Christ's teachings but from an ancient Babylonian "Mystery" religion that was centered on Nimrod, his wife Semiramis, and a child Tammuz. This book shows how this ancient religion transformed itself as it incorporated Christ into its teachings....

Religion/History   **Pages:358**

ISBN: *1-59462-010-5*   **MSRP** *$22.95*

QTY

The Go-Getter
Kyne B. Peter
The Go Getter is the story of William Peck.He was a war veteran and amputee who will not be refused what he wants. Peck not only fights to find employment but continually proves himself more than competent at the many difficult test that are throw his way in the course of his early days with the Ricks Lumber Company...

Business/Self Help/Inspirational   **Pages:68**

ISBN: *1-59462-186-1*   **MSRP** *$8.95*

QTY

The Power Of Concentration
Theron Q. Dumont
It is of the utmost value to learn how to concentrate. To make the greatest success of anything you must be able to concentrate your entire thought upon the idea you are working on. The person that is able to concentrate utilizes all constructive thoughts and shuts out all destructive ones...

Self Help/Inspirational   **Pages:196**

ISBN: *1-59462-141-1*   **MSRP** *$14.95*

Self Mastery
Emile Coue
Emile Coue came up with novel way to improve the lives of people. He was a pharmacist by trade and often saw ailing people. This lead him to develop autosuggestion, a form of self-hypnosis. At the time his theories weren't popular but over the years evidence is mounting that he was indeed right all along...

New Age/Self Help   **Pages:98**

ISBN: *1-59462-189-6*   **MSRP** *$7.95*

Rightly Dividing The Word
Clarence Larkin
The "Fundamental Doctrines" of the Christian Faith are clearly outlined in numerous books on Theology, but they are not available to the average reader and were mainly written for students. The Author has made it the work of his ministry to preach the "Fundamental Doctrines". To this end he has aimed to express them in the simplest and clearest manner..

Religion   **Pages:352**

ISBN: *1-59462-334-1*   **MSRP** *$23.45*

The Awful Disclosures Of
Maria Monk
"I cannot banish the scenes and characters of this book from my memory. To me it can never appear like an amusing fable, or lose its interest and importance. The story is one which is continually before me, and must return fresh to my mind with painful emotions as long as I live..."

Religion   **Pages:232**

ISBN: *1-59462-160-8*   **MSRP** *$17.95*

The Law of Psychic Phenomena
Thomson Jay Hudson
"I do not expect this book to stand upon its literary merits; for if it is unsound in principle, felicity of diction cannot save it, and if sound, homeliness of expression cannot destroy it. My primary object in offering it to the public is to assist in bringing Psychology within the domain of the exact sciences. That this has never been accomplished..."

New Age   **Pages:420**

ISBN: *1-59462-124-1*   **MSRP** *$29.95*

As a Man Thinketh
James Allen
"This little volume (the result of meditation and experience) is not intended as an exhaustive treatise on the much-written-upon subject of the power of thought. It is suggestive rather than explanatory, its object being to stimulate men and women to the discovery and perception of the truth that by virtue of the thoughts which they choose and encourage..."

Inspirational/Self Help   **Pages:80**

ISBN: *1-59462-231-0*   **MSRP** *$9.45*

Beautiful Joe
Marshall Saunders
When Marshall visited the Moore family in 1892, she discovered Joe, a dog they had nursed back to health from his previous abusive home to live a happy life. So moved was she, that she wrote this classic masterpiece which won accolades and was recognized as a heartwarming symbol for humane animal treatment...

Fiction   **Pages:256**

ISBN: *1-59462-261-2*   **MSRP** *$18.45*

The Enchanted April
Elizabeth Von Arnim
It began in a woman's club in London on a February afternoon, an uncomfortable club, and a miserable afternoon when Mrs. Wilkins, who had come down from Hampstead to shop and had lunched at her club, took up The Times from the table in the smoking-room...

Fiction   **Pages:368**

ISBN: *1-59462-150-0*   **MSRP** *$23.45*

The Codes Of Hammurabi And
Moses - W. W. Davies
The discovery of the Hammurabi Code is one of the greatest achievements of archaeology, and is of paramount interest, not only to the student of the Bible, but also to all those interested in ancient history...

Religion   **Pages:132**

ISBN: *1-59462-338-4*   **MSRP** *$12.95*

Holland - The History Of Netherlands
Thomas Colley Grattan
Thomas Grattan was a prestigious writer from Dublin who served as British Consul to the US. Among his works is an authoritative look at the history of Holland. A colorful and interesting look at history....

History/Politics   **Pages:408**

ISBN: *1-59462-137-3*   **MSRP** *$26.95*

The Thirty-Six Dramatic Situations
Georges Polti
An incredibly useful guide for aspiring authors and playwrights. This volume categorizes every dramatic situation which could occur in a story and describes them in a list of 36 situations. A great aid to help inspire or formalize the creative writing process...

Self Help/Reference   **Pages:204**

ISBN: *1-59462-134-9*   **MSRP** *$15.95*

A Concise Dictionary of Middle English
A. L. Mayhew
Walter W. Skeat
The present work is intended to meet, in some measure, the requirements of those who wish to make some study of Middle-English, and who find a difficulty in obtaining such assistance as will enable them to find out the meanings and etymologies of the words most essential to their purpose...

Reference/History   **Pages:332**

ISBN: *1-59462-119-5*   **MSRP** *$29.95*

The Witch-Cult in Western Europe
Margaret Murray

The mass of existing material on this subject is so great that I have not attempted to make a survey of the whole of European "Witchcraft" but have confined myself to an intensive study of the cult in Great Britain. In order, however, to obtain a clearer understanding of the ritual and beliefs I have had recourse to French and Flemish sources...

QTY

Occult   Pages:308

ISBN: *1-59462-126-8*   MSRP *$22.45*

Philosophy Of Natural Therapeutics
Henry Lindlahr

We invite the earnest cooperation in this great work of all those who have awakened to the necessity for more rational living and for radical reform in healing methods...

QTY

Health/Philosophy/Self Help   Pages:552

ISBN: *1-59462-132-2*   MSRP *$34.95*

The Science Of Psychic Healing
Yogi Ramacharaka

This book is not a book of theories it deals with facts. Its author regards the best of theories as but working hypotheses to be used only until better ones present themselves. The "fact" is the principal thing the essential thing to uncover which the tool, theory, is used...

New Age/Health   Pages:180

ISBN: *1-59462-140-3*   MSRP *$13.95*

A Message to Garcia
Elbert Hubbard

This literary trifle, A Message to Garcia, was written one evening after supper, in a single hour. It was on the Twenty-second of February, Eighteen Hundred Ninety-nine, Washington's Birthday, and we were just going to press with the March Philistine...

New Age/Fiction   Pages:92

ISBN: *1-59462-144-6*   MSRP *$9.95*

Bible Myths
Thomas Doane

In pursuing the study of the Bible Myths, facts pertaining thereto, in a condensed form, seemed to be greatly needed, and nowhere to be found. Widely scattered through hundreds of ancient and modern volumes, most of the contents of this book may indeed be found; but any previous attempt to trace exclusively the myths and legends...

Religion/History   Pages:644

ISBN: *1-59462-163-2*   MSRP *$38.95*

The Book of Jasher
Alcuinus Flaccus Albinus

The Book of Jasher is an historical religious volume that many consider as a missing holy book from the Old Testament. Particularly studied by the Church of Later Day Saints and historians, it covers the history of the world from creation until the period of Judges in Israel. It's authenticity is bolstered due to a reference to the Book of Jasher in the Bible in Joshua 10:13

Religion/History   Pages:276

ISBN: *1-59462-197-7*   MSRP *$18.95*

Tertium Organum
P. D. Ouspensky

A truly mind expanding writing that combines science with mysticism with unprecedented elegance. He presents the world we live in as a multi dimensional world and time as a motion through this world. But this isn't a cold and purely analytical explanation but a masterful presentation filled with similes and analogies...

New Age   Pages:356

ISBN: *1-59462-205-1*   MSRP *$23.95*

The Titan
Theodore Dreiser

"When Frank Algernon Cowperwood emerged from the Eastern District Penitentiary, in Philadelphia he realized that the old life he had lived in that city since boyhood was ended. His youth was gone, and with it had been lost the great business prospects of his earlier manhood. He must begin again..."

Fiction   Pages:564

ISBN: *1-59462-220-5*   MSRP *$33.95*

Advance Course in Yogi Philosophy
Yogi Ramacharaka

"The twelve lessons forming this volume were originally issued in the shape of monthly lessons, known as "The Advanced Course in Yogi Philosophy and Oriental Occultism" during a period of twelve months beginning with October, 1904, and ending September, 1905."

Philosophy/Inspirational/Self Help   Pages:340

ISBN: *1-59462-229-9*   MSRP *$22.95*

Biblical Essays
J. B. Lightfoot

About one-third of the present volume has already seen the light. The opening essay "On the Internal Evidence for the Authenticity and Genuineness of St John's Gospel" was published in the "Expositor" in the early months of 1890, and has been reprinted since...

Religion/History   Pages:480

ISBN: *1-59462-238-8*   MSRP *$30.95*

Ambassador Morgenthau's Story
Henry Morgenthau

"By this time the American people have probably become convinced that the Germans deliberately planned the conquest of the world. Yet they hesitate to convict on circumstantial evidence and for this reason all eye witnesses to this, the greatest crime in modern history, should volunteer their testimony..."

History   Pages:472

ISBN: *1-59462-244-2*   MSRP *$29.95*

The Settlement Cook Book
Simon Kander

A legacy from the civil war, this book is a classic "American charity cookbook," which was used for fundraisers starting in Milwaukee. While it has transformed over the years, this printing provides great recipes from American history. Over two million copies have been sold. This volume contains a rich collection of recipes from noted chefs and hostesses of the turn of the century...

How-to   Pages:472

ISBN: *1-59462-256-6*   MSRP *$29.95*

My Life and Work
Henry Ford

Henry Ford revolutionized the world with his implementation of mass production for the Model T automobile. Gain valuable business insight into his life and work with his own auto-biography... "We have only started on our development of our country we have not as yet, with all our talk of wonderful progress, done more than scratch the surface. The progress has been wonderful enough but..."

Biographies/History/Business   Pages:300

ISBN: *1-59462-198-5*   MSRP *$21.95*

The Aquarian Gospel of Jesus the Christ
Levi Dowling

A retelling of Jesus' story which tells us what happened during the twenty year gap left by the Bible's New Testament. It tells of his travels to the far-east where he studied with the masters and fought against the rigid caste system. This book has enjoyed a resurgence in modern America and provides spiritual insight with charm. Its influences can be seen throughout the Age of Aquarius.

Religion   Pages:264

ISBN: *1-59462-321-X*   MSRP *$18.95*

www.bookjungle.com *email: sales@bookjungle.com fax: 630-214-0564 mail: Book Jungle PO Box 2226 Champaign, IL 61825*

QTY

The Rosicrucian Cosmo-Conception Mystic Christianity *by Max Heindel* ISBN: *1-59462-188-8* **$38.95**
The Rosicrucian Cosmo-conception is not dogmatic, neither does it appeal to any other authority than the reason of the student. It is; not controversial, but is; sent forth in the, hope that it may help to clear,.. New Age/Religion Pages 646

Abandonment To Divine Providence *by Jean-Pierre de Caussade* ISBN: *1-59462-228-0* **$25.95**
"The Rev. Jean Pierre de Caussade was one of the most remarkable spiritual writers of the Society of Jesus in France in the 18th Century. His death took place at Toulouse in 1751. His works have gone through many editions and have been republished... Inspirational/Religion Pages 400

Mental Chemistry *by Charles Haanel* ISBN: *1-59462-192-6* **$23.95**
Mental Chemistry allows the change of material conditions by combining and appropriately utilizing the power of the mind. Much like applied chemistry creates something new and unique out of careful combinations of chemicals the mastery of mental chemistry... New Age Pages 354

The Letters of Robert Browning and Elizabeth Barret Barrett 1845-1846 vol II ISBN: *1-59462-193-4* **$35.95**
by Robert Browning and Elizabeth Barrett Biographies Pages 596

Gleanings In Genesis (volume I) *by Arthur W. Pink* ISBN: *1-59462-130-6* **$27.45**
Appropriately has Genesis been termed "the seed plot of the Bible" for in it we have, in germ form, almost all of the great doctrines which are afterwards fully developed in the books of Scripture which follow... Religion/Inspirational Pages 420

The Master Key *by L. W. de Laurence* ISBN: *1-59462-001-6* **$30.95**
In no branch of human knowledge has there been a more lively increase of the spirit of research during the past few years than in the study of Psychology, Concentration and Mental Discipline. The requests for authentic lessons in Thought Control, Mental Discipline and... New Age/Business Pages 422

The Lesser Key Of Solomon Goetia *by L. W. de Laurence* ISBN: *1-59462-092-X* **$9.95**
This translation of the first book of the "Lemegton" which is now for the first time made accessible to students of Talismanic Magic was done, after careful collation and edition, from numerous Ancient Manuscripts in Hebrew, Latin, and French... New Age/Occult Pages 92

Rubaiyat Of Omar Khayyam *by Edward Fitzgerald* ISBN:*1-59462-332-5* **$13.95**
Edward Fitzgerald, whom the world has already learned, in spite of his own efforts to remain within the shadow of anonymity, to look upon as one of the rarest poets of the century, was born at Bredfield, in Suffolk, on the 31st of March, 1809. He was the third son of John Purcell... Music Pages 172

Ancient Law *by Henry Maine* ISBN: *1-59462-128-4* **$29.95**
The chief object of the following pages is to indicate some of the earliest ideas of mankind, as they are reflected in Ancient Law, and to point out the relation of those ideas to modern thought, Religion/History Pages 452

Far-Away Stories *by William J. Locke* ISBN: *1-59462-129-2* **$19.45**
"Good wine needs no bush, but a collection of mixed vintages does. And this book is just such a collection. Some of the stories I do not want to remain buried for ever in the museum files of dead magazine-numbers an author's not unpardonable vanity..." Fiction Pages 272

Life of David Crockett *by David Crockett* ISBN: *1-59462-250-7* **$27.45**
"Colonel David Crockett was one of the most remarkable men of the times in which he lived. Born in humble life, but gifted with a strong will, an indomitable courage, and unremitting perseverance... Biographies/New Age Pages 424

Lip-Reading *by Edward Nitchie* ISBN: *1-59462-206-X* **$25.95**
Edward B. Nitchie, founder of the New York School for the Hard of Hearing, now the Nitchie School of Lip-Reading, Inc, wrote "LIP-READING Principles and Practice". The development and perfecting of this meritorious work on lip-reading was an undertaking... How-to Pages 400

A Handbook of Suggestive Therapeutics, Applied Hypnotism, Psychic Science ISBN: *1-59462-214-0* **$24.95**
by Henry Munro Health/New Age/Health Self-help Pages 376

A Doll's House: and Two Other Plays *by Henrik Ibsen* ISBN: *1-59462-112-8* **$19.95**
Henrik Ibsen created this classic when in revolutionary 1848 Rome. Introducing some striking concepts in playwriting for the realist genre, this play has been studied the world over. Fiction/Classics/Plays 308

The Light of Asia *by sir Edwin Arnold* ISBN: *1-59462-204-3* **$13.95**
In this poetic masterpiece, Edwin Arnold describes the life and teachings of Buddha. The man who was to become known as Buddha to the world was born as Prince Gautama of India but he rejected the worldly riches and abandoned the reigns of power when... Religion/History/Biographies Pages 170

The Complete Works of Guy de Maupassant *by Guy de Maupassant* ISBN: *1-59462-157-8* **$16.95**
"For days and days, nights and nights, I had dreamed of that first kiss which was to consecrate our engagement, and I knew not on what spot I should put my lips..." Fiction/Classics Pages 240

The Art of Cross-Examination *by Francis L. Wellman* ISBN: *1-59462-309-0* **$26.95**
Written by a renowned trial lawyer, Wellman imparts his experience and uses case studies to explain how to use psychology to extract desired information through questioning. How-to/Science Reference Pages 408

Answered or Unanswered? *by Louisa Vaughan* ISBN: *1-59462-248-5* **$10.95**
Miracles of Faith in China Religion Pages 112

The Edinburgh Lectures on Mental Science (1909) *by Thomas* ISBN: *1-59462-008-3* **$11.95**
This book contains the substance of a course of lectures recently given by the writer in the Queen Street Hall, Edinburgh. Its purpose is to indicate the Natural Principles governing the relation between Mental Action and Material Conditions... New Age/Psychology Pages 148

Ayesha *by H. Rider Haggard* ISBN: *1-59462-301-5* **$24.95**
Verily and indeed it is the unexpected that happens! Probably if there was one person upon the earth from whom the Editor of this, and of a certain previous history, did not expect to hear again... Classics Pages 380

Ayala's Angel *by Anthony Trollope* ISBN: *1-59462-352-X* **$29.95**
The two girls were both pretty, but Lucy who was twenty-one who supposed to be simple and comparatively unattractive, whereas Ayala was credited, as her Bombwhat romantic name might show, with poetic charm and a taste for romance. Ayala when her father died was nineteen... Fiction Pages 484

The American Commonwealth *by James Bryce* ISBN: *1-59462-286-8* **$34.45**
An interpretation of American democratic political theory. It examines political mechanics and society from the perspective of Scotsman James Bryce Politics Pages 572

Stories of the Pilgrims *by Margaret P. Pumphrey* ISBN: *1-59462-116-0* **$17.95**
This book explores pilgrims religious oppression in England as well as their escape to Holland and eventual crossing to America on the Mayflower, and their early days in New England... History Pages 268

www.bookjungle.com *email: sales@bookjungle.com fax: 630-214-0564 mail: Book Jungle PO Box 2226 Champaign, IL 61825*

QTY

The Fasting Cure *by Sinclair Upton*　　　　　　　　ISBN: *1-59462-222-1*　**$13.95**
In the Cosmopolitan Magazine for May, 1910, and in the Contemporary Review (London) for April, 1910, I published an article dealing with my experiences in fasting. I have written a great many magazine articles, but never one which attracted so much attention... New Age/Self Help/Health Pages 164

Hebrew Astrology *by Sepharial*　　　　　　　　　　ISBN: *1-59462-308-2*　**$13.45**
In these days of advanced thinking it is a matter of common observation that we have left many of the old landmarks behind and that we are now pressing forward to greater heights and to a wider horizon than that which represented the mind-content of our progenitors... Astrology Pages 144

Thought Vibration or The Law of Attraction in the Thought World　　ISBN: *1-59462-127-6*　**$12.95**
by William Walker Atkinson　　　　　　　　　　　　　　　　　*Psychology/Religion Pages 144*

Optimism *by Helen Keller*　　　　　　　　　　　　ISBN: *1-59462-108-X*　**$15.95**
Helen Keller was blind, deaf, and mute since 19 months old, yet famously learned how to overcome these handicaps, communicate with the world, and spread her lectures promoting optimism. An inspiring read for everyone... Biographies/Inspirational Pages 84

Sara Crewe *by Frances Burnett*　　　　　　　　　　ISBN: *1-59462-360-0*　**$9.45**
In the first place, Miss Minchin lived in London. Her home was a large, dull, tall one, in a large, dull square, where all the houses were alike, and all the sparrows were alike, and where all the door-knockers made the same heavy sound... Childrens/Classic Pages 88

The Autobiography of Benjamin Franklin *by Benjamin Franklin*　　ISBN: *1-59462-135-7*　**$24.95**
The Autobiography of Benjamin Franklin has probably been more extensively read than any other American historical work, and no other book of its kind has had such ups and downs of fortune. Franklin lived for many years in England, where he was agent... Biographies/History Pages 332

Name	
Email	
Telephone	
Address	
City, State ZIP	

☐ **Credit Card**　　　　☐ **Check / Money Order**

Credit Card Number	
Expiration Date	
Signature	

Please Mail to:　Book Jungle
PO Box 2226
Champaign, IL 61825
or Fax to:　　　630-214-0564

ORDERING INFORMATION

web: *www.bookjungle.com*
email: *sales@bookjungle.com*
fax: *630-214-0564*
mail: *Book Jungle PO Box 2226 Champaign, IL 61825*
or PayPal *to sales@bookjungle.com*

Please contact us for bulk discounts

DIRECT-ORDER TERMS

20% Discount if You Order Two or More Books
Free Domestic Shipping!
Accepted: Master Card, Visa, Discover, American Express